LELA IN BALI

Cameroon Studies

General Editors: Shirley Ardener, E.M. Chilver and Ian Fowler, Associate Members of Queen Elizabeth House, University of Oxford.

Volume 1
Kingdom on Mount Cameroon
Studies in the History of the Cameroon Coast 1500–1970 – Edwin Ardener. Edited and with an Introduction by Shirley Ardener.

Volume 2
African Crossroads
Intersections between History and Anthropology in Cameroon
Edited by Ian Fowler and David Zeitlyn.

Volume 3
Cameroon's Tycoon
Max Esser's Expedition and its Consequences
Edited by E.M. Chilver and Ute Röschenthaler.

Volume 4
Swedish Ventures in Cameroon, 1883–1923
Trade and Travel, People and Politics
Edited and with Commentaries by Shirely Ardener.

Volume 5
Memoirs of a Mbororo
The Life of Ndudi Umaru: Fulani Nomad of Cameroon
Henri Bocquené, translated by Philip Burnham and Gordeen Gorder.

Volume 6
In Search of Salt
Changes in Beti (Cameroon) Society, 1880–1960
F. Quinn.

Volume 7
Lela in Bali
History through Ceremony in Cameroon
Richard Fardon

LELA IN BALI

History through Ceremony in Cameroon

RICHARD FARDON

Berghahn Books
New York • Oxford

First published in 2006 by

Berghahn Books

www.berghahnbooks.com

©2006 Richard Fardon

Library of Congress Cataloging-in-Publication Data
Fardon, Richard.
Lela in Bali : history through ceremony in Cameroon / Richard Fardon.
   p. cm. -- (Cameroon studies ; 7)
Includes bibliographical references and index.
ISBN 1-84545-215-1 (hardback : alk. paper)
   1. Bali (African people)--Social life and customs. 2. Bali (African
people)--Rites and ceremonies. 3. Lela (Festival) 4. Cameroon--Social life
and customs. I. Title.

DT571.B33F37 2006
305.896'36--dc22

2006019689

British Library Cataloguing in Publication Data
A catalogue record for this book is available from the British Library
Printed in the United States on acid-free paper

ISBN 1-84545-215-1 (hardback)

Contents

Preface

A cutting of Chamba ethnography surprised me by taking root and growing into this book. It had started on its lengthy pre-publication career as a draft chapter in a monograph on Chamba religion. That book, I decided finally, worked best as a comparison between two Chamba communities (with some broadening when dealing with the impact of world religions); however, earlier drafts had contained comparative chapters, including discussion of resemblances between ceremonies in the Bali kingdoms of the Bamenda Grassfields (North West Province of Cameroon) – of which Bali Nyonga is one – and the Chamba communities hundreds of miles to the north, straddling the Cameroon–Nigeria border, from which the Bali royal families nowadays claim descent. One ceremony in particular caught my attention: Lela, a hugely popular street performance taking place once or twice annually in the Grassfields, takes its name from bamboo flutes that Chamba living around the Cameroon–Nigeria border would call *lera*. The flutes are not the only elements of this ceremonial complex with clear Chamba precedents; however Lela also contains much that lacks Chamba parallels. Where had it all come from?

It is fortunate that my earlier attempts to confront this problem did not find their way into print: my analysis relied upon a rather static comparison between Bali and Chamba ceremonials with an underdeveloped account of the historical relation between them. Only as my appreciation of the available historical sources improved, especially those authored by Basel missionaries, was I able to work towards what I think is a more satisfactory and nuanced account that pivots about the particularly detailed testimony we have on the circumstances of Lela for the year 1908. Reassembling the photographic and textual record from that period proved an intriguing challenge, with all the thrills and spills to which investigation is prone. The story of who witnessed Lela, and how and why they did so, itself transpired to be part of the history of the ceremony's change. European presence at Lela has now been routine for well over a century and, albeit more so at some times than at others, has been an important consideration in the modified reproduction of the ceremony. In consequence, there is a good deal of direct testimony about Lela from the last decade of the nineteenth century onwards. Before this, at least a further century of Lela's history – from the late eighteenth century – can be reconstructed more or less conjecturally on the basis of comparisons between communities. My analysis tries to demonstrate the stages by which a ceremony similar to Lela first developed among Chamba before their diaspora and then changed as the future founders of the Bali kingdoms accumulated people and practices on their migration southwards. Bali Nyonga especially – as the most ethnically diverse of Bali kingdoms – continued strategically to incorporate people, artefacts and performances (and sanctioned exegeses of all three) as state policy. The characteristic inventiveness of material ornamentation and display – that makes the Grassfields home to one of Africa's great sculptural traditions in wood – typifies Grassfield performative culture generally and the Bali parvenus' take on Grassfield mores particularly.

Contrasting Grassfield aesthetic preferences with those at the eastern end of the Middle Belt (from where Chamba and their early allies set off) throws into relief the baroque style of the former by comparison with the latter's comparative austerity. Eastern middle-belt stylistic preferences pare material objects to simple forms, fusing their parts, and making references outside the objects themselves difficult to detect and impossible to stabilise. Masks and statues alike are deceptively simple forms freighted with ambiguities in their handling of such constitutive categories as male/female, living/dead, domesticated/wild, and their correlates: for instance, human head/hair/skull/scarification and animal head/horns/skull/colouring (Fardon & Stelzig 2005; Fardon 2006: in press). Most middle-belt statues and masks are esoteric objects, seen under conditions of secrecy, or by some people and not others, or seen obliquely and momentarily. Consistent with their role in cultic societies, these elements of material culture were meant to produce an evocative surplus, an intimation of undisclosed meanings and occulted powers, rather than referential closure. In comparison to these, Grassfield forms strike one as more straightforwardly referential: the symbolism they employ is elaborate but it is overtly and publicly figurative. If an ancestral figure holds a decapitated head or a horn filled with palm wine, or if masks evoke the aggression of wild carnivores or the brute cunning force of the buffalo, if a throne is decorated with leopards, spiders or chameleons, it is because these are specific and lisible symbols about capacities to those who see them (Knöpfli 1999). The public material culture of the Grassfields is predominantly about the display of power. Even the exceptions prove the rule: masks of the regulatory societies sent out to chastise malefactors – masks that one should not or would not wish to see – lose this ready lisibility. The Lela ceremony – aside from its inception rite – is public, participatory and accumulative.

Thus a series of reflections prompted by a Chamba ethnographic offcut has led me into a comparative analysis encompassing a substantial part of the eastern Middle Belt and Cameroon Grassfields. My initial intention was ethnographic, and my argument still relies heavily on the material evidence about history that has been reproduced – though not entirely unchangingly – over the years into present performances; however, as presentation of my provisional analysis brought me into contact with specialists in regional art history, museum collections, photographic archives and so on, I became increasingly drawn to the variety of evidence derived from encounters (more or less ethnographic in purpose) previous to my own. In interpreting these sources I draw upon my familiarity with at least part of the region as an ethnographer, but this book cannot lay claim to being ethnography – in the sense of a written account of eye-witnessing and participation. An extensive list of acknowledgements gives the reader some idea what kind of research it is based upon.

Acknowledgements

Local research in Nigeria and Cameroon, amounting to about three years, was carried out from 1976 to 1978, and in 1984, 1985 to 1986, 1987 and 1990. Within this, my experience of Cameroon's North West Province amounted to less than three months at the end of 1984 that was supplemented by three weeks during the 2004 Christmas vacation. My earliest, and longest, period of research in Nigeria was supported financially by the Social Science Research Council and the Central Research Fund of the University of London; the second, and second longest, period in Cameroon by the former's later incarnation, the Economic and Social Science Research Council. Later and briefer African researches were made possible by the Hayter Parry and Staff Travel Funds of the University of St Andrews, the Carnegie Foundation for the Universities of Scotland, and the British Academy. I am grateful to all these bodies and to the many individuals and institutions – acknowledged previously – who variously made things feasible and bearable, enjoyable and memorable, or both.

An unrecognisable formulation of this analysis of Lela was presented in the early years of Dick Werbner's Satterthwaite Colloquium on Religion and Ritual and again at the LSE departmental seminar. A revised version was given to the African History Seminar at SOAS as long ago as 1991, after which I decided, helpful advice notwithstanding, to consign it to a drawer indefinitely. In 1993 the situation changed when Christraud Geary and I planned to author an account jointly. Work schedules did not allow this, but my references to her work make clear how far my approach has been inspired by Christraud's use of early photographic sources (particularly in her Bamum reconstructions, Geary 1988b, 1990c, 1995). In 1998 I was able to combine an invitation (and generous hospitality) from Carola Lentz and Karl-Heinz Kohl to deliver a seminar paper in Frankfurt with brief research in the Frobenius-Institut; my interest was predominantly in masquerades, but I also saw Frobenius's photographs from Koncha, one of which is included here. In 1999 a British Academy grant allowed me to undertake research for a week in the Basel Mission Archive; Paul Jenkins was both inspirational guide through the sources and considerate host; I had the good fortune to meet Hans Knöpfli and benefit from his years of experience of Bali Nyonga; Michael Chollet, doing his national service in the Basel Archive at the time, made most of the arrangements for me to copy texts and photographs. In late summer 2000, again predominantly in search of masks, I enjoyed a triangular tour of German museums in Berlin, Dresden and Leipzig. At the Ethnologisches Museum in Berlin, Hans-Joachim Koloss guided me through the Grassfields collection and his own knowledge of Oku and Bali Nyonga; Marie Gaida facilitated my access to the archives. I would describe Christine Stelzig's intellectual generosity to me as extraordinary had I not learned better what she considers normal. Many of the photographs reproduced here are from the Berlin collection. Another research trip took me to the Linden-Museum in Stuttgart, where I benefited both from Hermann Forkl's custodianship of the Africa collection and photographs, and from his wide knowledge as a scholar of northern Cameroon and Nigeria. The materials from Basel, Berlin and Stuttgart formed the basis of a seminar delivered at the University of St Andrews in late 2000. The invitation to teach a two-day seminar at the University of Basel in association with the Basel Mission Archive during May 2001 was invaluable since it gave me the chance to rehearse a version of the account offered here before a well-informed audience (I must particularly thank Paul Jenkins and Hans Knöpfli, again, as well as Barbara Müller for her organisational skills, Ulrike Sill for an uncanny facility with handwritten sources shared selflessly, and Hans-Peter Straumann, Andres Wanner, and Ernst Elsenhans – among too many participants to thank individually – for their illustrative materials, some of which appeared in Fardon 2005). Paul Jenkins's retirement in 2004 was the occasion of an inspiring gathering in Basel, papers from which were published later that year as *Getting Pictures Right: Context and Interpretation* under the editorship of Michael Albrecht, Veit Arlt, Barbara Müller and Jürg Schneider (Köln: Rüdiger Köppe Verlag). A revised version of my contribution to that volume (Fardon 2004), which benefited particularly from comments by Veit Arlt, Elizabeth Edwards and Adam Jones, appears with permission as Chapter 2 of the present work. Paul's successor, Guy Thomas, has splendidly upheld the Basel tradition of intellectual generosity. Andreas Merz's 1997 Lizentiatsarbeit at the University of Basel, from which I have profited greatly, deserves particular mention and wider circulation.

As someone marginal to the charmed circle of Grassfield specialists, it has been a comfort never to have embarked on Bali materials without E.M. (Sally) Chilver's advice; this account is no exception. Jean-Pierre Warnier, Mike Rowlands and Nic Argenti have all been good enough to answer queries. Shirley Ardener's encouragement and Ian Fowler's detailed comments as a Grassfield specialist have added to the pleasure of publishing this account in Marion Berghahn's 'Cameroon Studies' series, itself a brave initiative for a publisher faced by the realities of the smallness of such niches in the book market.

My debts to the School of Oriental and African Studies are numerous. Glenn Ratcliffe, SOAS's photographer, has helped cheerfully with photographs that arrived at a dribble in different formats over a period of years. SOAS research committee supported some of my research trips to Germany and Switzerland, and also made grants towards illustrative materials. My departmental colleagues rallied round when the Leverhulme Trust awarded me a Research Fellowship of nine months during the 2000–2001 academic year. Without both these estimable bodies I would probably never have brought this overlengthy saga to a conclusion. I thank my son Tom for his company during the brief visit we made to Bali Nyonga in the 2004 Christmas vacation with the almost-completed manuscript and illustrations. Our trip was facilitated and made memorable by – among numerous others – His Majesty Dr Ganyonga III and his palace officials, Professor Emmanuel Chia, Dr Mathew and Mrs Helen Gwanfogbe, Drs Elias Nwana, Francis Nyamnjoh, and Ben Page, Mayor Christopher Nyansenkwen, and retired Sergeant Gaso Fonyonga.

Richard Fardon
London, November 2005

For Sally

caretaker of the Bali road and its travellers in both directions

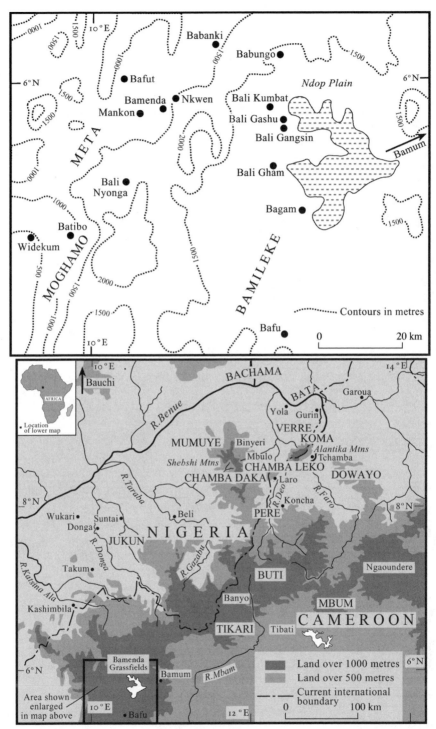

Map. The eastern end of west Africa's Middle Belt between the Benue-Faro-Deo river confluences and the western Grassfields

CHAPTER 1

Lela: Past Present, Present Past

Lela in the Early Post-Colony

Bali Town, the capital and largest part of the Kingdom of Bali Nyonga, sits on top of a commanding hill in the rolling Grassfields of Cameroon's North West Province. The kingdom is accustomed to outside interest: host, tool, beneficiary and intermediary of early German imperialism and Protestant evangelisation, Bali's fate has long depended on astutely squaring international links with local politics. Twenty-odd years ago, Bali was again made to play a representative role outside Africa when it became the subject of a lively illustrated book for British students in the middle years of their secondary school education (Green 1982).

One of a series sharing the title 'Through the year', *Through the Year in West Africa* was devoted to the yearly round of events in Bali where its author had spent some of the years between 1977 and 1981 as headmaster of the Self Reliance Comprehensive College. By 1980, Bali people's own renewal of interest in their past was a couple of decades old; the past had been put into some semblance of good order for present purposes, and Malcolm Green was well placed to absorb the importance of the Lela ceremony to this local renaissance. In deference to Bali ideas, Green's account of the West African year starts not in January but with the completion of Lela during December.

> The Lela festival is a time when all Bali people live their tradition. The four-day festival is the climax of the Bali year. The old year dies and the new comes with an eruption of colour and music.
>
> Bali people arrive from far and wide to their homes and relatives in the village, some walking from their farms, others arriving by plane or taxi. The night before, all houses are swollen with people and at midnight a sacrifice is made by a secret society on a small stone pyramid in the palace of the Fon (chief) of Bali. Meanwhile, oblivious of the nocturnal happenings, children scramble for one of their father's traditional dancing gowns, which they iron in preparation for the 'big day'. [...] The present Fon, Galega II, seldom appears in public and, when he does, it is as an almost mystical father-figure. [...]
>
> During Lela the Fon is supreme. On the first day, he leads his people on horseback to a stream on the boundary of Bali, kicking up a haze of red dust from the parched, dry-season ground. At the stream he is surrounded by his noblemen. The priests (*nwanas*) enter the water to consult with Nyikob (God) through the Fon's ancestors, and a white cock is offered to them as a sacrifice. People stand around and watch in silence as the

officiating priest cuts its throat and allows the blood to drip before releasing the animal. The headless chicken leaps and bounds across the ground. The way it dies and its position at death tell the people whether their relationship with the ancestors has been good or not. If the sacrifice is rejected, the people believe that there will be much hardship and suffering over the course of the following year. If it is accepted, the women ululate, guns fire and everyone returns happy, running or galloping their horses. They watch the children engage in mock battle, throwing long, dry elephant grass stalks at each other and singing 'hilo halo' as they throw.

On the second day of the festival, there is not a man without a gun. The wealthy have modern shot guns; the majority have their locally made flint-lock dane-guns, which they fire as they re-enact wars of conquest with a vigour that is something more than pure theatre.

On the third and fourth days, people come in their most magnificent robes of all colours. Dark blue, embroidered with red and yellow, is traditional, but anything goes, and people play music, dance, sing and drink until they are tired. (Green 1982: 9–10)

The ceremony evoked by Malcolm Green is immediately recognisable as that described by Basel missionaries between 1905 and 1913, and by the German artillery lieutenant Franz Hutter in 1891. The procession to a stream where the priests enter the water, the flapping of the white cockerel they sacrifice, the firing of guns and dancing in choicest clothes … all these were established features of Lela a hundred years earlier. Before then we lack written records, but inferences drawn from the distribution of ceremonies resembling Lela in one way or another allow recuperation of a probable past stretching back a further century to the end of the eighteenth century. In greater or lesser detail, then, we can trace a history of Lela through two hundred years, an unusually long period for a ceremony in a middling-scale inland West African society. Over that time, both the ceremony and the people who carry it out have done a lot of identity work; yet who the Bali are, and what Lela means, have remained intimately tied concerns. Lela has always been an occasion to suture past and present and, in this sense, has been remarkably unchanging; however, what past, what present, and what relations there should be between the two have been subject to ongoing revision. These triangulations of ceremony, history and identity have needed renewing, in large measure, for other people's eyes: new allies, Grassfield neighbours, German colonialists, Swiss missionaries, expatriate teachers, aid workers, Cameroonian officialdom, ethnographic researchers, tourists, visiting members of the Bali diaspora community, and so on.

My account means to look at reflections around Lela in two senses. In a straightforward sense, Lela has been a barometer of the state of play in Bali politics: a ceremony that has adjusted to reflect the changing composition and external relations of the community. But Lela has also been a thoughtful performance, an active musing about those relations, conjoined with subsequent reflections that their experience of the ceremony has prompted in both observers and participants (categories between which no clear line can be drawn). Malcolm Green's description already indicates something of Lela's cellular construction: in late twentieth-century, canonical form its opening rite is succeeded by four days, each with its own distinctive types of practice, paraphernalia and nomenclature. Each of these elements in its turn also has an interpretable past. There is no evidence for reluctance to graft on more elements as the opportunity arose. Lela has an additive, baroque aesthetic. This may be characteristic of Grassfields performative culture more generally where, contrary to the 'less is more' dictate shared by many elements of classicism and high modernism, in style terms more – almost always – really is more.

We shall return to the late twentieth century only in closing, but knowing the recent past differently is the purpose of an account that, for reasons of method, will consist of a set of recursive transections of the historic past. Malcolm Green's evocation of Lela has given the reader sufficient idea of what Lela is to get us started. The reader will also need an introductory thumbnail history of the people known as Bali, which I provide shortly. The next part of my account concentrates on a particular period of Lela performance, centred around the year 1908 which is more extensively documented (in words and pictures and sound) than any other. It is practically impossible to dissociate what the various accounts tell us about their authors from what they say about the ceremony they are documenting. To do so would be undesirable anyway, not just because of the generally conceded argument that all description is invested with a range of more or less self-conscious interests, but more urgently in this instance because Lela was intended to make an impression on observers (both African and European). That observers and participants should be elated or cowed, impressed or threatened, revealed as ally or enemy ... was and is no secondary or accidental feature of Lela.

Having described Lela in 1908, and in less detail during the years immediately before and after, my account employs a reverse chronology – working backwards from the first decade of the twentieth century – to analyse the contexts sedimented into Lela ceremonies: German–Bali alliance, the kingship complexes of the Grassfields, the heritages that Bali Nyonga shares with the other Bali chiefdoms of the Grassfields, and those the Bali chiefdoms share with Chamba in diaspora, and finally – thus earliest – the features of Lela which may well have come from the Adamawan homelands of the Bali founders. A conclusion reruns this chronology forwards and past 1908 to the late twentieth century to summarise how and why Lela developed in the ways it has.

Bali Nyonga: A Thumbnail History

Most probably it was during the early years of the nineteenth century that the last parties of Chamba warriors – mounted, armed apparently with bows and arrows, spears and swords and buffalo hide shields, and accompanied by their dependants – abandoned a homeland just east of present-day Chambaland close by the current border between Cameroon and Nigeria (see **Map** p. xiii). Although we may never know the immediate cause of their leaving, we can infer a mixture of motives: that they quit their homeland definitively suggests they went under some duress; but apparently they left in good fighting order, so in all likelihood they were not physically expelled, at least not routed. The effectiveness of these marauding Chamba bands as fighting forces makes it likely that they were not new to the business of raiding; and the impression of pillaging as a not wholly innovative means of livelihood for them is reinforced both by the bands being quite numerous, and by evidence that these Chamba-led bands may have been following paths pioneered by others. Putting together a couple of the not very many things we know about the area around the confluence of the Rivers Faro and Deo in the late eighteenth century, perhaps our best guess is that Chambaland suffered with the rest of the Middle Belt from the recurrent drought-induced famines of the middle and last quarter of the eighteenth century (Sargent 1999: 18–20, 71). This duress coincided with the intensification of the Atlantic slave trade and the shift of its most important supply chains eastwards along the West African coast, so that European traders increasingly took slaves from ports that would have been supplied from the upper Benue River hinterland. Small local raids and kidnappings, judicial procedures leading to expulsion from the community, and pawning of kin for food, may have shaded by degrees into a dependence on raiding for livelihood and a growing affection for the sorts of treasure purchases (such as gowns and imported horses) that were affordable only to those who participated in the slave trade.

The onset of the Fulbe jihad at the very beginning of the nineteenth century was the catalyst that accelerated transition to a marauding way of life. The historical testimony given to early European visitors – whether to the missionary Keller, the cartographer Moisel, the trader Esser, or the soldier Hutter (discussed in detail later) – by a generation of Bali informants who could well have been grandchildren of those involved, consistently gave avoidance of the Fulbe or Hausa wars of the jihad as the main reason for their migration. Before they reached the Grassfields, direct evidence for the passage of these raiders southwards is scanty, but we do know that when they ascended the Grassfields their bands contained contingents of people who would – in twentieth-century terms – have been drawn not just from Chamba, but from Bata, Pere, Mbum, Buti and Tikari as well (Chilver & Kaberry 1968: 16). Contingents of BaTi, from around Bamum, had also joined up before the main Chamba-led war party arrived on the Bamenda Plateau during the 1820s and, thanks to their unprecedented means of warfare and startling ruthlessness, swept through the less centralised Grassfield communities with devastating speed. Operating out of warcamps that they moved periodically, they eventually reached the edge of the Grassfields where their progress was arrested by larger scale, and probably better organised, Bamileke forces near Bafu Fondong in a battle usually dated around 1835. The technology of warfare may have played a role here too: Bali horses were suffering from proximity to the forest with its tsetse fly, while Bamileke may have received supplies of firearms from the coast. Defeated, the leader of their alliance killed, the Bali split into five, six or seven groups which went on to found the communities Bali informants know are related to them. Backreckoning has been built into these recollections so as to allow all the Bali identities of current importance to trace their origin from this dispersal of Gawolbe's alliance. Events were in all likelihood less neat. But, to follow for now the conventional account, those who were later to found Bali Nyonga, with today's Bali town at its centre, made their way north-eastwards under the leader Nyongpasi who would give his name to the later kingdom. Nyongpasi's Bali were expelled after sojourning (as had Gawolbe) on the borders of the powerful and expanding Bamum kingdom, but not before they incorporated a second large contingent of BaTi from whose language the Mungaka now spoken in Bali derives. It is likely that they completed their transition from mounted bowmen to foot soldiers, with some use of musketry, around this time. Nyongpasi brought his forces to a Meta marketplace close to the present site of Bali Nyonga, where he died in the 1860s. His successor, Galega I, shifted to the more defensible site that became Bali Nyonga. It was here, on 16 January 1889, that a meeting occurred between the Bali king, or Fon as Grassfields kings are usually known in English writing about the region, and the German explorer Eugen Zintgraff, which cast its shadow over the whole of twentieth-century Bali history.

Zintgraff's expedition represented the vanguard of German colonial expansion into Northern Kamerun. Zintgraff and Galega were much taken with one another: Zintgraff decided that Bali Nyonga would make an ideal centre for German administration of the hinterland, and Galega astutely reckoned that the Germans might be useful to his own search for power and wealth. This interlacing of their ambitions marked the beginning of Bali's attempts to exert sub-imperial control on behalf of the Germans.

German-supported Bali hegemony had its fits and starts and lasted little more than two decades from start to finish. It was inaugurated when Zintgraff returned to Bali in 1890 and led a – to his mind if not Galega's – disastrous expedition against Bali's powerful neighbour Mankon, which had allied with Bafut. When he next returned, in August 1891, Zintgraff was accompanied by the young artillery lieutenant Franz Hutter who set enthusiastically about raising and training a two-hundred-strong local Balitruppe and arming them with Mauser M71 breech-loading rifles that were significantly more lethal than the muskets that were the fire-power of neighbouring chiefdoms. The Bali station may have been closed in 1893, but Leutnant Hutter left his well-drilled and well-armed troop behind him, and they became the Fon's local militia.

Bali then disappears from our view again for three years until 1896 when Zintgraff next returned, this time in the company of the plantation manager Max Esser. By 1899 Bali was raising a levy of labour for the coastal plantations not just from Bali itself but from such neighbours as the Meta. Direct German colonial, rather than narrowly commercial, intervention in Bali resumed in 1901. In April, the month before the long-reigning Galega I died, Leutnant Strümpell set out with two European officers and fifty African troops to reopen the Bali station. Late the following year, an expeditionary party from the Basel Mission arrived in Bali and was as captivated by Fonyonga II as Zintgraff had been by his father Galega I. In 1903 Bali became the first centre for proselytising and schooling in the Grassfields, and its adopted language (Mungaka, derived, as noted above, from the language of the BaTi rather than from Chamba sources) was chosen as the idiom of basic education and religious observance. Missionary (translating the German courtesy title *Missionar*) Ferdinand Ernst was to become a particular friend of the palace and adviser on foreign affairs. Fonyonga II's stock was rising fast. In 1905 the redoubtable Hauptmann Glauning became military commander of the Bamenda Bezirk and, thanks to his firm advocacy, in that same year the Fon of Bali was officially recognised as regional paramount in an elaborate ceremony of investiture. Also that year, Bali was able to supply as many as a thousand irregulars to assist their German ally's campaign of pacification and to buttress their own paramountcy in the process. Thanks to the prominence of its market, the name Bali Nyonga featured often in the records of accession of Grassfield sculptures to German ethnological museums. The Director of the Berlin Museum für Völkerkunde, Felix von Luschan, was a particular friend of Hauptmann Glauning who, among his other interests,[1] was an avid collector of material culture, most of which he donated to the Berlin Museum. At one time a new wing of the museum was planned simply to house his donations (Geary 1994). It was probably through these two intermediaries that the ethnologist Bernhard Ankermann was despatched (with his wife) in 1907 to carry out the better part of two years research based in Bali Nyonga. While living in Bali Nyonga, his accommodation was supplied by the mission, which took another step forward in November 1908 when Ferdinand Ernst baptised thirty-two schoolchildren.

Fonyonga should have been most gratified by his position at the start of 1908: he was recognised as paramount ruler over a large area to which his 'traditional' claim was shaky. Substantial parts of it he had plundered rather than annexed; and while 'tradition' provided the grounds for German implementation of their version of indirect rule, a favourable interpretation of 'tradition' in the light of Bali's mobile nineteenth-century history was helped by having well-placed friends. Learning presumably from his father, Fonyonga already cultivated such friends in the colonial administration and the Basel Mission, and his kingdom was about to attract the attention of Berlin's cultural apparatchiks. This, in fact, was to be the pinnacle of Fonyonga's, and Bali's, success: Hauptmann Glauning would die, shot through the head in an attack on the Tiv, in March 1908 (anon. 1908; Marquardsen 1908); before the end of 1909, Missionary Ferdinand Ernst, his closest European friend, would succumb to blackwater fever while on home leave accompanied by one of the Fon's sons (K.H. 1909); during his lifetime, the ethnologist Bernhard Ankermann published almost nothing – merely a research report and a slim note on religion – from his Bali researches, and added more to the lustre of Bamum than he did to Bali. A seachange in German attitudes towards Bali paramountcy would see the beginning of the erosion of the Bali Fon's administrative fiefdom as well as the freewheeling military role he had enjoyed in pre-colonial and pioneer colonial times alike. The decimation of Grassfield youth in the coastal plantations would compromise the lucrative business of sending labour to the coast and permanently sour relations between the Bali and the peoples they had pressed into labour. During skirmishing around the British invasion of Kamerun, German forces would set fire to the palace that had been the backdrop to past Germano–Bali pomp, causing the Fon to transfer his allegiance despite, so local authors tell us, his practical support for the German war effort (Nwana & Ndangam 1981b: 8). Although it is unlikely that Fonyonga realised it then, 1908 was close to the highwater mark in his affairs.

This is where I shall leave my thumbnail sketch of the sequential history of Bali Nyonga; the story has been well told by others on whose accounts I have drawn.[2] My immediate concern is less with this history than with the ways we may interpret elements of the performative and material culture of some Bali ceremonies in light of it. From hereon I shall proceed evidentially rather than sequentially. The national festival of Lela is Bali's best-known and best-documented annual event. Lela in 1908 was particularly well documented thanks to the simultaneous presence of several European witnesses: the ethnologist Bernhard Ankermann (and presumably his wife), the novice missionary Jonathan Striebel, in all probability Ferdinand Ernst, the experienced missionary and confidant of Fonyonga, and perhaps some others of his colleagues.[3] The happy concurrence of so many witnesses to this late apogee of Bali's affairs, at a date roughly mid-way between the Fulbe jihad of the early nineteenth century and the present, provides a fulcrum to this account from which our attention can be pivoted

Notes

1. There are several references in the *Deutsches Kolonialblatt* to collections of zoological specimens which reached Germany as a result of Glauning's exertions.
2. Chilver (1963, 1967) covers the administrative history masterfully; Russell (1980) brings the story forward a further quarter of a century. Merz (1997) is particularly insightful on the local politics of the pre-First World War Basel mission. O'Neil (1987, 1996) provides an account of Bali history from the viewpoint of dominated neighbours, the Meta. Some of the broader context of this period of Kamerunian history is well covered by Michels (2004).
3. The longserving Jakob Keller was in Germany during the 1908 Lela; however, several other missionaries are recorded as being in Bali that year: Adolf Vielhauer had arrived in 1906, inaugurating a relation with the Grassfields which would be resumed after the First World War and last until 1938; Rudolf Widmaier and Georg Lösch could have been present but were not substantial contributors to the Basel ethnographic record. Since Martin Göhring came from Bamum for the 1905 investiture of Fonyonga, one wonders whether missionaries from other stations might not have come for Lela too.

CHAPTER 2

Lela in 1908: The Photographic Record

Lela and Voma in Bali

Bali Nyonga possesses two ceremonial complexes with Chamba names and credible Chamba antecedents: Lela and Voma. Voma is the Chamba Leko (and hence Mubako)[1] term inclusively for a secretive cult grouping, its cult place, rites and paraphernalia. Cult institutions with similar characteristics were a shared feature of the area where Chamba lived (Fardon 1991, 2006: in press; Knöpfli 2002: 60). I shall discuss the Bali variants of Voma in Chapter 5; enough for now to say that, compared with the variety of their Adamawan originals, these emigrant Chamba trajectories of Voma appear to have collapsed into single institutions. Particularly in Bali Nyonga, the organising contrast between Lela and Voma has lost much of its force. But the original opposition between the two has not been dissipated entirely: Voma may be performed in public space, but some of its stages drive away the uninitiated public, and others involve non-initiates on restricted terms: as, for instance, when women dance with their backs turned to the cult instruments. By contrast, Lela not only incorporates the public into its main performance but constitutively is a collective and public performance. The moment the Fon himself can no longer forbear from dancing and shooting is one of the epiphanies of the performance. This is not to deny that there are more private passages of events during Lela, but these serve to enable the public performance. An obvious but important point follows about our evidence for Lela and Voma: European presence at Lela has been normal for more than a hundred years. Lela is meant to be witnessed. To the best of my knowledge, no Europeans have been encouraged to present themselves other than at the most public elements of Voma; Lela, by contrast, has been another of the means – including gift-giving, especially of clothing, and the conferment of titles – by which Europeans have been incorporated into the social sodalities and politics of Bali. In the case of the 1908 Lela, our remarkably full account includes not just textual analysis, but also photographs and even audio recordings of *lela* flute music and singing on wax cylinders. That these Europeans were in Bali is testimony to the successful incorporative strategy of the state; that they were at Lela reveals the role public culture played as part of that strategy.

The Ethnologist and the Missionaries

Bernhard Ankermann, to begin with the ethnologist who is one of the main protagonists of the 1908 documentation, strikes the investigator as a man of punctilious habits (Schachtzabel 1938; Prinz 1989; Stelzig 2003). A proponent of the *Kultur Kreis* method (which proceeded though exhaustively mapping the distribution of culture traits, particularly material ones), Ankermann devoted himself on his return from the Grassfields to detailed listings of the holdings of Berlin's Museum für Völkerkunde, identifying items by type and style. The surviving, meticulously inscribed, bundles of thematically organized fiches (masks, shields, spears ...) must represent several years work. However, Ankermann published little that was wholly devoted to his time in the Grassfields: only, immediately upon his return, a chronologically organised research report and a two-page note on Grassfield religion (1910a, 1910b). He shouldered a burden of museum administration later in his life, but the fact that ethnological analytics encouraged an inventorial and comparative approach to the records he amassed, rather than an ethnographic sense of a local descriptive whole, may also have had a bearing on his failure, or lack of desire, to write more on the basis of what was a substantial body of material.

We know from a pre-Second World War account that Ankermann took more than 800 photographs in Cameroon (Schachtzabel 1938: 25). On 7 April 1908 he had written from Bamum to his superior – Felix von Luschan,[2] the Director of the Africa and Oceania Department of the Museum, who had despatched him on his mission – asking for permission to extend his researches by several months in order to visit various villages before attending the Lela festival in Bali at the end of the year (I/MV/798: 109).[3] Ankermann's 1910 report reiterates this intention to make a comprehensive record of the 1908 Lela (and there would have been no incentive for him to have mentioned an unrealised plan in a report written after the event). He had caught the tail end of the 1907 ceremony on his arrival with his wife that year and, like other visiting Europeans before and after him, had apparently been fascinated by the combination of religious ceremony, military parade, and general public entertainment that Lela was, and still is. The year-long wait for the ceremony to come round again would have given the meticulous Ankermann ample time to prepare himself and his equipment. Such evidence of intention and opportunity can leave us in little doubt that Ankermann should have made a substantial photographic record of the 1908 Lela.

When the Museum für Völkerkunde, then in Berlin Mitte, was hit by incendiary bombs during the last days of the Second World War, not only were the negatives of Ankermann's photographs destroyed but their accession records burned too. Some of the photographic prints survived (Geary 1994) but it is difficult to tell what original materials perished and what their original documentation might have added to our appreciation of the photographs that remain.[4] Ankermann's fieldwork diary also survived the bombing to be edited for publication in 1959 by Hermann Baumann and László Vajda; but thereafter it too disappeared. Among the few substantial items of Ankermann's original documentation still in the possession of the successor to the Museum für Völkerkunde, the Ethnologisches Museum in

Dahlem, Berlin, are his listings of audio-recordings and a small, hardcovered black notebook under the title 'Aufnahmen mit dem Stativ-Apparat 13 x 18', '[photographs] taken with the tripod camera 13 x 18 centimetres [dimensions slightly larger than 5 x 7 inches]'. This book contains 433 numbered entries itemising photographic subject, place, date, lens used, length of exposure and weather conditions. Some of the numbered entries are sub-divided into a) and b), and a quick count of these suggests that the notebook enumerates 456 images in all, or a good half of the total that Ankermann is estimated to have taken in Kamerun. The other, probably lesser, half of the images were almost certainly taken on a second camera: a smaller format travelling model (9 x 12 centimetres, that is slightly under 4 x 5 inches). No original listing – such as that of the larger plates – survives for these smaller pictures, but the Berlin Ethnologisches Museum has a collection of some of the images themselves, including a few hitherto unrecognised depictions of aspects of the 1908 Lela. It will assist our examination of the photographs themselves if we first explore such evidence as we have for Ankermann's photographic practice.

In his contribution to the 1914 edition of *Anleitung zum ethnologischen Beobachten and Sammeln* – the German equivalent to the British fieldwork manual *Notes and Queries in Anthropology* – Ankermann recommended the use of drawing and, preferably, photography by fieldworkers.[5] He urged fieldworkers to equip themselves with both a large-format, mounted camera for plates, as well as a hand-held camera for snapshots (Ankermann & von Luschan 1914: 14). Presumably this advice drew upon his recently completed researches (see also Geary 1986: 11 fn31, 1990b: 295) and, in all likelihood, Ankermann's own practice had been influenced by his reading of the *Anleitung zu wissenschaftlichen Beobachtungen auf Reisen* edited in its third edition by Georg von Neumayer in 1906. The section on photography, contributed by Gustav Fritsch, makes several recommendations on cameras, suppliers and equipment that Ankermann seems to have followed. For instance, when Ankermann writes to von Luschan from Bali on 21 December 1907 (BEM I/MV 798: 54–55), he asks him to order film from either Stegemann or Braun, the photographic suppliers in Berlin who also appear as the first two recommendations in Fritsch's list of stores (Fritsch 1906: 813). Von Luschan sources Ankermann's order from Stegemann's, a company which also enjoyed a particularly good reputation for travel cameras (Fritsch 1906: 797; Lederbogen 1989: 496).[6] Hence, there is a reasonable likelihood that Ankermann's smaller camera was one of Stegemann's.

After Ankermann and his wife arrived in Kamerun in October 1907, his first large-format photograph was entered into his black notebook at Bombe – a mission station where travellers from the coast via Buea broke their journeys – on 19 November 1907. He did not arrive upcountry in Bali Nyonga until 10 December 1907, where he found Lela was just being completed for the year (the festival probably lasted from 7 to 10 December in 1907). In his honour either the final day was extended or, more likely, a fifth day added, and this allowed Ankermann to take six large-format photographs which he entered in his notebook as numbers (6) to (11). To judge by ticks entered in a different hand against them in the notebook, all but number (8) survive in Berlin.[7] The five photographs that remain (**Figures 19** to **23**) show a throng of people around a pile of large stones set in the palace forecourt. The camera is placed at some distance from the action, perhaps befitting Ankermann's newly arrived status; his 1908 record was to be far more intimate. Even these few shots contain interesting details, although discussion of them is best deferred until we have followed the sequence of photographs from 1908, which lack a record of the final day. There is no reason to believe the events of this day would have materially differed in the two years. No small-format photographs of the 1907 Lela survive, and it is probable that none was taken, since Ankermann had little time to have enlisted the services of a second photographer.

Ankermann saw the 1908 Lela in its entirety; his published report of 1910 records that he was alerted to the ceremony beginning by a summons from Missionary Ferdinand Ernst. This time, Ankermann had every opportunity to take the comprehensive photographic record mentioned in the same report; and we do indeed have photographs of the 1908 Lela, but they are in Basel rather than Berlin. Could the Basel photographs be the record that Ankermann had intended for Berlin? Our trail ought to begin with that meticulously maintained little notebook in which Ankermann logged his large-format photographs; but this proves a cold trail. Here we read that Ankermann was away from Bali and took large-format photographs in the chiefdoms of Bafut and Banding (on 26 and 27 November 1908); Ankermann's written report tells us that he returned to Bali on 28 November. Yet no further photographs are recorded until 21 December 1908, three weeks after the ceremony had closed when, at 9 a.m., he recorded two pairs of beaded posts belonging to the Lela apparatus (**Figures 4** and **6**). Given that he took these pictures after the event, it seems inconceivable that Ankermann would have taken no large-format photographs during the 1908 Lela. Yet none such survive in Berlin, nor is there any specific record pointing to their previous existence. Perhaps Ankermann made a separate list of large-format photographs of Lela, and list and photographs were lost together during the Second World War? Of Ankermann's surviving small-format photographs in Berlin, at least four record moments from the 1908 Lela, and these complement a collection of twelve photographs of the same occasion lodged at the Basel Mission Archive, eight or nine of which were sent by the young missionary Jonathan Striebel.[8] Internal evidence from two of the photographs may illuminate what was going on.

Ankermann and the Missionaries Photographed: The Second Photographer

'King of Bali enquiring of the oracle' (**Figure 16**) is an image taken on a large-format camera which was published at least twice in *Der Evangelische Heidenbote* – the more popularly oriented of the magazines produced by the Basel Mission for its supporters – to illustrate accounts of Lela by Jonathan Striebel (in 1909) and Jakob Keller (a decade later in 1919). I shall discuss the stage of the ceremony it illustrates shortly. For now, I want to draw attention to the two Europeans standing to the left of Fonyonga (the caption's 'King of Bali'). The figure immediately left of Fonyonga wearing a pith helmet is, I suggest, the ethnologist Ankermann.[9] Although we cannot see his features clearly, his slight stature and the thinness of his face match that of the older Ankermann (Schachtzabel 1938, portrait photograph). Quite what Ankermann carries – supported by his right hand and shaded by his left – is difficult to see: but the way he holds it is consistent with his photograph having been taken as he looked down into the viewfinder of a travelling camera. The figure standing to Ankermann's right can confidently be identified as Jonathan Striebel on the basis of his photographic studio portrait preserved in the Basel Mission Archive (**Figure 25**).

A second photograph important to identifying our European protagonists (**Figure 13**), which is in Berlin's Ankermann collection, could have been taken from the very position in which Ankermann stands: it shows a third European behind a large-format tripod camera and (if the reader accepts my construal) he is about to take the photograph discussed previously, or one of two others similar to it (see below). The features of this second photographer are even more difficult than Ankermann's to discern. Might the hint of the beard – or is it simply a shadow – identify him as the missionary Ferdinand Ernst whom the Bali dubbed 'King Beard'? It was Ernst who had written to Ankermann alerting him to the start of Lela. Ernst was also the missionary closest to the king, Fonyonga, hence best positioned to make practical arrangements for Lela to be recorded. But there are also contrary indications: the second photographer wears white, while portraits of Ernst invariably show him dressed in dark suits that seem to be made of heavy cloth. Perhaps this anomaly can be explained away as a concession to the dominance of white on the first day of Lela when the Fon himself wears a white gown?[10] But in addition to entering a question mark against the second photographer's dress, we have no evidence for Ernst being even a competent photographer, and the same can be said of Missionary Dorsch – most cited of Ankermann's missionary informants after Ernst – who was also present on the occasion of Lela in 1908.[11] The outstanding missionary photographer in the vicinity of Bali that year was Martin Göhring. Had he perhaps been summoned by letter from Bamum at the same time as Ernst wrote to tell Ankermann that Lela was about to begin? The second photographer's dress and physique resemble Göhring's, but there is no evidence to take us further. To judge from missionary descriptions of the event (especially that of Jakob Keller discussed below) by 1908 missionary presence at Lela may have become – in the course of the five years since their arrival – anticipated by the Fon and missionaries alike. Whoever the second photographer, it seems unlikely he was not a missionary.[12]

The general involvement of the mission community is attested by the panoramic **Figure 19**, taken on the larger of the two cameras. This photograph would not obviously be of Lela but for its original caption in Basel, 'Abmarsch der Leute vom Lela'. Which procession, what people, and where are they leaving to? The buildings in the background are the mission school of the time, passage in front of which is lined by the Fon's (apparently unarmed) soldiers. The only figures processing appear to be Europeans: two short individuals in pith helmets (who might be Ankermann and his wife), and a noticeably taller figure in dark clothing, who may be Adolf Vielhauer. He (with Jakob Keller, whom we know to have been absent) stands out as the tallest of the 1908 crop of missionaries. Three European hats visible above the heads of the soldiers to the right of the photograph suggest other Europeans might be processing right to left hidden from our view. The stage of the ceremony is difficult to determine. Since we know that the school was built close by the palace, it could be the departure of the procession from the palace, past the school, to the river site of sacrifice. In this case 'Lela' would mean the dance of the first morning, and we might be looking at a photograph of Ankermann's party going on ahead to await the procession at the river side. However, if the river site was close by the mission school this might instead be a record of return *following* the sacrificial rite of Lela. The position of the original mission school relative to the nearby palace in Bali town – which might help us distinguish coming from going – has proved difficult to reconstruct. But either leaving for the river or returning from it, why would the soldiers be unarmed when photographs at the river show them armed? A third alternative suggests that the 'people' of the photograph's caption are simply those Europeans who attended some later phase of Lela dancing, and they are leaving the palace forecourt to return, past the mission school, to the mission house. For want of evidence of where to place it, I leave this photograph at the end of the 1908 sequence, where it was placed by its original accession number in Basel.

The surviving photographic reportage of the 1908 Lela results not just from the combined efforts of Ankermann, Ernst and Striebel, and a second photographer who is also likely to have been a missionary, but also benefited from the more general presence and perhaps assistance of the missionary community. Like other German allies, by 1908 Fonyonga himself was very accustomed to being photographed, and there are poses which suggest he is happily playing to the camera (**Figure 3**). Rather than speak of a photographer, it is more productive to think about all those circumstances which made the surviving photographic record of Lela possible: among which, someone in particular releasing the shutter may not be the most significant.

The Texts and the Photographs

The authorship of textual sources repays similar contextualisation in the local Bali community. Three Basel missionaries published accounts of Lela before the First World War: Jakob Keller's Annual Report for 1905 made brief mention of Lela in general, and that year's in particular, and this was excerpted for inclusion in the Basel Mission's published annual report (BMA E-2.20.394; *Jahresbericht* 1906). Keller could not have witnessed the 1908 Lela since he was on leave between December 1907 and April 1909. He left Bali for the last time to embark from Douala on 25 March 1914, and thereby had the good fortune to avoid internment along with those missionaries still in station when war broke out. Keller's extensive report on Lela was published in 1919 and drew explicitly upon festivals that took place between 1910 and 1913. Jonathan Striebel was the first of the missionaries to publish a descriptive account based on his eye-witnessing of the 1908 ceremony. Unless he visited Bali from his subsequent posting in Bagam, this would have been the only occasion Striebel witnessed Lela. Eduard Lewerenz definitely saw Lela just once (in 1910); he also composed an account that was published in 1912 following heavy editorial emendation in Basel. The fact of both Striebel and Lewerenz completing accounts of Lela during their *Sprachstudium* suggests the festival may have become akin to a recycled examination question. The accounts by Keller, Striebel and Lewerenz are clearly not independent of each other. Passages of text are recycled verbatim between Striebel and Keller, and there is more generally a sense that the published texts are only a small indication of conversations going on between the missionaries: including others who, like the well-placed Ernst, published no account under their own name. The local mission station, with its small documentary archive and lamplight conversations, was also able to produce its own illustrative materials. We know that Ankermann produced prints in the field, since he ordered supplies of collodian paper and fixer from von Luschan (see Note 6). The surviving photographic record of the 1908 Lela derives predominantly from at least eight (possibly nine) photographs Striebel submitted with his manuscript.[13] Three further photographs which are demonstrably of the same occasion were accessioned later: Lewerenz's manuscript makes reference to two photographs of the 'oracle' which must be **Figures 14** and **15**;[14] **Figure 18** (which is evidently a close-up of events depicted in **Figure 17**) came into the Basel collection as late as 1916.[15] No donor is specified, but the date corresponds with the likely period that the lately returned Jakob Keller would have been working up his account of Lela for publication. In sum, twelve of the photographs of the 1908 Lela in Basel were sent there to accompany written accounts of the ceremony.

The missionaries' published accounts of Lela supplement description with their sense of the ceremony's significance, but we need to be cautious in assuming that they were sole authors of the accounts published under their names since comparison of written and printed texts suggests otherwise. For his part, Ankermann left only an incomplete description of Lela in his diary with no indication what, if any, analysis he might have proposed. There are only four small-format photographs of 1908 Lela in the Berlin Ethnologisches Museum's Ankermann collection, and no large-format photographs at all.

What, to return to the question, is the likely relation between the photographs in Berlin and those now in Basel? The question of 'the photographer' has come to seem less pressing. We know that photographs were taken on two cameras: and perhaps by several hands. It strikes me as a strong likelihood that Ankermann would have kept his travelling camera in hand to react to whatever caught his ethnologist's eye (this is what we seem to see him doing in **Figure 16**). Three pictures of the 1908 Lela in the Basel archive also appear to have been taken on a small-format camera (**Figures 5, 7** and **18**). In the absence of evidence for a 'third camera', one assumes this to be the same as the camera on which the four Berlin small-format photographs were taken. A total of seven small-format photographs does seem a rather modest record, but perhaps others were lost (or are yet to be identified). When Jonathan Striebel submitted his description of Lela for publication, he definitely enclosed both large- and small-format photographs, none of which, in all likelihood, he took himself.[16] All this suggests that the local mission station, equipped with its small archive of texts including copies of materials sent home, was capable of producing texts with reference to previous texts. Moreover the mission station also retained original negatives, or copies of negatives, so that it could produce prints some years after the event. Living with the missionaries, and benefiting from their access to the palace, Ankermann found himself happily situated in the equivalent of a well-equipped small research station: scant wonder that his notes are full of references to conversations with the better informed missionaries like Ernst, Dorsch and Vielhauer.

The sum of these links, some of them individually tenuous, suggests that we need to assess the record of the 1908 Lela – and of other Lela ceremonies between 1905 and 1913 – as the unevenly preserved results of collaboration on the occasion between at least the mission house, a compliant Fon and his officials, and the visiting ethnologist and his wife. Quite who was participating and who observing is a matter of opinion. The ethnologist presumably thought he was observing; some of the missionaries were discomfited by the apprehension that their attendance at a pagan rite might be construed as participation in it; Fonyonga, I would surmise, felt pleased that Europeans participated in his ceremonies (without necessarily believing in them) just as he participated selectively in European ceremonies.

An Inventory of the Photographic Record of the 1908 Lela

I use the order of the K (= Kamerun) accession numbers of Striebel's original donation as a skeleton in terms of which to present the surviving record in its entirety (K 1535–43). I have inserted materials from three other sources – most already mentioned above – as seems appropriate.

1) On the basis of their subject matter, three photographs of the 1908 Lela subsequently accessioned in Basel (two via Lewerenz in 1913, and another probably via Keller in 1916) belong with others that arrived earlier.

2) Berlin's four, small-format, Ankermann photographs are readily fitted into the 'action' of the 1908 Lela. As noted earlier, Ankermann had taken photographs of the last day of the 1907 Lela but apparently did not do so again in 1908; these I have simply appended to the 1908 record. On 21 December 1908, subsequent to the event, with his large-format camera Ankermann photographed two types of wooden post associated with Lela: the Lela posts themselves, and the ornate entrance posts to the palace.

3) Clara Schultze-Reinhardt donated two photographs taken around Lela time to the Basel archive. Given the dates of her stay in Bali, if she were the photographer then these must be from either 1909 or 1910; if she were simply the donor then these also might belong to the 1908 series.

The K-series numbers do not, however, correspond to the order of the Lela ceremony. I shall attempt to reconstruct this in the course of describing the materials. The photographic record begins with depictions of the two sides of the entrance to the chief's compound:

Figure 1 'Decorations on the outer wall of the King's compound in Bali' (BMA K 1535/E-30.27.003; previously published in Geary 1988a: 20). Lela was, among many other things, the occasion for an exhibition of royal prestige and royal treasure. From the orientation of the Fon exiting his palace, the treasure display is to the right of the palace entrance. Other photographs of the period show this as the spot where the throne was placed when the Fon (whether Fonyonga II or Galega I before him) gave an audience in the palace forecourt. The treasure display is interesting in itself: the 'skins' appear to be cloth simulacra, but this is not for want of real leopard skins since the throne rests on a leopard skin. There seems implicitly to be a rule at work: skins are royal floor coverings, but cloth is a fencing cover. Rather than taking the place of actual leopard skins, these cloth-made skins are strung over two layers of cloth. The upper layer appears at first sight to be plain (although it is not), and under that is an elaborately patterned blue and white-figured cloth, called in local English 'King's cloth', that is usually said to be produced either in the Jukun town of Wukari or in the Ndop plain.[17]

Another photograph of the same period, **Figure 2** 'The Bali King's thrones' (BMA probably K 1569/E-30.27.008) – if correctly attributed to Clara Schultze-Reinhardt as photographer as well as donor to the Basel archive – must have been taken in either 1909 or 1910 (the only years that Schultze-Reinhardt was in Bali during December).[18] A figurative print hangs over the same patterned display cloth we see on the chief's fence in 1908. Its middle panel is an elephant (facing the viewer's right), while a lion (facing left) can be discerned on the right – visible only as a pair of eyes in this photograph; the striped animal on the viewer's left is a tiger (facing left) – of which only the tail and rear are visible. Keller refers to these hangings – accurately it seems – as European carpets in his 1919 description of Lela (see Chapter 3). The tapestry's exotic fauna are all of Indian inspiration (tiger, small-eared Indian elephant and, presumably, Asian, lion). Under computer enhancement it becomes apparent that the same three panels are present also in the 1908 photograph (**Figure 1**). On this earlier occasion, the leopard was hung to the viewer's right – behind the right-hand cloth 'leopard skin'; a lion (facing right) was made the central panel – behind the left-hand 'leopard skin'; and the elephant was to the viewer's left.[19] The tapestries were still in use during Lela in 1963, 1975 and 2002 (as evidenced from film and photographs taken on these dates by Hans-Peter Straumann, Hans-Joachim Koloss and Ernst Elsenhans, see Fardon 2005), and they hung permanently pinned to the walls of the palace entrance chamber in late 2004 when I had the opportunity to visit Bali. The animal figures are picked out against a background of bright red which contrasts with the blue of the patterned cloth below. Perhaps the tapestries were another of those exchanges of treasure goods of one kind and another which typified early relations between Bali Fons and Europeans.[20] Between 1993 and 1994, the Bali artist David Louis Musi created a mural on the palace walls for the new Fon, HRH Dr Ganyonga III: at its centre is a tiger on a red background, framed by a blue and white frieze modelled on the cloths over which the tapestry used to hang at Lela.[21] In a striking continuity through changing media, the tiger is flanked by panels depicting an (Asian) elephant and two lions (Fardon 2005). Another substitution of this sort is visible in the 1908 photograph of Fonyonga's treasure: the box-like object with a protruding horn was apparently a foghorn[22] from a European ship that added its voice to Lela music (Keller also mentions a phonogram, but this was kept with the Lela standards). Fonyonga's curious throne – with its backrest of two standing figures respectively holding a drinking horn and a severed head – appears in both photographs. The stool and figures are in different styles and may have been stuck together relatively recently, certainly by the time of Fonyonga's installation as paramount in 1905 (see Chapter 4). In Schultze-Reinhardt's photograph of 1909 or 1910, a set of *lela* flutes has been placed on top of this throne, suggesting that hers was a posed scene taken at the time of Lela. The throne and treasures are placed directly on cow hides in Schultze-Reinhardt's print. Two extra stools (also present in the next photograph, and one of which apparently reappears in the 1963 photographs) are in the same style as the throne base; while a pair of male and female freestanding figures seem to resemble the backrest of the throne stylistically.

Figure 3 'King of Bali in dance costume in front of his house' (BMA K 1536 lost/QE-30.010.S.30.3), the second of the photographs that Striebel sent to Basel, now exists only as a half-tone (produced for publication with Striebel's article in *Der Evangelische Heidenbote*). The Fon occupies the foreground of the scene also pictured in **Figure 1**. Because we have no original print or negative, we cannot be entirely sure what camera the picture was taken on. However, the proportions of the published illustration are those of a large-format photograph. **Figure 1** could have been photographed at almost any time during the ceremony; however, **Figure 3** is unlikely to come from the first day of Lela (when the Fon wears white until his return from the river). Evidence from Striebel's account (examined in Chapter 3) suggests this may be the second day of Lela. The alignment of the upper edges of the various cloths suggests that they have been rehung between the two photographs. Our best guess is that the two photographs were taken with the same camera but not at the same time. The Fon's costume is elaborate, including an abundant feather headdress, capacious gown,[23] a sword in a rich scabbard (festooned with what might be horse hair) and a horsetail fly whisk which he carries in his right hand. Behind his right shoulder is what we can recognise from other photographs as a long, beaded pipe-stem. Aside from his umbrella bearer, he is accompanied to his left by a figure who may be a woman carrying his pipe. She (if indeed female) wears a garment that looks like a dressing gown. Just behind her we glimpse the finial of one of a pair of beaded posts that were erected on either side of the palace entrance. These are clearly visible in a photograph that Ankermann took shortly after the 1908 Lela (**Figure 4** 'Two tu ntsubo' BEM VIII A 5398; previously published by Geary 1988a: 24, Plate 3).

Figure 5 'Decorations on the outer wall of the King of Bali's compound' (BMA K 1537/E-30.27.002; previously published by Geary, 1988a: 25) records the other side of the palace entrance (the left for the exiting Fon) in what, despite apparently being taken on the small-format camera, is one of the technically most accomplished of the photographs that Striebel sent to Basel.[24] At the left edge of the photograph is the pair to the beaded post visible to the extreme right of **Figure 3**. Just as it was to the other side of the entrance, the palace fence is hung with patterned cloth. Several spear bundles (perhaps seven are visible, although

Ankermann later specifies nine), their tips protected by covers of various designs, lean against the fence. From two elaborately beaded horned poles are hung a variety of weapons and instruments: a bow is wedged between the two poles; from the left pole (as we view it) hang two leopard-skin bags (at least one of which may contain *lela* flutes), a sword in its scabbard, a large powder horn[25] (rather than a drinking horn to judge from its hinged lid, and possibly imported), a cloth (perhaps a flag), and maybe a horse tail; the right hand pole also carries two skin bags (made either of smaller leopards or civet) in which stand what appear to be horns made from (or at least in the shape of) elephant tusks. The two poles are said to be decorated anew before each Lela ceremony.[26] Ankermann again photographed these poles at the same time as he recorded the entrance posts (**Figure 6** BEM VIII A 5397). His picture confirms that each of the posts had four horns in 1908. I shall discuss the functions and symbolism of the posts later.

The next photograph in Basel's K-series turns our gaze through 180 degrees from the palace entrance to its forecourt.

Figure 7 'The cairn on the market place in Bali' (BMA K 1538/E-30.27.004), a second small-format photograph in Basel's collection, shows the palace plaza which served a number of purposes. 'Market place', as the caption suggests, was one of them; but elsewhere it is referred to as the 'palaver ground' where people came to have their grievances referred to the Fon; it was the kingdom's main public ceremonial space. I shall call it the palace plaza or just plaza: which conveniently means both market place and square. While considerably diminished in size by subsequent extensions to the palace compound, this remains the plaza of the palace today, so we know that someone exiting the palace would be heading roughly north-east. The direction of the short shadows in this photograph indicates it to have been taken early in the afternoon. Like the plaza, the 'cairn', or stone pile, also had various significances. Most mundanely, the Fon mounted it to make public announcements; mounting the cairn also formed part of the Fon's installation rites: as it did when Fonyonga was installed as paramount chief by the Germans in 1905 (see Chapter 4). The stones are reported to have been reddened with kaolin during nocturnal preparations for Lela; but the casual attitude of men (and a boy, perhaps a schoolboy, with shirt and white stick) sitting on them in this photograph does not suggest any aura of inviolable sacrality. I shall need to return to the likely significances of the stone pile later. To the right of the photograph we are looking at a rear view of the *lela* flute players (as becomes apparent from the next photograph, albeit not of the same players): one drummer is seated on a stone just to the left of them, the man standing beside him in a Bali robe is playing a standing drum that may be supported by the boy facing him. Three apparently senior men are circling the stones at a speed that the small-format camera cannot quite freeze as it does the motions of the flute players (the seated drummer's hands are also a blur). A child passes the stone pile in the opposite direction behind them. The palace fence is to the rear left, and we get a sense of the encircling crowd: its first rank made up of seated men behind whom is a larger rank of women occupying the slight elevation that makes the palace plaza into an amphitheatre. There is a small gaggle of men and boys in the centre of the photograph (three in traditional dress face the flute players, a pair to the left are in European clothing:

the man closer to us appears to be African, but the further figure in white tunic and homburg hat may be European). Perhaps, together with the two boys beside them wearing shirts, they belong to a mission party.

Figure 8 'Wind musicians at the Lela festival' (BEM VIII A 6736): on grounds of format, it looks as if this frontal photograph of *lela* flute players[27] was – like the last – taken on Ankermann's travelling camera. To judge by the shadows, it was snapped at around the same time of day as the last, albeit the four flute players are not the same individuals as in the previous photograph. To our right, a figure observes them in profile (at first glance, the outline of his hat in this photograph distorts the shape of his head); to our left, the circular object in the hands of the man wearing a feather headdress is probably a coiled whip: he is a scout or *gwe*, of whom there is another in the right middle ground. Three of the men wear large white (probably ivory) bangles on their left wrists; the leader of the *lela* flute players (second from left) has a leopard-skin bag which may be the container for the flutes (such as was hung from one of the prongs of the post in **Figure 5**).

Figure 9 'Cairn on the market place, with the assembled people' (BMA K 1539/E-30.27.005) was taken from much the same position as **Figure 7**, but apparently on the other, large-format, camera. The shadows have lengthened indicating that it is later in the afternoon. Contingents of warriors, many of whom – like the pair in **Figure 7** – wear feather headdresses, are processing from left to right. The third flute player from the left in the previous photograph (**Figure 8**), wearing a distinctive checked and short sleeved gown, may appear here in rear view. The boy wearing a white shirt, whom we saw in **Figure 7**, also reappears here.

Figures 3, 7, 8 and **9** are difficult to place within Lela because the kinds of moments they show us – dancing, flute playing, military parade – recur during the ceremony. All might be of the first day, illustrating Ankermann's description of the events taking place then, but they could equally belong to the second day as Striebel describes it (see Chapter 3). The sequence that now follows can be related securely to the passage of the Lela celebration from the palace plaza to the riverside where a sacrifice takes place. All this occurs during the middle of the first day of Lela.

Figure 10 'Lela festival' (BEM VIII A 6737): around a score of warriors wearing plumed headdresses, with muskets slung over their left shoulders, make their way through the dry-season grasses.

Figure 11 'Parade (*Aufmarsch*) during the Lela festival' (BMA K 1540/E-30.27.011): roughly fifty 'soldiers' (to distinguish them from the 'warriors' in Bali costume) stand to attention on the left of the photograph. On closer inspection their European-style uniforms differ more than initially seems the case. Bolts are visible on their weapons; these are breechloading rifles not muskets. Further contingents of armed men in Bali dress sit in the long grass. One of them, in the centre of the photograph, approaches the uniformed troops, gun in hand, quickly enough for his image to have blurred. Fonyonga sits under his umbrella, dressed in a white robe, pipe to his mouth. His umbrella bearer is likely to be the same individual as in **Figure 3** taken at the palace, and the pipe bearer from that photograph may now stand behind him, a horsetail fly whisk in her (or his) right hand. A soldier in full equipment faces Fonyonga, apparently at attention. Just to his left, two standing men (one bare-chested) may be blowing whistles and, further right, I count eight spear bundles with covered points (although Ankermann's description suggests nine, see Chapter 3). Another spear, differing in design, may be that with the special function of representing the chief at the oracle (see Chapter 3). Unless the lines are no more than scratches on the photograph, some kind of framework seems to have been erected to the back right, perhaps to hang cloths. Two more of Ankermann's small-format photographs from Berlin belong here in the sequence.

Figure 12 'Two men fishing' (BEM VIII A 6744): although captioned as men fishing, what we see here are the *lela* spears being washed by two men who have stripped down to their loin cloths. In 2004, palace informants told me it was the responsibility of Nyagang to wash the spears, and he would later hold both of them when saluting the Fon. The white object in the foreground is presumably one of the *lela* flags.

Figure 13 'Lela festival' (BEM VIII A 6743): the *lela* flags fly in the left foreground, while the *lela* spears (which were washed in the previous photograph) occupy the middle of the photo. The 'second photographer' whose image is captured here presumably took the next three photographs (*Figures 14, 15* and *16*). He stands amidst a contingent of warriors.

Figure 14 (BMA K 1541c/E-30.27.013) and the next photograph were added to the existing Basel series in 1913 after Lewerenz's account of Lela was published: on internal evidence I am presenting them in the reverse order of their alphabetic cataloguing (i.e. K 1541 c,b,a). Three men clad only in loincloths are crouched. The man at the rear appears to be unwinding a thread which has been attached to the fowl being decapitated by the nearer man whom we see in back view. In addition to the two flags, three spears are stuck into the ground. It is still the case, so I was told in 2004 when this photograph prompted me to ask, that the fowl is attached by a thread to prevent its straying too far after decapitation. The decapitation is performed by the same official who washed the spears, Nyagang. Partially obscured by the flag, a man in a white gown looks on with a leopard-skin bag over his left shoulder and an oliphant in his right hand; presumably the oliphant is one of those hung in a leopard-skin bag from the horned pole by the palace entrance in **Figure 5**.

Figure 15 (BMA K 1541b/E-30.27.012): spectators look on attentively as the white fowl beats its wings. At the rear of the photograph, the man in the white gown sounds his oliphant. The thread by which the fowl is attached is barely discernible. The significance of the two calabashes placed on the ground at the foot of the flags becomes apparent from the textual accounts of Lela.

Figure 16 'King of Bali enquiring of the oracle' (BMA K 1541a/E-30.27.014/QE-K3410):[28] I earlier proposed that the two Europeans standing to Fonyonga's left in this photograph are the missionary Jonathan Striebel (compare **Figure 25**), who is bearded and wears the relatively flat, wide-brimmed hat some missionaries favoured, and Bernhard Ankermann, the moustachioed European in a pith helmet whose left hand supports a square object, shaded by his right hand, into which he is looking as if into a viewfinder: presumably that of the portable camera on which **Figure 13** was taken (as well as **Figures 5, 7, 8, 10, 12** and **18**). We see again the flags, spears and calabashes; the white bundle lying to the front right at the feet of the man in a checked wrapper is the dead fowl; Fonyonga beats a double gong. The man in the foreground could be caught in the action of saluting the Fon with his musket. Like **Figure 13** (and unlike **Figures 14** and **15**) this photograph shows two rather than three spears stuck upright into the ground by the flags. According to Bali opinion in 2004 this absent 'third' spear should be decorated with a ram's mane, and is particularly associated with the Fon. The photographic evidence indicates it has been removed from the ground in the time between the fowl ordeal taking place, and the signal of its successful outcome: the Fon's coming forward to strike the double gong. What might well be a tuft of animal fur is indeed visible around the middle of the shaft of the 'third' spear in **Figures 14** and **15**, and we may see it in **Figure 16** just behind the man with the musket in the left foreground of the photograph.

To judge by the order of original accession, the Basel K-series next returns us to the palace forecourt.

Figure 17 'Interval during Lela dancing in Bali' (BMA K 1542/E-30.27.006): there is little to suggest where this photograph might fit sequentially, although it is full of interesting detail. We are on the plaza, and the palace fencing at the rear is hung with patterned cloth. The shadows have lengthened suggesting it is late afternoon. To the left of the stone pile a group of women face the *lela* flute players. Two of the six women standing with their backs to us wear large buttock covers in the form of lizards decorated with fur; their headgear looks like European straw boaters. The other four women wear smaller aprons. Their finery suggests they may be a party of the Fon's or other dignitaries' wives, or 'princesses', daughters of the palace. In the right background of the picture, a matting enclosure has been erected and is guarded by a couple of soldiers.

Figure 18 'Grassfields – the Bali or Banja area' (BMA E-30.27.007) is a small-format photograph, which entered the Basel collection during 1916 and was accessioned with only a general geographical designation. It has been printed on paper with rounded edges – quite unlike any other pictures of the 1908 Lela – and I noted earlier that its accession followed the return of Jakob Keller from Kamerun. Despite this unpromising provenance, we can be certain from internal evidence that this is a member of the 1908 series. It shows much the same scene as **Figure 17**, albeit taken closer and with the other, compact, camera. Four elaborately dressed women in the left foreground stand in the same relation to one another as they do amongst the six women of the previous photograph (a fifth must stand outside the left-hand frame of the photograph, and the sixth is obscured by the two women in boaters). Facing us to the right of the *lela* flautists are three figures, of whom two – those closest to the stone pile – appear to be women although wearing men's robes. They resemble women elsewhere identifiable as wives of the Fon, and the woman with basin-cut, dark hair may be the Fon's favoured wife (see, BMA E-30.26.034). Close re-examination of **Figure 17** in the light of this image directs our attention to a female figure, standing in the same position but not wearing a gown, who is apparently identical to the woman who wears a gown in **Figure 18**. If they are indeed the same person, then Ankermann may have intended to record the moment when two Bali women were attired in men's gowns to the accompaniment of *lela* flutes and in the presence of other important women. It is a disappointment, then, not to discover mention of such a scene in the published version of his fieldnotes which might explain its significance.

Figure 19 'Procession of people from (*Abmarsch der Leute vom*) the Lela dance' (BMA K 1543/E-30.27.009 & 010):[29] this final photograph in the Basel K-series, which has already been discussed on account of the presence in it of Europeans, is difficult to place because we cannot be sure what the caption writer meant by Lela. If Lela meant the display in the plaza on the first day then we might be looking at the departure of the party *en route* to the ordeal at the river. However, if Lela referred to the ordeal at the riverside then the photograph may depict the party returning to the palace. In that case, the original captions would contrast the *'Aufmarsch'*, of people setting off to the 'ordeal' (**Figure 11**), with the *'Abmarsch'* that was their return. However, Lela might just refer to dancing on any of the days of the celebration. The buildings in the background are almost certainly those of the Basel Mission School (see **Figure 44**, BMA E-30.26.023). We know that these were built near to the palace, but the precise relation between the palace, school and river has proved difficult to reconstruct. The route has been lined by soldiers of Fonyonga's *Basoge* – the Bali irregulars modelled on Hutter's Balitruppe, of whom there seem to be about a hundred. They appear not to be carrying the rifles of the soldiers in **Figure 11**, and the motley character of their European-style uniforms is apparent. Although the figures on the left of the photograph are difficult to make out, I speculated earlier that the couple dressed in white with pith helmets might be Ankermann and his wife, and the tall figure preceding them in a darker jacket and wearing a broad-brimmed hat resembled other portraits of Adolf Vielhauer. Three European hats are just discernible above the heads of the soldiers to the right; presumably they belong to people – whether or not Europeans is impossible to tell – processing from left to right. The cattle in the foreground might well be part of the mission's own herd. My null hypothesis about this photograph would be that it simply recorded the mission party and ethnographer leaving the plaza to return to the mission compound, rather than a stage in the Lela ceremonial in any stricter sense.

Overall, were it not for the original caption to **Figure 19**, we would be hard put to know that it was from Lela ceremony at all. The other photographs we have examined so far clearly do derive from Lela, but only those concerned with the river-side sacrifice are readily placed within the four day ceremony. In 1908, as seven decades later in Malcolm Green's time, three further days were devoted to music and dancing, and to military manoeuvres, much of which activity took place on the plaza. There is no reason to believe that the images Ankermann took of the final day of Lela in 1907 would have differed greatly from what transpired in 1908. So I add them here to represent the final day of the festival.

Figures 20 to **24** (BEM VIII A 5304-8; originally numbered 6 to 11 in Ankermann's notebook, of which number 8 is probably the one missing): again we are looking towards the palace fencing hung with cloths. Contingents of men in Bali dress with muskets are demonstrating military manoeuvres; the Balitruppe is lined up under the trees against the palace fence (**Figures 20, 21**, and **22**). A large group of women is apparent in the left half of **Figure 23**, and they predominate in **Figure 24**. The women may be watching the Fon himself leading the warriors since the tips of covered spear bundles are visible above their heads. This pattern – of women joining the dancing in a celebration that men initiate – is also found in the installation ceremony of 1905 examined in Chapter 4.

Conclusion

Methodologically it might be desirable entirely to separate the written and pictorial evidence of Lela, but this is not wholly practicable. Nevertheless, I have sought to make the photographic record immediately comprehensible, without anticipating the detailed contemporary written record of early twentieth-century Lela performance. The photographs seem to demonstrate a practical convergence of interests during the performance of Lela. Galvanised by Ankermann's presence, the missionaries, presumably with the assistance of the Fon and his palace, cooperated in producing what is by far the most extensive record of any Lela celebration in the early twentieth century.

Sadly, we know almost nothing of the circulation of these images beyond what is reported here. For instance, we lack any evidence for the Lela photographs with which Ankermann returned to Berlin ever being seen beyond the Museum für Völkerkunde (whether through publication, as copies, or as illustrations to lectures). Copies reaching Basel did so directly from Kamerun. As noted already, the Basel Mission published two images from Lela, but we have no grounds to believe that the mission found a wider audience for the record of the ceremony. Given Fonyonga's attachment both to the missionary Ferdinand Ernst and to the German colonial projects of the time, copies were presumably given to the palace. But we do not know this was the case. In short, subsequent circulation of the photographic record as a material artefact remains – so far – a closed book to later investigation. The photographic record can be made to speak to its own times but tells us little, except negatively, about its own subsequent history as a material artefact (prior, that is, to Paul Jenkins's project to make the Basel Archive's collection amenable to analyses such as this).

Bernhard Ankermann had chanced upon Bali at a moment when the relations not just between palace and mission, but also with the German colonial administration, still basked in the afterglow of their most harmonious period. But Hauptmann Hans Glauning was already dead, and Missionary Ferdinand Ernst would not survive home leave the following year. Fonyonga found himself losing control of the African mission community he had encouraged when some of its members began to agitate, amongst other things, against participation in Lela. Although they may not have known it, in 1908 the missionaries, the ethnologist, the Fon and his Bali people were enacting their military manoeuvres and religious rites at the very apogee of Bali power. The fault lines in these relations are more apparent from the textual reflections on the event than they are from its performance.

Notes

1. Mubako is the dialect of Chamba Leko still spoken in the four Bali chiefdoms of the Grassfields other than Bali Nyonga. The names of both languages – Mubako and Mungaka – are explained as deriving from the phrase 'I say that'.
2. A decade earlier von Luschan had himself been described as a skilled photographer interested in photodocumentation of museum collections by a visitor from the British Museum (Edwards 2001: 54, 59–60).
3. The Berlin Ethnologisches Museum's surviving legacy of Ankermann materials is listed in the *Findbuch* of the archival project undertaken by Christine Stelzig (Stelzig & Johannes Röhm 2000: 234–41, and 210–11 for Ankermann's trip to Kamerun). Christine's irreplaceable assistance with this section is particularly acknowledged.
4. Geary examined 542 surviving Ankermann photographs to produce a breakdown of their subject matter (Geary 1986: 98–9). The largest category in her classification is accounted for by 'African elite' (nearly 40 percent); just under 30 percent, consists of '[physical] anthropological portraits'; a fifth of the photographs could be categorised as concerning rituals and belief (10 percent), and artistic activity (under 10 percent). While Geary demonstrates that this last category constitutes a high proportion of Ankermann's collection relative to other photographers of the same area and time, it is perhaps not as high as one might anticipate of a museum-based ethnologist.
5. Ankermann's contemporary, Bronislaw Malinowski, had lately turned to a revised version of A.C. Haddon's article in the 1912 edition of *Notes and Queries* for guidance in his own photographic endeavours (Young 1998: 4, and Note 14).
6. Some indications of Ankermann's photographic work can be deduced from his surviving letters and bills. On 21 December 1907, shortly after photographing the close of the 1907 Lela, Ankermann asked von Luschan for various photographic supplies including 25 dozen 13x18 Agfa-Chromo plates; 12 dozen 9x12 Agfa-Chromo plates; 15 dozen 9x12 Agfa-Chromo packs of flat, cut film (BEM I/MV/798: 54–55). Fritsch noted in 1906 that some travelling cameras allowed the photographer to switch between plates loaded into cassettes and cut film held in metal frames, as well as roll film which we have no evidence of Ankermann using (1906: 805). Ankermann's order was sent by von Luschan to Stegemann on 27 February 1908 and acknowledged two days later. Had all these photographs turned out, these supplies alone would represent 624 shots. It was Ankermann's habit to print at least some of his photographs in the field. On 7 April 1908 he wrote to von Luschan from Bamum asking for 100 sheets each of 13x18 and 9x12 photographic paper (BEM I/MV/798: 106–7). On 10 June 1909, Ankermann despatched two boxes of negatives from Bamenda to Berlin; later that year, and in 1910, there are bills from Johan Nöller for printing 340 13x18 and 318 9x12 photographs on 15 November, and 66 13x18 and 65 9x12 on 16 January 1910 (BEM I/MV/799: 49–50). This makes a total of 789 prints, which is broadly consistent with Schachtzabel's report of 800 photographs repeated above.
7. Presumably, some time since the Second World War, someone working on the collection has ticked off the surviving prints.
8. Striebel has previously been credited as the photographer (Jenkins & Geary 1985: 60–1). But, as its creator Paul Jenkins himself insists, the Basel database should be read as a record of the donors of photographs who need not perforce themselves have been the photographers.
9. Christraud Geary has noted that the Berlin photographs contain no portrait of Ankermann or his wife in the field (1986: 10), so there is no obvious source for comparison.
10. See Jenkins (1996) for an analysis of the political implications of the missionaries wearing local Bali clothing gifted to them by the Fon. Given this understanding of social context and appropriate behaviour, it seems plausible that the missionaries might adapt their European clothing to reflect the gravitas of the events in which they participated, or in this case the association of the first day of Lela with the colour

white. Jenkins (2004) documents the flipside of this: Bali appropriations of European clothing as signs of alliance, or even as signs of their annexation of European power.

11. I have revised my earlier view (Fardon 2004) that Ernst was the likeliest of the missionaries to have been the second photographer, not least because Ernst is not credited in the Archive's database with a single photographic donation to Basel.

12. Observers familiar with European women's dress in African photographs of this period discount the likelihood of Ankermann's wife being the second photographer.

13. Striebel's manuscript contains references to photographs he enclosed with it: after describing the display to either side of the palace entrance he writes 'the accompanying pictures show this' (presumably **Figures 1** and **5**); the scene at the riverside of Fonyonga and his soldiers, Striebel references as 'picture number 5' (see **Figure 11**); finally he refers to 'pictures 7 and 8' in the context of a concluding descriptive passage about the Fon leading his warriors on the plaza (perhaps **Figures 3** and **9**). We cannot know from this that Striebel enclosed only eight photographs; in fact nine photographs were accessioned together under his name. The photographs were subsequently glued onto cards which carry their captions, so the likelihood that they were numbered on the back cannot be checked without affecting their condition.

14. Because they showed the same subject as K1541, in 1913 these photographs were accessioned into the 'Striebel series' as K1541b and K1541c. From seeing the originals, the later two were printed onto different paper from the original Striebel series (and they have deteriorated a little more).

15. Even more obviously than with Lewerenz's photographs, **Figure 18** results from a separate occasion of printing (on paper with rounded corners). The dimensions suggest the photograph was taken on a small-format camera, which would explain how it could have been taken simultaneously with **Figure 17**.

16. The Basel photographic database suggests that these prints also differed in that some were printed on silver gelatine and others on collodian papers.

17. Hans Knöpfli differs from most authors in arguing that the name *ndzi ndob* in Mungaka means not Ndop cloth but cotton cloth. He further argues that both cotton and weaving were introduced to the Grassfields by the Bali. In Mubako, the cloth is called 'death cloth' because of its use to bundle the corpses of royals (Knöpfli 2002: 177–84). It is indeed the case that Chamba preferred cotton shrouds to the skins used by some of their neighbours.

18. Mrs Schultze-Reinhardt appears to have been among the keener missionary photographers to judge by attributions to her in the Basel collection. A shot of the Fon at Lela (with umbrella, oliphant and supporters) may have been taken on the same occasion as **Figure 2** here (see BMA E-30.27.020).

19. This means that when **Figure 2** was taken, in 1909 or 1910, the lion panel was hung with its reverse side on display. Because it is the case in all the photographs I have seen, I assume this arrangement was dictated by a wish that the two animals on the right face one another. In photographs from the 1960s and 1970s, Fonyonga's successor, Galega II, had the tapestries hung left to right in the sequence lion–elephant–tiger behind his throne. Fonyonga's sequence in 1908 was elephant–lion–tiger; but by 1910, he too placed the elephant centrally: tiger–elephant–lion. Knöpfli (1999: 33, Figure 3) reproduces a 1993 photograph of the current Fon enthroned with his feet on a leopard skin and the elephant panel alone pinned to a background of 'King's cloth' behind him. Hence, although it would have suited my argument, I failed to notice in my 2005 essay, 'Tiger in an African palace', that the tiger panel did not achieve its central position until the tapestries were translated into murals by Fonyonga's grandson, Ganyonga III.

20. The tapestries could have been the gift of a trader or labour recruiter, or even a returning labour migrant. Had they been from the mission, Keller might have been expected to mention the fact. Seeing the tapestries first-hand in December 2004 allows me to add descriptive detail to the account I published in 2005. The animals are picked out in yellow and white on a red background; details in black appear to have been

overpainted. The tapestries have a cut pile surface for display, hence a rough outline of the figures also appears on the reverse but without pile or overpainting. At some time after 1910, when it was still possible to display the reverse of the lion panel, the tapestries have been backed with blue material, presumably for reinforcement. Since the prominent red patch on top edge of the elephant panel (visible in 1963) continues under the backing, perhaps these two repairs were done at the same time.

21. Before the 2003 Lela, Buma, a Bali artist to whom I spoke in December 2004, together with a visiting Ghanaian whose name he recalls as Bobo, remodelled the murals, which had been rather crudely retouched in the meantime, among other things doubling the tiger figures on the central panel.

22. Dr Mathew Gwanfogbe recalled the foghorn adding its voice to Lela celebration in the 1950s and perhaps as late as the 1960s; its whereabouts is now unknown.

23. Fonyonga's son, Galega II, was to wear the same gown on his accession to the throne in 1940, as is evident from a photograph taken by Missionary Zürcher in the Basel collection (see **Figure 27**). Retired Sergeant Gaso Fonyonga, one of twelve sons of Fonyonga living at the end of 2004, described this as the most expensive of his father's gowns. The present Fon, HRH Dr Ganyonga III, claims the gown still to be in his possession.

24. Striebel's published account was apparently meant to carry this illustration: there is a reference to our **Figure 5** – 'see the second illustration' (1909: 82, left hand column, at the end of paragraph 2) – at the point where Striebel's manuscript had referred to the photographs of both sides of the entrance. However, neither **Figure 5** nor **Figure 1** appears with Striebel's account which carries two illustrations: **Figure 16** on its first page (1909: 41), and the photograph of Fonyonga in dancing costume (**Figure 3**), which is not specifically referenced in the text and appears on a page following the article (1909: 84).

25. Bali opinion in 2004 also supported this object being a powder horn.

26. The poles are clearly unadorned in 'Front of Fonyonga's Palace' (see BMA E-30.26.041) a photograph taken by Mr. Wilhelm Trautwein between 1902 and 1905. From Trautwein's known movements, Andreas Merz is able to narrow down the dating as shortly after 22 January 1904 (Merz 1997: 193), demonstrating that the beading had been removed soon after the end of Lela that year.

27. Previously published in Schindlbeck (1989: 123, Abb. 125), described as 8.1 x 11.4 centimetres on 'Silbergelatinpapier' (1989: 149). It seems likely that all the surviving Berlin photographs were amongst those printed onto silver gelatine paper immediately after Ankermann's return.

28. This photograph – which has been retouched – also exists as a half tone, having twice been published in *Der Evangelische Heidenbote* as an illustration to accounts of the ceremony by Jonathan Striebel and Jakob Keller. Photograph and cliché are, other than technically, identical; so it is likely that the lost original of K 1536 (**Figure 3**) would also have been close to its surviving half-tone version. (For a contrary example from the Basel Mission Archive – of an engraving differing markedly from its photographic original – see Jenkins & Geary 1985: 60.)

29. The two E-catalogue numbers represent two prints from the same negative which found their way into the Basel archive; the second of them is inferior.

CHAPTER 3

Lela: The Texts, 1890s to 1960s

In skeletal outline, Lela has remained strikingly unchanged during its recorded history. By Lela, reporters usually meant the major ceremony held in late November or early December which lasted several days and had numerous stages, some open to all and others to memberships restricted in one way or another.[1] The earliest indications we possess of the ceremony are to be found in the writings of the first Europeans to live in Bali (Eugen Zintgraff and Franz Hutter, both discussed later); neither of these, however, offers the substantial description of the ceremony that we can gain from the German-speaking Swiss and southern German Presbyterians of the Basel Mission.

The Missionaries' Version 1903 to 1913

So far as I know, three Basel missionaries published accounts of Lela as it was before the First World War. Of these, two were neophytes and one a seasoned campaigner. The archive of the Basel Mission houses the original manuscript versions of all three published texts.

1) Jonathan Striebel's account – based upon having witnessed the 1908 Lela together with Bernhard Ankermann (whom he stood alongside during the Lela sacrifice, as we have seen from the photographic evidence of **Figure 16)** – was published in 1909. The visual testimony to such close collaboration is made the more valuable by Ankermann's presence going unmentioned in Striebel's description.

2) Jakob Keller's account, published in three parts, explicitly drew on his observations between 1910 and 1913 – although Keller had also witnessed Lela before 1907 – and was not published until 1919, after the Basel Mission had been expelled from Kamerun during the First World War. Parts of Keller's account may have been written earlier and subsequently revised for publication. Trained as a baker, Keller had additionally been a missionary since 1890. His experience and position as head of the Bali mission make it likely that shared points of interpretation in the three accounts were initially his.

3) Eduard Lewerenz saw Lela once only in 1911; he published a description of it in the following year.

Keller's is the only one of the three accounts to demonstrate a detailed working knowledge of Mungaka and is much the most comprehensive in its scope. However, the accounts are interesting read together for what they tell us about a developing missionary line in exegesis of Lela. All three missionaries wrote confidently that Lela had lost its inner meaning, and was in the course of losing most of its functions too. But the truth is likely to have been more complex, and missionary participation itself was playing a role in redefining what Lela was and how Bali people thought of it.

Biblical comparisons played a key role in this. Editors at the mission's home in Basel supplied Striebel's early account with a title, 'The secret oracle of the Bali Negroes' in order to compare Lela with the oracle of the King of Babylon, but they otherwise changed it only stylistically in minor respects. Striebel was writing in Keller's absence and does not make the parallels between Bali and Israelite practices to which Keller seems to have been drawn. Keller's own account, which was published with minimal editorial changes under its original title, compared the washing rituals at Lela with the Israelite practice of washing atonement sacrifices. This was not the first time he had drawn the parallel: the mission's published annual report on 1905 (*Jahresbericht* 1906: 87–8) contained an excerpt from Keller's manuscript report to Basel (BMA E-2.20.394, 12 January 1906) under the title 'Eine merkwürdige Sitte in Bali' ('A remarkable custom in Bali') which noted how reminiscent this New Year festival was of the '*Versöhnungsfest*' ('reconciliation festival') of the Israelites. Reference was made to Leviticus Chapter 16, which details the Lord's commandment to Moses to make purification offerings: sending away the scapegoat, bleeding sacrificial animals and putting their flesh in the fire, bathing and wearing fresh vestments.[2] The editors subtly changed Keller's report to accentuate the similarities between Lela and its Israelite counterpart, for instance moving to a censorious conclusion Keller's initial statements about the drinking of palm wine and beer, and the dancing that formed part of the festival. Most significant is the prayer that Keller claimed was pronounced while the King laid his hand upon the sheep's head, 'God, my Father, forgive me all my sins and bless me richly in future with earthly goods (*Gütern*)'. Evidently, much depends upon the close translation that has been given to Fonyonga's words. The 1905 Lela would have been one of the earliest that the missionaries were in a position to witness, and Keller's published note confirms that the mission – both in Kamerun and Switzerland – inclined towards an inclusive reading of Lela, or at least of the sacrificial rite taking place on its first day, from the outset of their relationship with Bali. Heinrich Dorsch's annual report for 1907 (BMA E-2.25.55, dated Bali 21 January 1908 in Keller's absence) introduces events following what he calls the '*Lela-Sühnopfer*' ('Lela atonement offering') virtually without comment, as if this usage would be familiar to the committee receiving his account (transcribed in Merz 1997: 114).

Eduard Lewerenz's account has been the most remarkably transformed by Basel editing. Lewerenz's manuscript (BMA E-2.37.50) is simply entitled 'Das Lelafest der Bali' and makes only generalised reference to the Old Testament parallel already familiar from Keller: 'Little is known with certainty about the origin or meaning of [the Lela] festival, but it seems in several respects similar to the reconciliation festival (*Versöhnungsfest*) of the Israelites.' This comparison was likely to have been encouraged by Jakob Keller who had returned as head of the mission station and countersigned Lewerenz's description before its submission. Lewerenz's published text (1912: 41–3) had mutated into a catalogue of correspondences between Bali and Israelite practices, with point-by-point references to verses in Leviticus Chapter 16. Provided with the title 'Der grosse Versöhnungsfest der Balileute' ('The great reconciliation festival of the Bali people'), the article is also expanded by inclusion of materials from Keller's brief report on 1905 (notably the prayer Fonyonga speaks over the sacrificial animal, which was a cockerel rather than a ram in 1911) and from Striebel (particularly the parallel drawn with the oracle of the King of Babylon in Ezekiel).

How far, one wonders, did these conversations between the missionaries in Kamerun and Switzerland also include Bali interlocutors? And could this conversation have sparked off changes in Bali – and particularly the Fon's – understandings and actions (which, we shall see, were hypersensitive to influences from whomsoever seemed powerful in their environment)? At the prompting, one presumes, of the palace, missionaries consistently set Lela in the context of a decline in Bali's historic power; this, despite their writing when Bali had only recently reached the summit of its influence as a German sub-imperialism. What one wonders, was the influence behind-the-scenes of the Fon's intimate adviser, Missionary Ferdinand Ernst, a man who apparently accepted Bali's broadest claims to power as well-founded, commended to his flock the compatibility between submission to Godly and Kingly power, and taught his schoolboys songs extolling the Fon's power?[3]

Now to look at the missionary accounts of Lela with closer regard to what they tell us about the festival itself. Like many of the Basel missionaries, Jonathan Striebel (**Figure 25** '1907 portrait of Jonathan Striebel', BMA QS-30.001.1243.01) was a skilled manual worker, a weaver. Born in 1879, he had entered the mission in 1902 and been sent to Kamerun in 1908. It was while undertaking his *Sprachstudium*, or obligation to learn a language during his first year abroad, that he stood alongside the ethnologist Ankermann at the fowl oracle during the 1908 Lela (see **Figure 16**). Striebel's account, published in a magazine designed for mission supporters, introduces its subject by remarking an apparent absence of the signs of heathenism confronting the 'young missionary' first walking the streets of Bali. Knowledge of the language permits deeper insight into heathenism, but it remains the case that little of the people's religious life is apparent from their everyday behaviour. The religious '*Kultus*' appears in festivals such as Lela, but even here it is difficult to learn much about the original sources or current meanings of the rites. In a passage that Lewerenz will echo and amend, Striebel writes, 'Little is yet known about the origin and actual meaning of this festival' (1909: 81); neither the mission's school pupils nor the run of people can enlighten him, and those few who are initiates will not do so. This circumstance leads Striebel to conclude that although Lela was originally a religious celebration (*Freudenfest*) over time it has lost most of its religious character. Striebel does not attempt to fill in possible meanings by reference to biblical parallels but provides a description largely based, it seems to the reader, on his observations.

On a night at the end of November or beginning of December, depending on the phase of the moon, around midnight the leader of Lela reddens the stone pile in the middle of the palace plaza with (what Striebel, erroneously according to other sources, believes to be) camwood (*Rotholz*) and announces the inception of Lela by blowing on a large horn. The following day preparations begin: Bali women soak maize to start the process of brewing beer; sub-chiefs bring in palm wine and palm oil as a tax; men carrying palm wine and women carrying comestibles throng the roads into Bali. Two days before the festival begins the Fon slaughters two oxen and several sheep and goats to feed his subjects. On the day of the festival people are summoned to the plaza by a blast on an oliphant. By the stone pile stand several large drums, and Striebel expatiates at some length on how the people abandon whatever task they have in hand to flock irresistibly drawn to dance to the music of the flutes (Striebel 1909: 82, left column, reproduced almost word for word in Keller 1919: 117, left column). The Fon's riches are displayed to both sides of the entrance to the palace. Striebel writes as if he had Ankermann's photographic illustrations before him: to the (viewer's) left is the Fon's stool, to either side of which hang two beautiful pelts decorated with beads (oddly he does not remark that these are cloth simulacra). In front of the stool lie two elephant tusks which serve as horns. Left of the stool are two wonderful figures (Striebel's editor substitutes '*wunderlich*' for the less exoticising '*prächtig*', splendid, of Striebel's manuscript BMA E-2.30, 59). To the right of the entrance hang spears, drinking horns (more likely a powder horn), and decorated posts (*Schmuckgegenstände*). (Here the reader is told to 'see the second picture', evidently a reference to **Figure 5**, although there is no second illustration in the published article's page range. The original manuscript refers the reader simply to pictures.) In the reception rooms of the palace are assembled the great of the kingdom, and within the palace several big pots have been filled with meat.

While the people sing and dance, one of the scouts[4] goes into town to find a white hen (in fact, a cockerel) and a white billy-goat (in fact, a ram). Around midday his Majesty appears in the festival place to be received with tumultuous enthusiasm. The festival procession is now under way: in the vanguard are the scouts with two flags, they are followed by the Fon surrounded by his soldiers. The rear of the procession is made up of other men, each armed with his flintlock. The procession wends its way through the narrow streets and out towards the river (we have already wondered, without being to resolve the question, whether this is what **Figure 19** depicts). The long grass is trodden under foot. The soldiers station themselves near the place prepared for the Fon; one stands as look out, meanwhile a servant holds his umbrella (Striebel's manuscript refers to picture number 5, which I would assume is our **Figure 11**). The scouts have installed themselves a slight distance away; the head priest comes from among them and takes some fetish objects to the nearby river to wash them. The leading people wash, and two men swim in order to fill two calabashes with sand. Meanwhile the head priest has stuck the fetish spear in the ground and everyone gathers around him. He cuts the head off the fowl and leaves it to flap (here the reader is referred to our **Figure 16**). If the fowl jumps around at length, then God has accepted the sacrifice and all is well. When it has bled to death, the head priest divides it and places its innards next to the fetish spear (here Striebel's Basel editor refers his readers to Ezekiel's description of the King of Babylon's oracle). His helper empties the sand from one of the calabashes over the intestines. Water that has filled the oliphant is sprinkled onto the Fon, whereupon the horn is blown. On this signal all the scouts discharge their flintlocks. Electrified, the King rises from his stool and gives the signal to return home. They stop at the compound of the King's mother who gives beer to the scouts. Some try their skill at shooting. After a short pause the King and his company resume their procession and draw near the plaza where people are singing, dancing and shooting as expressions of joy. The oxen killed two days previously are now consumed and, with the exception of the scouts, all go home to recover from their exertions. At dusk the people reassemble to dance by the moonlight.

Early next day (Striebel's editor adds, contrary to evidence of the importance of the first day, 'the main day of the festival'), the trumpet again summons the people together and they go to the river to bathe. Clothes and jewellery are removed. At midday there is a stately procession from the plaza. A halt is made a quarter of an hour outside the town. As on the day before, the grass is trodden down. The King sits on his stool and, with those around him, he consumes a large calabash of beer. Everyone taking part has his weapon to use in war games: some make as if to attack – crawling through the long grass and shaping to shoot – then in the blink of an eye dancing back. Others follow their example. After two or three hours they return. Back on the plaza the festivities reach their highpoint. The King seizes his own flintlock and, positioned at the head of a group of warriors, shows off some elegant footwork as he jumps around the plaza discharging his weapon. The warriors follow his example, cries of rejoicing succeed the guns' discharges. This takes place several times until the chief installs himself by his stool and looks upon his milling subjects with pleasure. (Striebel's manuscript refers here to pictures he numbers 7 and 8; perhaps our **Figure 3** of the Fon in dance costume and **Figure 9** of processing warriors.) Again there is dancing late into the night. There were fewer participants on the third day; the people, Striebel suggests, had had enough; the leader of the festival had found difficulty getting people to dance the previous year (something Striebel must have been told since he was not present in person). The festival ended early on the fourth day thus completing within a week a festival which had once lasted two or three weeks. Striebel concludes on a note of satisfaction: Lela has been losing meaning year by year and, God willing, he hopes that it will soon drop away and with it the chief bulwark of 'heathenism' in Bali (this latter an editorial emendation of Striebel's far stronger manuscript allegation of 'Satanism').

In content and prognosis, Striebel's brief description of Lela concurs with the lengthier description Jakob Keller published a decade later in 1919. Close textual correspondences suggest that Keller even had Striebel's account to hand when composing his own. But this is not to deny Keller's preeminent position as interpreter of the ceremony: Keller had first witnessed Lela three years before Striebel and sent a note based on this experience to Basel in January 1906. Thanks to the publication of that note, as well as to the conversations around the mission station, Striebel is likely to have been briefed on Lela before he witnessed it (as was certainly the case for Ankermann in the same year).

Keller's published account is prefaced by an introduction, itself perhaps a late addition, that provides dates only for Lela between 1910 and 1913. The dates themselves are suggestive. In 1910 and 1911 Lela began on a Monday, and would have lasted until Thursday; in 1912 and 1913 the festival ran from Tuesday to Friday; Ankermann's indications of the closing date of Lela in 1907 and its opening date in 1908 suggest that it occupied Saturday to Tuesday in both years; I have been unable to find dates for 1906 or 1909, but the 1905 Lela also began on a Saturday.[5] This changing weekday correlation seems too regular simply to have resulted from concurrence with Bali criteria (the lunar month and eight-day week).[6] Between 1910 and 1913 the four-day Lela festival never included a Sunday, yet in 1905, 1907 and 1908 it apparently began on a Saturday: as if the second day were deliberately timed to be a Sunday. Was there a move to avoid the Lord's Day out of deference to the mission? If so, the innovation might have resulted from a fracas in 1908 reported by Missionary Rudolf Widmaier (BMA 1909 E-2.30, 57), which involved schoolboys fighting among themselves when those who had taken part in Lela dancing were confronted by those who had not done so. The newly qualified Bali teachers[7] insisted that Christians should not attend the dancing at Lela, although the religious aspects of the festival were apparently of less concern to them. Reflecting, I shall argue later, their different relationships with the palace, the African teachers appear to have been more exercised by participation in Lela than were the European missionaries.

At least when addressing the mission supporter readership of *Der Evangelische Heidenbote*, Keller, like Striebel, considered Lela – in common with Bali's other main festivals – to be losing most of its former religious content and seriousness, an eventuality he explained by a combination of the 'easy-going attitude of Negroes and the frequent changes of settlements by the Bali. The ceremonies have degenerated into merrymaking consisting of eating and drinking, music and dance. Lela lasts longest of these festivities and had the deepest kernel of religious content, which has a certain validity' (1919: 63). Keller claimed the term Lela could not be glossed, and this prevented any conclusion being drawn about the original religious kernel to which he had referred. He concluded nonetheless that the concept of sacrifice was bound up with the meaning of its content.[8]

Keller's ensuing description of Lela adds much circumstantial detail to Striebel's account, particularly about the material culture of the event and some aspects of its terminology (all of which I leave in his transcription). Keller begins by evoking the preparations for Lela: once the King has decided to inaugurate Lela, the women are told to 'moisten the maize' and beer brewing begins. At midnight when the new moon waxes, the 'chief of Lela' reddens the pile of stones (or 'speaking platform') in the palace plaza with camwood pulp [more likely kaolin] and beats a large carved drum. With him are four stave bearers who beat small drums. All pray to God putting men's curses before him to adjudicate which are just. Then final preparations are in hand for Lela: foreign chiefs arrive with gifts to the Bali King, beer brewing is completed, palm wine brought in, animals killed to feed the crowds. Organised by residential quarter, the King's subjects renew the matting fence around his palace and smooth the plaza. The fence is draped with blue and white fabrics ('ndzi ndob', cloth from the Ndop plain, north-east of Bamenda), and the entrance ornamented with European carpets with woven animal figures: elephant, tiger and lion. Posts symbolising kingly rule, surmounted with three to six protuberances, stand to the right of the palace entrance, and these are decorated with beads in which lizards are picked out in special colours. A similar post, about three metres high, is erected for decoration by the stone piles in the middle of the plaza. During the festival, a bead-covered stool is placed to the left of the palace entrance, where the King normally sits; there is also a peculiar box here: the foghorn of a sailing ship gifted by a European which has been added to the royal treasury, the growl of which heightens people's joy during their merrymaking.[9] The German flag, inscribed with 'Fonjonge', flutters on a tall post during Lela days alongside the white flag of Bali. Nearby are four staves ('song ntsöng') planted in the ground by their iron ferrules. These have symbolic importance: two of them terminate in peculiarly wrought iron decorations and are carried into war next to the flags. The other two are wooden, their iron points covered with part of the mane of a ram. These are the 'fu' medicine staves. 'Perhaps, according to heathen animistic conceptions, they are the seat of the secret deity which is supplicated through the ceremony of Lela to assure victory in the next war. Lela was previously celebrated without surrounding ceremony when marching into war' (1919: 66).

On another part of the plaza are locally-made, beaded calabashes and decorated European pottery and porcelain, as well as a gramophone which has been added to the royal treasures. The town elders who earlier had supervised preparations and beer drinking now reappear in their festival dress of pleated burnous ('tope'). Young people appear, flintlock in hand, wearing war attire ('vandara' a shirt with short, wide sleeves, and a fantastical hat with long hen and bird feathers). Clowns ('bagwe') make the people laugh. 'One finds oneself at a summit of foreign, *echt* African, heathen life' (1919: 66).

Keller introduces the main part of the festivities with the now familiar reference to Leviticus and atonement. In the afternoon of the inception, the King appears in a white toga carrying a white cockerel or leading a white ram (these animals must be male and alternate year on year). Surrounded by his male subjects only, he hands over the sacrificial animal and receives a calabash of water, kneels in front of the threshold and murmurs over the water,

> All evils that have happened in the town during the last year be expiated [*sühnen*], all curses ('ndon') which lie heavily upon us be done away with. Good fortune be ours in the new year, plenty of food and the blessing of many children. All evil and every type of sickness that has reached here, turn around and get on its way. (Keller 1919: 78)

Water is poured thrice into the channel in the threshold. Once the King would have spoken words over the water to departing warriors,

> Go out to war for me. God grant that the eyes of the enemy be blinded while yours remain clear. Come back as victors! (Keller 1919: 79)

Then, as previously described by Striebel, the procession leaves to the river: the boys holding mock battles with grass spears, the King's bodyguard wearing fantastically feathered headdresses, the two flags ('titnan') swung in front of the King. Others carry the magic staves ('song ntsöng'); then come the sacrificial animals, spearmen and musketeers. The King strikes, what Keller describes as a peculiar bell-like iron instrument (a double gong), which he tells us is acknowledged to have been the cult instrument typical of heathen Kameruners from ancient times. Its single-tone, clanging sound signifies one's presence at a very holy rite: a standing in self-judgement before the deity to see how things stand between them, and finally through sacrifice gaining the deity's goodwill, assistance, victory and blessing. This deep significance may have been the foundation of the ceremony, but for people today the clanging of the hand gong ('mukongkong') may hold only the significance of pealing bells for us.

Keller's description of washing the staves adds little to Striebel's (although Keller insists, contrary to the photographic evidence from 1908, that the iron staves are not washed lest they rust). 'The uninitiated are not allowed to watch this washing ceremony, but they do not dare refuse the watching European. After this purification (*Reinigung*), other elders bathe to show that their sins are taken away and a newer, purer part of life begins' (1919: 79). Sand from one of the calabashes is daubed in stripes of equal width onto the iron ferrules of the flags and staves, and over these some maize meal is sprinkled. The other calabash of sand is returned to the palace to be sprinkled over the threshold during the year for other cult ceremonies. The beautiful elephant tusk is washed and filled with water which is splashed against the king.

Next the sacrifice is offered: the fowl is made to drink and is washed before cutting off its head. Should its fluttering be prolonged this is a good omen. Should the sacrifice have been a ram then the stomach contents are daubed on the staves and on the sacrificers, and more of the same is used to bleach the ram's mane, which is used to cover the points of the spear bundles. The sacrificial meat is placed on the fire and eaten before reaching home. On the passage homewards, the procession stops for refreshment at the King's mother's compound and feasts on the King's plaza; then begins the Lela dance.

The following day people reassemble in the plaza around midday and join a procession to a place a quarter of an hour out of town. Simulated warfare takes place (although 'now' – since the government banned importation of gunpowder – there is only the occasional shot whereas previously there was cacophony). Returning to the plaza, the King himself dances and discharges his musket at the head of his troops. He exchanges his warrior's costume for costly robes and everyone, attired in their finest, dances. For women this means either striped cloth aprons, or beaded aprons consisting of a bottom half of strung beads and a stiff upper half on to which beads have been sewn in patterns (stars and rosettes); some of the last type include a small round mirror in which the following dancer is able to watch her own elegant movements with great pleasure. 'Lela is now become a pure fancy dress or costume festival' Keller observes sniffily (1919: 117 left). There are necklaces, belts, sashes, knee bands and to European observers the comic and ridiculous: one year the King's wives wore German infantry helmets back to front; the head wife donned a white cuirassier's helmet; another wore blue glasses. Dancing and singing continue to exhaustion. Keller reaches his conclusion.

Such rejoicing and dancing used to last eight to ten days, but thanks to political and missionary influences the festival has lost some of its meaning, so that recently it has been completed in four to six days. With the passage of time, some of the inner content has been lost. The several moments of religious truth that it hitherto contained, have been pushed into the background and given way to complete abandonment in enjoyment and good living. In recent years even the King has no longer attended the offering of sacrifices. Outwardly and inwardly the old Bali grandeur is paling. New times, with European and other influences, knock too strongly on the door of old heathenism in Bali and overcome it. (Keller 1919: 118)

Aside from the corroboration it adds to our previous textual and photographic record – for instance with respect to the hanging cloths and foghorn in the treasure display (**Figure 2**) or the costumes worn by the Fon's wives (**Figures 17** and **18**), Keller's version is interesting for its 'editorial' line. Although Keller suggests in places that Lela was originally a martial rite preceding war, the significance he claims it to have lost is hardly related to its military function at all. Instead he detects a kernel of religious truth in sacrifices made to the deity, and he invokes concepts of sin, self-judgement, expiation and purification to explain how the ceremonial achieves its aims. This may not simply be an outside construction placed upon the event, Lela practice and understanding might itself already have been moving in a 'christianised' direction: having absorbed so many other influences why not this too? However, the immediate effect of Keller's reading is to render the more hedonistic and materialistic aspects of Lela both recent and degenerate. Beaded calabashes and oliphants may be described positively, but the foghorn and gramophone, decorated European china, and most of all the women's taste in military headwear and glasses are described as absurd features of those influences 'knocking on the door' of Bali's 'heathenism'.

Eduard Lewerenz, described in Basel records as a mechanic from Berlin, remained in Kamerun until the outbreak of war when he was interned. For reasons already adumbrated, his account may best be treated as a pendant to Keller's; of the three missionary authors, he adds the least by way of substantive detail to our knowledge of the event. However, we do learn from Lewerenz that Fonyonga was absent from the Lela sacrifice because of ill-health in 1911.[10] In common with Striebel and Keller, Lewerenz claims that the contemporary ceremony is reduced from a previous eight days; that it has lost much of its original meaning; and that this ceremony is waning. His Basel editors supplied detailed biblical reference to Lewerenz's text, echoing the citation of Leviticus 16 that had struck Keller. Analogies are pursued point-by-point with references to Leviticus on washing, clothing, the bleeding of the sacrifice, and the burning of the offering, as well as the scapegoat. The biblical reference Basel editors supplied Striebel is also echoed, 'At the parting of the ways where the road divides, the King of Babylon will halt to cast lots with arrows, consult household gods, and inspect the livers of beasts' (Ezekiel 21, 21). The upshot of taking omens was that the King of Babylon sent his 'command for slaughter' down the road to Jerusalem, which is in keeping with Striebel's relatively untheological gloss on the Lela ceremony. But these ramifications of the reference are not pursued in the Lewerenz's text. Instead, the Bali are cast as Israelites fallen away from their previous beliefs.

These accounts by Basel missionaries were written up for publication over a short period (between 1908 to 1918 at most), the first two just prior to and the third during the First World War. Although Keller was absent from Bali during Striebel's *Sprachstudium* in 1908, his early notes on the ceremony would nonetheless have been available; by the time of Lewerenz's *Sprachstudium*, Keller had returned as mission head; hence, we may expect to detect the influence of the older man in all three accounts. Read together, they suggest a preferred missionary understanding of Lela framed in terms of sin, sacrifice and purification. The military element of Lela was acknowledged, but missionaries believed it had declined and would continue to do so. More troubling were the drinking, dancing, and the material display: especially the apparently boundless appetite for novelty. This was portrayed as degenerate, or mildly ludicrous, or both. As we shall see, reading the sacrificial elements of Lela in christian terms was to become acceptable to Bali Presbyterians and Catholics in the later twentieth century, while the other elements of performance were shifted into the register of tradition (admitting, just as previously, a range of innovations thereby).

Following the internment of those missionaries in station when Kamerun was invaded, a hiatus in Basel missionary activity in Bali would ensue until 1926: a period of roughly the same duration as that of their preceding Bali mission, but about which we are able to say much less. Post-First World War resumption of Basel Mission activity saw renewed efforts to make the Bali language, Mungaka, a lingua franca of the Presbyterian church in the Grassfields. Ferdinand Ernst had pioneered such attempts before the war: an orthography and grammar had been put in place by 1905, and a Bali Primer published the following year. In 1915, a Mungaka translation of Bible stories became available. But it was not until 1933 that a New Testament translation was completed (Dah 1983: 301–2 for the remarkable contribution towards this of Adolf Vielhauer; see also Vielhauer 1951, Lima Sema 1988: 132–3). An extensive Mungaka–English dictionary was a protracted and collective labour: a dictionary was originally compiled in manuscript by Reverend Georg Tischhauser during the 1930s (drawing upon Ernst's foundational Mungaka–German work) and subsequently revised after 1986 by Reverend Johannes Stöckle with the help of Bali scholars and informants (Tischhauser 1993). The meanings of especially troublesome Bali words must have been debated extensively during this prolonged gestation. Lela is defined as '1) feast of redemption beginning of December; 2) dance after redemptive action' (1993: 161), which is a terse fulfilment of the thrust of Basel missionary thought in the early part of the century. Unlike Keller, who stated that the origin of the term Lela was lost, the dictionary correctly identifies the immediate source as the word for bamboo flute. This is the meaning of *lera* or *lela* in Chamba Leko: beyond which in etymological terms the name may simply be onomatopoeic.

The most substantial documentation of Lela by Basel missionaries in the mid-twentieth century derives from Tischhauser himself and from Wilhelm Zürcher, who took a series of photographs of a Lela festival some time during the 1930s.[11] The photographs add little to our knowledge of the festival, although one of the captions suggests continuity in the tradition of missionary exegesis, 'With this sacrifice [of cockerel or ram] they seek reconciliation with the deity and ask for power, success, health and protection from all evil … [Of the medicine staffs] It is believed they are the dwelling place of the deity on whom they call' (caption to BMA E-30.85.248). Tischhauser's typed notes on Lela in German and Mungaka (apparently belonging to a series of notes on Bali customs) are dated 20 December 1975, around the time of Lela, and carry the sub-title 'der grosse Versöhnungstag', the great day of reconciliation or atonement, a title familiar from the 'Versöhnungsfest' of Lewerenz's 1912 account, and with equally familiar reference to Leviticus 16, as well as to Leviticus 23, 27, 28 (BMA E-10.54, 17). The first day of Lela, according to this account, is a day to dispel guilt and curses from the town and people. Tischhauser's account conveys familiar detail about the sacrifice of the white fowl, and a description which suggests that the Lela posts with three or four horns had by his time been moved inside the Fon's palace, and only the forked poles were erected in the plaza. Perhaps the most interesting aspect of the text is the fact of its translation into Mungaka; however, I defer consideration of later twentieth-century reflections on Lela by the Bali educated elite until my conclusion.

Why had missionary interest in Lela intensified around 1908? Circumstantial considerations suggest two likely reasons. Immediate causes were: the death of Ernst, who had been the main channel through which the mission pursued its dealings with the Bali palace during the first five years of the mission, which shifted responsibility for relations with their royal host on to other missionaries; and perhaps the interest that Ankermann had taken in the 1907 and 1908 Lela festivals, just before Ernst's death, which persuaded the missionaries that this was a topic on which they might pen their own accounts: maybe even pre-empting the ethnologist's. Ferdinand Ernst had not himself been a frequent contributor to mission magazines, and his departure from the scene left others to write of those local customs about which he had known most. However, the broader context concerns the political order and its rituals: how to square and to dramatise the aims of palace, mission, emergent colonial elites and colonial regimes, each pair of which had the potential to run in complementary or oppositional directions or, indeed, both at once. We shall return to these issues but first need to address unfinished business with the 1908 Lela.

The Ethnologist's Version 1907 to 1908

What of the ethnologist? As it transpired, Ankermann himself published nothing whatsoever about Lela. However, it has already become apparent that written and pictorial accounts of Lela before the First World War were intimately related and hence, even if we are left guessing about details, we may be sure that our witnesses collaborated and discussed their thoughts both with one another and with some of their key Bali informants. Ankermann and his wife, who were apparently known to some of the missionaries from Berlin, were accommodated within an existing framework of relations: they lived in the mission (where a small new house had been built to await their arrival), they were taught Mungaka by the missionaries (primarily by Ferdinand Ernst and Heinrich Dorsch), and they wrote down stories told them by the mission's Bali students, as well as making audio recordings of their singing. Much of Ankermann's information came from the missionaries rather than from Bali informants. Not only was he summoned for the beginning of the 1908 Lela by Ernst's letter, but numerous accounts of local customs in Ankermann's fieldnotes were related to him by missionaries: including, in Vielhauer's case, a long letter sent to Berlin in answer to queries. Ankermann's access to the palace must have used the missionary channels which Ernst maintained. Tracing what influences his sources of information might have had on his conceptions is made difficult by the paucity of Ankermann's publications. We know that the missionaries' published accounts were written for a readership of mission supporters, but Ankermann wrote next to nothing for publication about his Kamerun research: his fieldwork report is predominantly a chronology of things done, and the brief paper on religion supplies only meagre generalisations about the Grassfields region as a whole. Ankermann's detailed observations of Lela come from the posthumous edition of his (lost, original) fieldwork notes I mentioned earlier.

Like the missionaries, Ankermann's interest was attracted primarily by the first day of the ceremony. This is not accidental since his notes briefly outline the events of the 1907 Lela (of which, recall, he missed all but the repeated last day) as retold by Missionary Ferdinand Ernst. In 1907 there had been a ram sacrifice at the river carried out by the King himself, who slit open the ram's belly with a small knife allegedly once belonging to Gawolbe, the leader of the united Bali, and tore out its stomach and then its heart and lungs. Ankermann also learns of the prominence of the *ba-gwe* (scouts and fools) who are licensed to steal during Lela in commemoration of their valour when the Bali left their homeland. Ankermann's description of the 1908 Lela accords in detail with the photographic record that Striebel sent to Basel: as if his text (like Striebel's) had been written with photographs to hand.

By 11 a.m. a crowd had gathered on the plaza; the *lela* orchestra (consisting of four flutes and three drums) was playing around the stone pile (perhaps **Figures 7, 8** and **9** if these are not of the second day). Ankermann notes the King's stool by the palace gate (**Figure 1**) and the various poles: two beaded poles with knobs hung with bags of entire leopard skin (**Figure 5**), two posts surmounted with animal images (**Figure 4**), and the two staves with ornamental iron tips (which he sketched). Ankermann went ahead of the procession to the river, but the party did not reach him until 2.30p.m. At its head came scouts and youths whose task it was to flatten the grass; there followed men in tall feather headdresses with flintlocks (**Figure 10**), then a boy with a fowl, Fonyonga, the two flags, nine spear bundles, the two staves with iron ornaments, and one of the beaded poles. Fonyonga wore a white robe and carried what Ankermann correctly identifies as not an iron but copper double gong. The soldiers brought up the rear. The King's stool was set on a leopard skin between the path and the river, and Fonyonga sat down. To his right stood his soldiers; to his left squatted men in feather headdresses; behind him were the spears (*kong so*); an umbrella was held over his head (**Figure 11**).

Not far from the river, a small area was cleared by the *ba-gwe*. Here the two flags and the staves with iron ornamentation were planted in a row: behind them lay the white fowl, and in front the two empty calabashes. The flags, staves and King's ivory horn were taken to the water, and the staves and horn washed while the flags were laid upon the bank and simply sprayed with water (**Figure 12**). With the items replaced, the King descended to the cleared area and sat. There followed the fowl sacrifice as previously described. Feathers were stuck into the wrappings and lower ends of the flags. Some pinion feathers were stuck upright in the ground in front of the flags. The fowl was put in a bag by a *gwe*, and water was poured in front of the standards. A number of the men made an attacking movement (in the direction of the pool above the river where the men had bathed) and returned to the chief who struck the copper double gong with which he gestured towards them (**Figures 13 to 16**). Ankermann notes the local term for these actions ('loti ne ndikan') which were repeated three times. Tischhauser's Mungaka dictionary defines *ndikan* as gun; *lo 'ti* (pronounced *lə'ti*), discussed in the next paragraph, roughly means salute. Little further detail emerges from Ankermann's brief description of the Lela party's return via the *Ma Mfon*'s (Queen Mother's) compound.

On the following day (29 November 1908), the King and his men set out in the direction of Batibe in what Ankermann describes as 'loti' style. Looking in more detail to Tischhauser's dictionary, the Mungaka noun *lo 'tì* means 'display, parade in front of a chief (firing guns along with a pantomime of war)'; the verb *lo 'ti* is presumably a cognate form since it means 'to present oneself before the chief as a kind of faithful submission; also at funerals as a sign of faithfulness to the deceased' (Tischhauser 1993: 170). Another verb, a homophone of the previous, receives a separate entry though it might have a related sense, 'to comfort, strengthen, calm, make happy'. 'Loti', as Ankermann must recognise in citing it among the few Mungaka terms in his description that are not simply names of things, is a term of art in relation to Lela. The senses of *lo 'ti* and *lo 'tì* recorded in Tischhauser and Stöckle's dictionary are the same as those entered in Ernst's first vocabulary (of which a copy is preserved in Basel) a text which would have been available to Ankermann. The term continues to appear in its Mungaka form in later, locally authored, English language accounts, an indication those writers feel something would be lost by its translation. Ankermann notes how, in earlier times, the war party sent out after Lela would always leave in the direction taken by this procession on the second day. Dancing ensued at midday on the second day of Lela.

The editors of Ankermann's papers could find no account of the third day, and their description of the fourth day is taken from Ankermann's account of the additional (fifth) day of Lela performed for him on 11 December 1907 (**Figures 20 to 24**). This would have been the first occasion on which Ankermann saw the matting-lined plaza in front of the palace hung with blue and white cloth, the stone pile, the King's stool with its backrest formed from two human figures and its leopard caryatid. A few wooden stools were set out for Europeans present (another indication that Europeans were as much a fixture for Lela as the rest of the material display). Ankermann describes the two 'leopard skins' ornamented with beads that we recognise from the 1908 photographs, but asks himself in a parenthesis, '(genuine or cut to shape?)'. The pair of large, beaded posts, each with four horns were also present in 1907, and Ankermann describes them elsewhere (Baumann & Vajda 1959: 243–4): their covering of cylindrical beads was composed of a red ground against which lizards were picked out; between these were diamond patterns, and the horns of the post were decorated in blue and white. Every 'big man' had such posts but with smaller horns than the King's. The King himself explained that they served as somewhere to lean the spear, or hang the knife, of anyone who came to the palace with a palaver. Because more people came to him than to other 'big men', his horns had to be bigger.[12] These posts were prepared newly for each Lela; Ankermann saw an old, undecorated pair in a corner of the palace; he records simply that the posts are called 'tu nganged' (according to Tischhauser's Mungaka dictionary, *tu* means tree, pole etc; 'nganged' might be *ngangyed* meaning bow: hence, perhaps, a pole for hanging bows and arrows). Together with these poles, Ankermann enumerates the spear bundles with their leather or bead ornamented covers, several large ivory horns and fly switches, one of them with a bird-headed handle. The opposite corner of the plaza – of which we apparently have no close-up photographs from 1908 (although this may be the enclosure visible at distance to the right of **Figure 17**) – was occupied by a fenced enclosure to contain the two flags (one white and one German imperial tricolour) and a pair of reddened, forked wooden posts with carved decoration, as well as a table with a collections of bead-covered calabashes and other valuables belonging to the King. Ankermann remarks that the forked poles were crudely carved with what struck him as indicating a head with protruding horns. Fonyonga tells him that these poles (**Figure 26**) must be set up at the beginning of a reign else the new King incur the curse of his father; they remain until the King dies (Baumann & Vajda 1959: 244). At the top of the square stood soldiers in khaki uniforms wearing Prussian helmets.

The festivities (**Figures 20** to **24**), which started at around 4p.m. and lasted for two hours, began with what Ankermann describes as an imitation battle (**Figures 20** to **22**). To the accompaniment of *lela* flutes, oliphants and drums, individuals or groups of warriors approached the corner of the plaza where the flags flew, fired their flintlocks and then returned. A blast on the oliphants signalled the emergence of the King from his palace to take part in the dance. The simulated charges now multiplied. The King, like some of his companions, wore an extraordinary feather headdress of cockerel and parrot feathers (like that depicted in **Figure 3** from the 1908 Lela). Next the women joined the dance. The King stayed by the stone pile with his small following, while groups of warriors formed rows, organised into ten town wards according to Ankermann's informant Missionary Dorsch. Mock fights alternated with single file processions around the plaza.

Eventually the warriors and women retreated to the edges of the plaza and the soldiers formed a circle in the middle of the plaza to fire off a salvo 'to German commands!' (Baumann & Vajda 1959: 265): an element of the festival that may, as we shall see shortly, have a specifiable origin. The King himself stepped forward, spoke a few words, and went to the pile of stones, where drummers were seated. The King and three notables then played the *lela* flutes while a single woman danced in front of him and another carried his train. The other women and warriors danced around him (**Figures 23** and **24**). Having reformed at the other end of the square, the soldiers discharged a further volley, at which the dancing ended. The King returned to the palace, changed clothes and reappeared in a tall red cap to stand before the gate smoking a cigar. Containers of palm wine were brought out from the palace and divided among the people who squatted in groups on the plaza and drank out of horns and gourd cups. Of the corresponding phase of the festival in 1908, Ankermann records only that the ceremony ended on the fourth day when the flags were returned to the palace in the evening. Dancing continued in smaller numbers for a few days, and he notes that during the four days sexual contact is forbidden.

As the reconstructed circumstances of Ankermann's research would have us suppose, there is a close correspondence between Ankermann's text and the photographic record annexed to the Basel Mission by Jonathan Striebel. Ankermann clarifies what was occurring in the photographs, and he answers some questions about the material culture of the event. However – to judge by the edited version of his subsequently lost fieldwork notes, which is our only source – he enquired little about what the festival might mean to local participants, and his ethnological priorities left him uncurious about the personnel involved. Other than Fonyonga, the King, only the European missionaries appear as named individuals rather than categories. For a very different, and very practical, sense of Lela's significance, we need to look back to the earliest descriptions of Lela.

The Soldier's and the Trader's Version 1889 to 1896

To the best of my knowledge, the only observer to record his impressions of Lela prior to Keller in 1905 was the artillery lieutenant, Franz Hutter, whom Zintgraff had brought to Bali to train a local soldiery in the aftermath of the mauling taken by a combination of expeditionary and Bali forces at the hands of Mankon and Bafut. As the mission's superintendant Eugen Schuler noted in his report of the very first Basel Mission visit to Bali, by mid-November 1903 Bali had been in direct contact with Europeans for fourteen years (Schuler et al. 1903: 191). By the 1908 Lela, the relationship was in its twentieth year: ample time for some accommodation to have been made to European sensibilities and expectations within the Lela ceremony, and for Bali to incorporate whatever potentials they perceived in some European material culture. How had Lela changed during this period?

Eugen Zintgraff had reached Bali for the first time on 16 January 1889 and, between his travels, was based there for much of that year initiating the early alliance between Bali and German imperialisms. At this point, Fon Galega I may have considered himself the more powerful of the two. Zintgraff's description of his column's first entry into Bali town sketches a scene similar to that in our later photographs: surrounded by its matting fence, the palace ran the length of an extensive plaza. To the (observer's) right of the palace entrance was a large assembly house open to two sides, and in the centre of the plaza a three-pronged pole was inserted into the stone pile. Lela must have occurred a month or so earlier, and so the palace fences would still have been in good condition. When Zintgraff was driven by rain into the assembly house, he met Galega's two oldest sons: Tita Nji and Tita Mbo (the future Fonyonga). Awaiting finalisation of his arrangements to continue northwards, Zintgraff came to realise the strategic importance of establishing a station in Bali. Once such an agreement was established by oath, Galega decided to publicise the impending presence of the white man in his town. As epitomised by Sally Chilver from Zintgraff's accounts, the events that ensued suggest striking parallels with some stages of Lela.

> People streamed in to the dance, for which hundreds of calabashes of wine were brought in by slaves. The general summons was given by ivory horns which were used to call the Bali to dance and to war. Garega [Galega] sat on a stone [i.e. throne stone], Zintgraff near him. The two hornblowers were on the left. Next to him was the Bali cloth of white native cotton, flown on a long lance, and the German red, white and black standard given by Zintgraff. These were with a guard of honour and nobody might approach the ground on which they stood. On the left of Garega stood his armed servants leaving a space free at the gate to the palace and round the flags. (Chilver 1966: 5)

This, presumably, would have been the first occasion on which Bali and German flags fluttered side by side in the guarded enclosure on the plaza: as they would for another two and a half decades.[13] What followed might well have described the climax of Lela around the same period: the King arose, bare-chested, cutlass on his left flank, holding his decorated dane gun, surrounded by trusted retainers,

> Towards him came first his own warriors, led by the eldest officer, while his retainers leapt forward and placed themselves in front of him. Guns and spears were swung and presented. The advancing party proclaimed their courage, pounding their chests. In answer, Garega's bodyguard shook their feather-crowned heads violently. There was a threefold rush back and forth and this time they took the chief between them and marched with him with long warlike strides till a halt was made in the middle of the marketplace. The hitherto confused crowd now divided itself into two long rows, with left knee bent, the right leg stretched out, guns raised and ready to spring. Some detached themselves, pretending to fight an imaginary enemy. Here and there shots rang out: cutlasses were drawn and imaginary enemies beheaded ... Now they came forward to greet the chief. (Chilver 1966: 5)

However they were organised at different times in Bali history, these wargames and salutes were a recurrent expression of the solidarity between the Fon and his contingents of troops. The incorporation of the Fon as both recipient of and participant in the military manoeuvres appears to have been a stylised feature of all such occasions.

After this auspicious beginning, Zintgraff returned to Bali with four other Europeans in December 1890. Led by scouts, warriors and a German flag, together they embarked upon the ill-fated attack on Mankon. To signal its willingness to fight, Mankon (Bandeng in Zintgraff's account) raised its own white flag (Chilver 1966: 26), and when the Bali initially overran the Mankon position, the German tricolour was stuck into Mankon's stone pile (Chilver 1966: 27), which suggests that a military syntax of flags and stone heaps had become diffused at least among Bali and its neighbours prior to direct European contact. The later stages of operation, however, degenerated into fiasco and humiliation for the Bali and

German forces. As a direct response, June 1891 saw the arrival of Leutnant Hutter with 2,000 M71 Mauser single-shot breechloaders to arm a Balitruppe; quickly trained to Hutter's satisfaction, they began to carry out punitive operations in the area.

In 1891, the 'Leda' dance – the great festival of arms of the Bali (*Waffenfest*) as Hutter describes it – began on 5 December (1902: 204–5, 431–4). Early that day a troop of warriors had waylaid two Bandeng (Mankon) men, which was a source of great joy. The Bali had already cut the head off one of them, and the same fate awaited the other at the great dance the following day. A 'howling, yelling, mob' brought the head to show it off at the German 'station': a liana had been threaded through the mouth and throat and the head swung back and forth; dripping with blood, the skull was hung in a tree and a war dance took place. That evening Hutter and Zintgraff went to Galega to ask for the release of the second prisoner but, when the latter failed to respond to questions, Fonte (a close friend of Galega's and apparently a blacksmith) unsheathed his knife and cut the man's ear off 'because the Bandeng understands so badly what the white says, it is necessary to cut off his ear so that he hears better …' (1902: 205). The next afternoon Hutter marched over with his own platoon to the dance; there were three thousand warriors there and delegations from Bagam and 'Bafuen' (Bafreng/Nkwen). Hutter's men discharged seven platoon salvos, and there was a murmuring among the assembly that this would be known in Mankon and Bafut the following day. The Bali and German flags flew over the stone throne of Galega. In addition to the (by now) two Bandeng skulls was a third, already eight days old. (Hutter did not eschew such trophies himself since he records in May 1892 that he had his troops present him with five right hands and a couple of skulls, 1902: 210.)

Returning to the subject of the 'Ledafest' and 'Ledatanz' later in his book, Hutter ties their timing to the ensuing grass-burning at the beginning of dry season which clears the way for the passage of arms: 'the dry season is also the war season' (1902: 431). It was Hutter who provided the yardstick by which later commentators were to claim that Lela had been truncated in their times: he tells us that both the Lela and Voma festivals lasted a week (Hutter 1902: 431), meaning presumably an eight-day Bali week, given later reference to the paraphernalia remaining in place until the following 'Bali-Sunday'.

The festival begins the Bali-Sunday[14] after the king espies the new moon when he leads an entourage to the river in order to wash the standards, his people and himself (Hutter puts 'wash' in inverted commas and glosses it as both 'cleaning' and 'atonement' [*Entsühnen*]). Hutter is told by Galega that the men who fell in war were remembered at this time, while Fonte confides in him that if the ceremony were not held many Bali would die in the next battle, but holding it correctly means the enemy will fail to kill any of them (1902: 428). This washing had to occur as the sun reached its zenith or else the blessing would turn into a curse (not something that later accounts reveal: indeed the 1908 party did not reach the river until mid-afternoon). Some of the water was brought back to the town in great bowls and poured on the threshold of the palace, on the houses, and on the paths to and from the plaza in order to keep evil influences at bay.

Parts of the paraphernalia of the Lela ceremony were very similar to that in use seventeen years later. Hutter describes a three-pronged post by the entrance to the palace (and this, or one like it, is illustrated in his Figure 46 facing page 348; it appears undecorated but the quality of the plate is too poor to be certain). The same illustration shows the stone throne on which Galega sat during the Lela festival (Hutter 1902: 432), confirming that the decorated, Grassfield style, stools of the 1908 Lela are later additions to the royal treasure. The single post was hung with spear bundles and a quantity of old skulls, augmented by new ones, should a war party have been successful (as we know was the case in 1891). A second holy pole, stuck into the stone pyramid in the middle of the plaza, was 'antler-shaped'; presumably this is the forked *letya*; it also is described as hung with spear bundles and skulls. Hutter's illustration of one of the two sacred spears is different in a number of respects from those photographed in 1908 (1902: 431). This may be simple inaccuracy (his illustrations of musical instruments might – charitably – be described as only approximate), however there is another likelihood: Sally Chilver's interviews with Lela officials (reported in the next section) reveal that one of the spears is a genuine heirloom while the other was said (in 1963) to be broken and replaced with another newly fashioned in each reign. Between 1891 and 1908, Galega had indeed been succeeded by his son.[15]

The 1891 war games were instigated by the King in wardress at the head of his palace guard, and then taken up by his sons leading two masses of warriors. The giant Tita Nji embraced the manoeuvres, and subsequent drumming, with manic energy, launching one of the spears from his spear bundle a considerable distance in the direction of his father into a roof. The other wing was led by Tita Mbo. This reflected real warfare since Galega's senior sons had led the wings of the army in the 1890 attack on Mankon reported by Zintgraff. Tita Nji, said to be the bravest of the Bali warriors, was to die before Zintgraff returned with Max Esser to Bali in 1896. Commentators had feared that he and Tita Mbo, the future Fonyonga II, would clash over the kingship on their father's death. Tita Mbo had been his father's favoured candidate and contemporary opinion, for instance Hutter's, that Tita Mbo was the most intelligent and courteous of Bali men, would suggest that Galega's sense of the qualities required to cope with changing circumstances was shrewd.

Musketry was much in evidence in 1891, but it could not always have been thus. Oral traditions relate that the Bali entered the Grassfields as mounted bowmen, and it is likely that they adopted firearms in substantial numbers only after the defeat at Bafu Fondong and the loss of their cavalry. This must have brought about a change in their organisation and, correspondingly, a change in Lela. From Jean-Pierre Warnier's researches (1980) we learn that firearms reached the Grassfields from about the mid-nineteenth century. Originally these are likely to have been good quality Birmingham-made guns, known locally as *tafanga*. But thanks to the use of local flint, poor maintenance, unpredictable powder composition, irregular projectiles and other circumstances the guns were more effective used in volleys than individually. In the Grassfields, musketeers were usually protected by spearmen. Although the gun was best used defensively, it did have offensive some capabilities. However, spears remained the standard offensive weapon, and dances by and large reflect this preeminence. (Warnier notes that spear dances might be performed while holding muskets, but never vice versa.) By 1891, Bali may have been increasing its use of guns over a forty-year period. But this in turn implies that the military manoeuvres of earlier Lela festivals would have been appropriate to an offensive force based on cavalry and footsoldiery. Later we shall have the opportunity to compare Lela with a counterpart celebration among Chamba-led raiders who did not lose their cavalry (see Chapter 6).

Hutter and Zintgraff's accounts of Lela and similar festivities in Bali Nyonga give a vivid sense of the relation between warfare and martial ceremony. Zintgraff remarked just how concerned were Bali about maleficent influences, which had to be dispersed (Chilver 1966: 10). *Nyikob*, which was to become the standard translation for the High God, struck Zintgraff as having the sense of a fearful bush demon. Lela emerges from these accounts as a mixture of precautionary practice and military demonstration; both of them designed as prelude to actual warfare.

Zintgraff was to return to Bali Nyonga in 1896 in the company of the future plantation manager, Max Esser, who stayed for six days. As in 1889, the party was greeted by a Lela-like performance and responded in similar style (Chilver & Röschenthaler 2001: 89–93). Esser, presumably on Zintgraff's advice although he does not admit as much, has his Vai soldiers dressed in red jackets and blue caps discharge a salvo from their Mauser M71 rifles. The European party trick themselves out in towelling dressing gowns, coloured turbans and weapons to impress their host. Foghorns are sounded to add to the impact (and, as noted earlier, one similar – if not indeed one of these – survived among the royal treasures in 1908 and for at least fifty years afterwards). The scene described from the palace plaza – of military manoeuvres, armed warriors, and scouts – is reminiscent of Hutter's description; however, only Tita Mbo (the future Fonyonga) survives to lead a column of troops. His older brother, Tita Nji, had died two months before the arrival of Esser's party.

Zintgraff, Hutter and Esser's observations in Bali during the reign of Fonyonga's father Galega suggest that earlier German visitors were minded to see Lela as a predominantly martial ceremony with ritual aspects designed to ensure success in arms. They participated enthusiastically on the basis that their own and Bali interests in the use of violence more or less coincided. Basel missionaries, understandably, were drawn to the aspects of Lela that struck chords with their knowledge of the Old Testament, and they also participated, although less enthusiastically, because Bali's ritual rootstock could serve only as something on to which the Christian message might be grafted. In both cases, the Lela festival gravitated towards the grounds of European participation. I shall suggest later that this was what Lela had always done so that while the incorporation of the ceremony into imperial and colonial contexts was in some respects unprecedented, it was not wholly so. The additive and cellular character of the ceremony provided a robust way of adapting to political environments that were never stable.

Interlude: The Bali Axis Unravels

The triangular relations between German colonial administration, the Swiss and southern German Basel Mission and the Bali palace which had served Fonyonga's interests well were already unravelling by the time of the 1908 Lela. Both policy and personnel were implicated. Hauptmann Glauning was already dead and Ferdinand Ernst was to die the following year; Fonyonga would continue to rule until 1940, dying when probably in his early eighties, without ever regaining his earlier importance.

To begin with the Bali–German axis: as Chilver has documented, Glauning's replacement as Head of the Bamenda Garrison, Hauptmann Menzel, began to question the extent that German administration had served to bolster Bali power. Menzel was particularly hostile towards the Basel Mission and towards Ernst's role as adviser to Fonyonga (Chilver 1967: 500–1; Chilver & Röschenthaler 2001: 154–6).[16] More general considerations stemmed from the need to introduce a head tax and to protect the smaller groups in the colony (Chilver 1967: 503). By 1909 measures were in hand to attempt collection of the breechloaders in Bali hands and to detach chiefdoms made dependent on Bali. The expenditure that Fonyonga required to maintain his position (help support the Basel Mission, provision his soldiers, sweeten his relations with sub-chiefs …) was beginning to outstrip his resources. When Adametz replaced Menzel in 1911 he decided that Bali had been given jurisdiction over peoples whom they had never subjected, and he began to take steps to rectify this situation even before receiving official approval (Chilver 1967: 504–8; Chilver & Röschenthaler 2001: 159–62). Eventually, powers of tax collection from vassal villages were removed from Bali. The supply of labour to the coastal plantations, in consideration of which Fonyonga received an income, was banned in 1913. In short order, Bali found German colonial support for its economic and political infrastructure pulled from under it.

Not unsurprisingly, relations with the Basel Mission deteriorated at the same time. The ties between Fonyonga and Ernst had been quite extraordinarily close: the missionary joked with his kingly friend and was permitted to touch him. Although supposedly in charge of education, Ernst spent long periods in the palace advising the Fon and apparently acted as his envoy in settlement of disputes.[17] The returning Jakob Keller described Ernst's friendship with the Fon as '*intimisten*' (most intimate),[18] and reports Fonyonga's words *in memoriam*, 'People of Bali, when you lie down think of King Beard [Ernst], and you get up, think of him then too. He loved us. He helped Bali town in every respect. He was our father. If something bad threatened the town, he averted it and threw it aside. Don't forget him, think of him' (Keller 1909b: 92). Elsewhere, Keller quotes the Fon as saying, 'Now I am abandoned, who will help me, who will advise me on domestic and foreign affairs?' (Merz 1997: 54, quoting Keller's 1909 *Jahresbericht*). While Fonyonga evidently felt his position weakened by Ernst's death, it was the conjuncture of this personal loss with Bali's deteriorating structural position that posed him challenges. Probably because he saw the expansion of Mungaka as part of the building of regional hegemony by Bali, Fonyonga had paid the salaries of teachers outside Bali town, and made spontaneous gifts to the school: for instance of 200 marks to Ernst in March 1907, to pay for the slates for the first intake of pupils to the 'folk school' about to be taught by those who had graduated to the upper school (*Jahresbericht* 1908: 64); and a further 160 marks the following year, when the Annual Report also noted his support of the church to which he sent his wives and soldiers on occasions (*Jahresbericht* 1909: 70). The report on the year 1908 concluded by noting the friendly relation between the Bali missionaries and the Military Station in Bamenda: the brothers were pleased to mediate the relations between the administrative authorities and the Bali '*Reich*' (*Jahresbericht* 1909: 72). However, Fonyonga's support for the school was curtailed as his income declined, and the mission came to seem a less valuable intermediary between himself and the Bamenda authorities.

Warning signs of deteriorating relations with the palace are apparent in the 1909 Annual Report with its note that even Keller had been unable to put his relation with the Fon on the same footing as Ernst (*Jahresbericht* 1910: XCIX). By 1910 the mission was in the throes of a 'crisis' (*Jahresbericht* 1911: 125). The grounds for this were several, but among them was the growing rift between Fonyonga and the Chief of BaTi. The latter had suffered severe burns during the 1907 Lela when a spark ignited a powder keg and set fire to his palace and ninety houses. At that time he is quoted as saying he would work in God's service if he recovered his health (*Jahresbericht* 1908: 64). The 1910 report records that the Chief indeed built a chapel on his marketplace as a thank-offering for his recovery, but then began to frequent it rather than the Bali church. The Chief of Bafu also had himself a chapel built locally (*Jahresbericht* 1911: 126). Ironically, given the Fon's attempt to annex missionary effort to his own hegemonising schemes, it seems that chapel building was fast becoming an expression of fissioning within the Bali Reich. The BaTi would leave Bali, with the approval of the administration and the support of the Basel Mission during the following year. Another challenge is apparent in the unpublished sections of Keller's Annual Report which recount the circumstances surrounding an outbreak of dysentery apparently caused by witchcraft. Initially, two suspected witches fleeing from Bande were expelled, then after pleading for peace during a distribution of palm wine and elephant meat to his people, Fonyonga was persuaded to allow an ordeal to be conducted (although excluding schoolboys and Christians from it); finally, there was resort to hanging all animals dying of unnatural causes (BMA E-2.34,56). A further problem had arisen over land: Fonyonga wanted to reclaim the valley section of the land he had given the mission – land which had never been built upon – so as to accommodate his expanding town (Merz 1997: 63). The list of conflicting interests was indeed extensive.

The Bali Mission's Annual Report for 1912 records that Fonyonga's star was waning: the Governor had allowed any of the sub-chiefs who so wished to take their tax directly to Bamenda (where the military station would apparently continue to pay Bali a 10 percent commission). Governor Ebermaier had made it clear that Bamum's stock was rising, and Fonyonga had taken this reversal to heart and embarked upon a plan to elevate his people to a higher cultural step (*Kulturstufe*), which he intended to enforce under pain of arrest: daytime use of camwood paste as a cosmetic was banned; men should clothe their wives (and clothed women should not be mocked for putting on airs and graces); and his subjects should build beautiful houses and enclose their compounds with mats. Fonyonga intended to support the mission's work as previously and had begun again to send his wives to church. 'Whether all this is more than a passing ambition will soon be apparent' (*Jahresbericht* 1913: 135). By 1913, however, relations seem to have adjusted to the changing situation: a new church was built in Bali and would be consecrated in the New Year; and the King was coming more often to church with his retinue (*Jahresbericht* 1914: 155). However, if palace–mission relations were on the mend, those between the palace and the christian congregation in Bali had now became less amenable. In his enthusiasm to provide children for the mission school, Fonyonga had his soldiers impress youngsters from the 'subject tribes' into education (Dah 1983: 128). We saw earlier that dissension arose within the first generation of Christians about participation in Lela. It seems likely that this amounted to more than a squaring of pagan and christian practices: given that the European missionaries continued to attend Lela, African refusal to do so, like the establishment of an independent BaTi chapel before their chief's secession from Bali, indicates that Christianity was becoming a justification for African dissent from the paramountcy. Fonyonga may have come to wonder whether in supporting the Basel Mission he had not accommodated a cuckoo in his kingdom's nest.

Exactly what occurred in Bali during the First World War is difficult to establish, although the immediate event of the British occupation appears not to have been traumatic.[19] 'On October 21st [1915] about 9 a.m. the British Army arrived in Bali. The Rev. Vielhauer went out to meet the troops and gave the officers tea in the mission' (Pefok 1962: 85). Fonyonga had the recently completed church locked and handed its keys to the new colonial authorities. Only a little earlier, he had planned to have his own palace rebuilt in the style of mission houses (Dah 1983: 121–2). In the event, the palace was torched, allegedly by the Germans during the final stages of their withdrawal. With the Basel missionaries interned, the responsibility for the young christian community devolved upon its African pastors. But Pastor Modi Din reported to his superiors in 1919 that Bali was the single place where permission to preach was withheld (Thomas 2001: 48). Pastor Johannes Litumbe Ekese's experience was the same, 'Only in Bale [Bali] I was absend (sic) to preach for their ungodly Chief instructed his villages that he will not hear any word speaking about Godspell' (Thomas 2001: 52, quoting a letter to Basel from Ekese). Whether Fonyonga's attitude was opposed to the mission, or whether he sought to curry favour with the British by denying access to pastors with known German links, is not clear. In either case, the effect was to hasten the decline of Bali as a mission centre in the Grassfields once the missionaries were allowed to return (Thomas 2001: 55–7).

When the Basel Mission resumed work in Bali in 1925 the missionaries discovered that Fonyonga had taken architectural modernisation into his own hands using a large quantity (39,000) of their stored bricks to rebuild the entrance chamber to his palace (near the mission's own brick-built and tin-roofed chapel completed a decade earlier). The dispute that ensued was eventually settled when the administration arranged compensation (BMA E-5–2.4,51, Vielhauer

Jahresbericht 28 February 1930). According to the 1931 report, Fonyonga attended church now and then, arriving with a cow hide on which a European chair decorated with beads was placed near the altar (this chair appears in photographs taken by Hans-Peter Straumann in 1963). That year he had been invested with a Certificate of Honour and Bronze Service Medal and had remarked 'like a child', according to Brother Steudle the reporting missionary, 'I am still a big chief' (BMA E-5–207,8, 11 Jan 1932). In the eyes of the missionaries the aged Fon was clearly not the figure to reckon with politically that he had been in his pre-war pomp: perhaps not in the eyes of his own people either. The few photographs of Lela from the inter-war years suggest it may have become a lower-key affair. Missionary Wilhelm Zürcher's photographs do not feature scenes of massed crowds, but the record is slight and it may be too easy for the later viewer to read into the scene of the aged Fon and his retainers a twilight hour of the kingdom. However, Adolf Vielhauer's report for 1929 notes that when the missionaries went to witness the Lela sacrifice on 6 December that year, they found Fonyonga grumbling about their having forbidden participation in the dance. Turnout was poor and the elders commanded few youngsters to arrange war games; the elders felt themselves to be in new times that were hostile to them (BMA E-5–2.4,51: 8). However, as noted earlier, the missionaries did not entirely abandon interest in Lela. Georg Tischhauser, who was in Bali from 1931 to 1933 and again during 1938, composed interlinear (German/Mungaka) notes on Lela: dated December 1975 in typescript, these may have been intended for a collection of Bali texts that never materialised and survive in the papers that entered the Basel Archive following his death (BMA E-10.54,17).

Fonyonga was to live another ten years, dying on the night of 29 August 1940, as his successor V.D.S. Galega II informed Missionary Zürcher by letter on 2 September (Zürcher BMA E-5.2,15, *Jahresbericht* 1940). The five-hundred strong Grassland Synod commemorated the old and greeted the new Fon on the palace forecourt on 1 February when, on the assumption that Zürcher's photographs indeed record this event, he wore the gown in which his father had posed in prosperous times under his capacious umbrella by the entrance to his old palace more than three decades earlier (compare **Figures 3** and **27**). During Galega II's reign there occurred a reinvigoration of Bali tradition and with it the Lela festival. Most of our evidence comes from the late colonial period onwards, and I shall deal with it in my concluding chapter. However, because they introduce kinds of information we have hardly met thus far, it is appropriate to conclude this résumé of accounts of Lela with the first, professional academic investigations carried out since Ankermann's time.[20]

The Anthropologist and the Historian: A 1960s Version

The historian Sally (E.M.) Chilver and social anthropologist Phyllis Kaberry did not witness a full-scale Lela in Bali Nyonga, but they were familiar with previous published literature and saw something of the festival elsewhere. Unlike most previous investigators, they were interested in all five of the Bali chiefdoms.

Chilver and Kaberry's main interview bearing on Lela was with the officials concerned, rather than with the Fon, as seemed to have been the case for such earlier investigators who looked for evidence beyond that of their own eyes. Chilver and Kaberry's unpublished notes add some esoteric and organisational detail to the existing record. Earlier accounts told us little about those who took part in the festival. Aside from the Fon himself, participants appear generically: as priests, soldiers, warriors, scouts and so forth. Yet participation in Lela is important in two senses: it is prestigious to have some prominent role in this largest-scale of the kingdom's annual celebrations, and the festival is itself about participation: individually and collectively people take part as a mark of belonging. In the later twentieth century, they belonged to a community represented in the person of the Fon; in Hutter's time, and hardly less so as sub-imperialists on behalf of the Germans in the early twentieth century, they had adhered to the kingdom's fighting menfolk and their women and, because this has not been forgotten, the festival retains its edge of menace.

Lela, as we have seen, was the major demonstration of support and esteem for the Fon, underwritten by personal valour and a capacity for violence, meanings that condense in the Mungaka term *lo 'ti*. In the late nineteenth and early twentieth centuries, the Fon reciprocated *lo 'ti* by distributions of food and drink (much of which came in as gift or tribute) and by his own participation in the dancing, music-making, and military display which, although anticipated of the event, must occur spontaneously as if in response to being willed by the crowd. Although recorded as homophonous verbs in Tischhauser's Mungaka dictionary, it does not seem contradictory that *lo 'ti* encompasses the senses both of comforting, strengthening, calming, and making happy, as well as of military salute to the Fon as a special instance of such support. Some of the gestural repertoire of *lo 'ti* is reminiscent of the salute of horsemen in northern muslim states at a durbar;[21] and it is likely that elements of Lela indeed derive from this source. This, like various European accoutrements, has become part of Lela on Bali terms, and the active demonstration of the Fon's credentials as warrior is one element of this change. Because Lela is a demonstration of loyalty to a warrior King, the who-does-what of the ceremony – who participates, in what capacity, and who directs that participation – looms constitutively large in the ceremony itself. Although earlier accounts allow us glimpses into the relation between the direction of Lela and military command, and participation in Lela and military organisation, before Chilver and Kaberry we learn little in detail about Lela's social organisation.

Chilver's 1960s Bali Nyonga respondents told her that Lela was in the custody of people called Sama. In those northern lands home to the earliest adherents of Bali – at the risk of anachronism, Chambaland – this term would have at least two senses: a patriclan name, but also one of the terms from which the ethnic term (Chamba) has been derived, probably in a Hausa pronunciation. Sama and custodians of Lela seem to have become synonymous in Bali Nyonga; however, there are indications that Sama retains a sense of 'royals' in the other Bali chiefdoms, or at least that the term designated the Adamawan core of the Bali confederacy. Descent relations are traced primarily through father–son steps in Bali Nyonga, the patrilineal descendants of someone being called '*nggöd* so and so'. However, members of patrilineages defined this way are additionally related to their daughters' children whom they call *mundzad* (sing.)/*bundzad* (pl.); the same term is apparently applied reciprocally by a man to his sisters' children.[22] Because the Ba'ni – descendants of the core Adamawan alliance which entered the Grassfields – intermarried by preference, the dominant people of the kingdom were networked by both patrilineal descent and matrilateral relations. The very high rate of polygyny, particularly on the part of the Fon, tended to reinforce the importance of a supportive mother's family to extremely numerous children who were competing for a father's attention. This is one of the reasons that matrilateral kinship appears to have grown in importance in Bali.

As an instance of this networking among the kingdom's elite, we could take the four principals of Lela identified in 1963: Tita Fonkwa (Sama, *nggöd* Nyongpasi), Tita Nji III (presumably a patrilineal descendant of Zintgraff and Hutter's Tita Nji, the oldest son of Galega I), Tita Langa (said to be of Kag-nebba), and Gwanlima (a Tikali and *mundzad mfon*, or matrilateral relative of the King). The first two were patrilineal descendants of former Fons but had not succeeded to the throne themselves: Nyongpasi became leader of the future founders of Bali Nyonga after the splitting of the alliance that had entered the Grassfields under Gawolbe. Tita Nji was the grandson of Nyongpasi, but predeceased his own father, Galega. Kag-nebba, to take the *nggöd* of the third principal, had been the earliest allies of the Sama; in Chamba Leko, Kaga is an ethnic term for Bata or Bachama (northern neighbours of Chamba) and -*nebba* simply a suffix meaning people. The Tikali (or Tikari) were one of the last groups to join Gawolbe's Ba'ni before they ascended the plateau; this fourth official is additionally, one assumes, descended from a daughter of a past Fon. All four Sama officials, therefore, not only belong to the Ba'ni (the core of the chiefdom whose alliance predates entry to the Grassfields) they are also, in different ways, descendants of Fons.[23]

The four principal Sama are said to watch the phases of the moon so that they can forewarn the Fon when they will gather the other Basama on the eve of the new moon and come to collect the *lela* flutes in their skin bag. The flutes are placed on seven bunches of a particular leaf.[24] The four Sama take the four flutes[25] and run the same water through them (from largest to smallest) and this water is then poured over the stone pile (*wolela*; according to Tischhauser's Mungaka–English dictionary, *wo* simply means stone). The Fon then sends a bowl of *kasi*, which the dictionary describes as a 'red stone' used for personal decoration. This must be what Chamba Leko would call *kasa*, a suspension of kaolin in oil. Anointing the flutes with this solution is the action properly designated *pob lela* in Mubako (as it is in Chamba Leko). The stone pile is also anointed with kaolin solution. The other Sama witness this, as does the Fon who sits for the occasion on a mat rather than his throne. Oil from a bowl is put on the navels of all present who then wash. This is followed by drinking until midnight when the four flutes are played to the accompaniment of drums (in Mubako *su-vaana* and *su-keena*, with respectively male and female suffixes, and the tension drum called *yamak*, or also *danga*, according to Nwana et al. 1978). This is the signal to begin brewing beer. A Sama sits on the stone pile to play the tall female drum, but only the Fon may ascend to the top of the pile.

From hereon the timing of the festival seems to be tied to market days rather than to the phases of the moon. On *Nggo* (the first day of the Bali eight-day week, see Nwana et al. 1981), the Sama assemble to dance for about two hours from 5 a.m. onwards, and fencing mats are replaced around the palace. The Fon feasts the matmakers and sends out five pots of meat and food.[26] The following day, *Ndansi*, the standard bearers (*tutuwan* in Mungaka, *wan-ding-ma* in Mubako)[27] are called to the compound of Tita Nyagang who leads them to the palace.[28] Once they have checked that the flags are in good order, the Fon clothes the men, who will carry his standards wearing new gowns. By now the scouts, *bagwe*, have arrived and the standard party can depart towards the river (Ntshi Nggo): the oliphant is sounded three times, the Fon presents a white cockerel to Tita Nyagang who also carries the two spears (*ding pasag*, the female spear; and *ding soga*, the male spear). The two flags lead the way: one white flag representing the men of Bali, another white flag, distinguished by its red border, representing the women (Chilver was told explicitly that neither flag was German).

Washing of the standards and oliphant takes place as described in earlier accounts; the leading role of Tita Nyagang in this – predictably given that he was her main informant – was particularly emphasised to Chilver. The sacrifice of the white cockerel is carried out by one of the *tutuwan* and, again, the description concurs with earlier accounts, except that the knife used is described as a circumcision knife, *sawa*, rather than Gawolbe's knife, as Ankermann was told.

The party makes its way back to the plaza (stopping en route at the compound of the *Ka* or royal mother) where the Sama are still playing *lela* flutes. Tita Nyagang and the flag party 'demonstrate' (translating *lo'ti*) three times to the Fon, who plays his double gong, and then to the Sama, before the spears and flags are erected next to the two *letya*, forked poles,[29] where scouts will guard them. At nightfall, beer and kaolin solution are again provided by the Fon, who takes his place on a mat to observe Tita Nyagang anoint the spears and *letya*. Beer is strained and the lees thrown thrice in front of the flags before all those present drink the liquid from a single calabash. The remaining beer is apportioned by groups that have been incorporated into the kingdom (named as Kufad, Tikali, Buti, BaKwen, Nggoulan and Fochu or Kenyan) each of which, following Tita Nyagang, in turn performs *lo'ti* three times before the Fon after 'touching' the spear bundles (saluting with one of the spear bundles might be intended here). All this while, the Sama continue to play *lela* flutes around the *wolela*, or stone pile; their *lo'ti* is made separately.

On the afternoon of the second day of Lela, (*ntsu lo'ti,* day to salute) men are summoned by beating a slit gong and they arrive decked out in their finery and carrying weapons. Again, Tita Nyagang salutes the Fon and then leads a procession to the big market place where a mock battle occurs between the *manjong* war lodges. All those present process back to the palace where individual lodges make their salutes. After dark, when all but the Sama and *bagwe* have dispersed, the Sama accompany Tita Nyagang to the palace gate nine times which signifies 'their handing over to him'. Together with Tita Langa, Tita Nyagang performs a libation at the palace gate.

There is dancing for two further days (*Ntanba'ni* and *Fontsam*) until the Fon makes his speech on the fourth day. That evening, after further salutes, the flags and *letya* are returned to the palace by Tita Nyagang. The fifth day, called *Ntunngwen*, sees the Sama take the flutes, oliphant, drums, one of the spear bundles and leopard skin to visit various important officials around the town. Chilver's informants culminate their account with a meticulous account of the rights and obligations of various Bali groupings in the ceremonial. In the early 1960s, the Fon continued to feed contingents of people attending Lela: the notables inside the palace and others outside. Otherwise, two things are particularly striking about this account. A consistent gendering of the materials and personnel of Lela has occurred. That this is not simply a matter of previous accounts having neglected this question is demonstrated by the gendering of the flags, which we know from several sources were previously Bali and German standards. Female equipment (flag, *letya*, spear as well as drum) has been aligned symbolically with the significance of female officials (especially the queen mother) and of matrilateral male relatives of the Fon among the Lela officiants. The gendering of the event has explicitly become a principle, and this corresponds to an increasing importance of matrilateral kinship to Bali. Thanks, one imagines, to the fact that Chilver's informants were officials of diverse origin, the account centres upon the demonstration of fealty through *lo'ti*. On the evidence of their testimony, questions of loyalty would appear to have preoccupied Bali informants, and this concern may have been accentuated by Chilver's account being gathered in the aftermath of another embattled period of Bali history. However, before outlining these circumstances in Chapter 7, I want to see how far comparative anthropology allows us to push the history of Lela beyond the reach of textual evidence.

Notes

1. A smaller Lela, held in May/June and called *Keti Nyikob*, barely features in the record.
2. I am indebted to Hans Peter Straumann for reference to Keller's (1926) more extended discussion of Old Testament parallels with Kamerunian practices: 'seeds of gold in heathen base-rock' (*Goldkörner im heidnischen Urgestein. Ein Vergleich der Sitten und Gebote Israels hauptsächlich im Pentateuch, mit denen der Heiden in Kamerun*).
3. Paul Jenkins drew my attention to this excerpt from the Mungaka language catechism, written by Ferdinand Ernst, cited in English translation by Jonas N. Dah (1995: 5–6). 'Question ... What does the word of God teach about kings? Answer: Kings are servants of God who care that you dwell in peace ... Question ... What does the word of God teach about the citizen? Everyone should obey the king because they do not enthrone themselves but are crowned by God ... Whoever is against the orders of a king is against the law of God.' In 1909 Ernst had his schoolboys sing 'Heil dir in Siegerkranz' ('Hail you in the victor's garland) in the Fon's honour (Moldenhauer 1909: 13).
4. In his manuscript, which is in most respects identical to the published version, Striebel writes of 'Vorkämpfer' or scouts, presumably translating the Mungaka *bagwe*. Striebel's Basel editors have changed his more precise usage to either 'Krieger' (warriors) or 'Hauptleute' (leading people). I have reverted to Striebel's terminology.
5. The inception dates given by Keller are 5 December 1910, 27 November 1911, 12 November 1912, 2 December 1913. In 1907 the ceremony began on 7 December (the

fourth day was prolonged into 11 December in honour of Ankermann who arrived on 10 December); in 1908 it began on 28 December. Keller's 1906 report states the Lela began on 30 December 1905. Corresponding weekdays have been taken from the useful Internet facility at <www.earth.com>. According to Mathew Gwanfogbe (1995: 185) and Werner Keller (1981: 140), Fonyonga declared Sunday a day of rest throughout his kingdom in June 1906, which suggests later reconsideration of the compatibility between Lela and the christian Sunday. .

6.   In 1891, festivals began the next 'Bali-Sunday' in the eight-day week after which the Fon saw the new moon (Hutter 1902: 429). There appears to have been two moves: from Bali to European calendars, then from a Saturday to a Monday start.

7.   The first *Knabenschule* had opened in 1907 with 130 students recruited from graduates of the Bali school. Because it served primarily to train catechists, it was dubbed *Katechistenschule* (Keller 1981: 141; Gwanfogbe 1995: 185).

8.   This material is contained in a preamble to Keller's first numbered section and might have been a late addition to the text.

9.   Max Esser mentions foghorns in a procession he mounted to impress Galega in 1896 (Chilver & Röschenthaler 2001: 90). Perhaps one of these was subsequently gifted to the Fon.

10. Of course Fonyonga's illness could have been strategic, and we don't know quite what Keller meant by an absence in 'recent years'. Presumably if he meant 'throughout the period 1910 to 1913', he could have said so; but we cannot rule out Fonyonga's absence also in 1912 and 1913.

11. Zürcher's photographs are dated only as between 1932 and 1938: six of them apparently relate to a single festival (BMA: E-30.85.247–8; E-30.85.274-5; E-30.85.280–1). The scene is not immediately familiar from the pre-First World War photographs because the palace had been substantially rebuilt in the interim.

12. Zintgraff had earlier noted that it was forbidden to approach the King armed (Chilver 1966: 9).

13. Stefanie Michels (2004: 99–101) notes the importance of flags and costumes to the imperial project generally, and particularly to this phase of relatively powerless German expansion.

14. Hutter (1902: 431) claims that the Lela festival begins on the same day, or the day following, the Fon sighting the new moon. However, he also claims that the festival would begin the next 'Bali-Sunday' (1902: 429). The latter seems the more plausible given the time needed to brew beer, and the reference to the week-long ceremony ending on a Bali-Sunday.

15. Of the two spears, the heirloom is that with a rattle top: fashioned rather like the leg rattles with which women dance (see **Figures 13** to **16**). The spear illustrated by Hutter has a hafted iron head which bifurcates into a rattle at its middle and terminates in a point; Knöpfli's illustrations suggest such a form might have been within the repertoire of Babungo smiths (1999: 109).

16. Chilver (personal communication) commented that it may be relevant both that Menzel was a Catholic and this was a period of antagonism between the churches in Germany.

17. When Fonyonga attended the opening of a sawmill in Bafotschu, Ernst asked the Fon en route, 'He alter, lebst du noch?' (Well old man, you're still living?), to which the Fon answered in German, 'Ja, ja freilich'. (Addressing the royal person as 'old man', or 'elder', may connote familiarity but lacks the overtones of disrespect the English translation 'old man' carries.) The machinery so startled the Fon that he had to be taken to a block of wood where he sat holding Ernst's hand in wonderment (Moldenhauer 1909). Merz quotes a letter from Ernst dated August 1908 to relatives demonstrating how discreetly Ernst shielded the other missionaries from full knowledge of the role he was playing in the palace (1997: 53–4).

18. Andreas Merz has turned up evidence, in the form of a report by President Lutz on his tour of the Grassfields, that Ernst accepted the gift of a housemaid from the Fon.

Apparently she also helped him with his language work. Merz notes that Robert Moldenhauer (author of the report on the opening of the sawmill quoted above) was himself expelled from the mission for taking a local wife (Merz 1997: 58 and Note 253). Fonyonga also entrusted Ernst with one of his sons, Sosiga, who accompanied Ernst on his last journey to Germany. Maxwell Fohtung mentions Susigah (Sosiga) as one of the first Bali to be baptised (Fohtung 1992: 222).

19. Fonyonga presented a leopard stool to George V in 1916, although the circumstances of the gift are presently unclear. The stool was subsequently loaned to the Liverpool Museum (7.3.1925 1).

20. A filmed record of Lela, once in the possession of the Pitt-Rivers Museum in Oxford, made during the 1950s under the auspices of the Commonwealth Development Corporation, is presently untraceable but may yet turn up.

21. See Apter (2005) for a very suggestive account of the genealogies of durbar in Nigeria.

22. Although pluralisation is by prefix in Mungaka (rather than by suffix as in Chamba Leko/Mubako), one nonetheless wonders whether the *mun-* of *mun-dzad* derives from the Chamba Leko *muna*, meaning mother's brother (and, with a diminutive suffix, also sister's child). If the Mungaka suffix *-dzad* signified something like 'relationship', then a similar derivation might be suggested of the term for joking relationship, *mang-dzad*, from the Chamba Leko term for such relations between clans or ethnic groups: *manjala*.

23. Stuart Russell's account, researched in the early 1970s, also cites four senior Sama, who are responsible for sacrifices at the initiation of the ceremony of Lela; they seem to be the same individuals serving ten years earlier: 'Tita Langa (or Gana) the senior Lela priest, and Tita Nji, who represents Galega I's issue', are the most senior Sama and also *nwana*, or Voma priests. 'The other senior Sama are Tita Fonkwa, representing Nyongpasi's side, and Gwandima, a Tikali *mundzad mfon* who represents the female side of the Bali community' (Russell 1980: 60). I shall discuss the developing representation of the 'female side' of Bali later.

24. This leaf is called *dzandzan* or *kila* in Mubako.

25. Named *le-nya* (mother), *le-samba*, *le-dinga* and *le-kasua* (see also Nwana & Ndangam 1981a).

26. Chilver itemises the recipients as Buti, Kufad, Tikali, Manded and Bedmfon: but she cautions that there are different realisations in other accounts. The *fonte* (sub-chiefs), *kom* (knights) and *bonmfon* (children of Fons) are fed within the palace.

27. The Mungaka term *tutuwan* surely derives from the Fulfulde *tutuwal*, flag. Bali practice has assimilated the flags with spears: the Mubako term for flag bearer, *wan-ding-ma*, is composed of Chamba Leko word for spear (*ding*) and *wan*, presumably derived from the Chamba Leko *nwana* (priest/ritual specialist). If this derivation is valid, then *tutuwan* (in the sense of flag bearer) would have to result from Chamba Leko speakers borrowing the Fulfulde term. The *tutuwan* complex would then have to predate the break-up of the Bali Chamba and the adoption of Mungaka by Bali Nyonga. In Chapter 6, I support this reconstruction with comparative evidence from the Donga Chamba, who did not enter the Grassfields, and from the area of Chambaland likely to have been the immediate origin of the Ba'ni where festivals called 'spear beer' are reported.

28. Nyagang occurs widely as a title among Chamba Daka and Leko, and is glossed by some informants as the leader of cavalry (though on the basis of a dubious etymology: *nyaan* horse, *gang* chief, Chamba Daka, which therefore could not hold in Chamba Leko).

29. Sally Chilver was able to meet the *letya* carver, a Kaga man belonging to the same family as Tita Langa. The two poles were said to be male and female; furthermore two pots, normally kept in the palace, were apparently buried under them for the Lela ceremony. These were called *mbangbena* and *nyingbungga*, which Chilver was told were Mubako terms. The Bafut customs at their equivalent of Lela, discussed in Chapter 5, probably help to explain this.

Chapter 4

Lela: Incorporation, Ascendancy and the Means of Violence

The snapshot of Lela in the early 1960s provided to Chilver by her informants makes apparent what missionary commentators a half century earlier apparently neglected. Those early observers were indulgently amused by the ebullient, extravagantly costumed, participation of Bali people both individually and as groups in Lela. Sober-minded Protestants, they saw Lela as a religious rite (largely confined to the first day) which had lately become the excuse for eating, drinking and partying. Looked at dispassionately, however, the politics and aesthetics of participation defined Lela just as much as did the rites. To participate, dressed up in finery, was to be incorporated as a member of some organisation that honoured the Fon and belonged to the kingdom: *lo 'ti* as a gesture both of submission to the Fon and of potential aggression towards his enemies was far from folkloric. During the nineteenth century, the Bali – like other raiders from Adamawa – had been socially fluid and militarised to a degree that was probably unprecedented. Thanks in part to their own activities they traversed what was fast becoming a degraded and dangerous – and ultimately depopulated – social environment. What Lela dramatised under such circumstances was an aesthetic of visible adherence to a predatory organisation and to its lifestyle. Lela exalted conspicuous wealth and the violent means of its acquisition. The consequences of not belonging among those who made Lela together – if these were not already obvious – would have become immediately apparent in the campaigns that Lela inaugurated annually.

The Ba'ni before the Germans

As a register of current social incorporation and political ascendancy, and a muster of the means of violence, some of the changes which Lela underwent through the nineteenth century would simply have reflected the changing composition, hierarchy and weaponry of the raiders. The historical narratives recorded earliest from the extant chiefdoms founded by Adamawan raiders consistently refer back to circumstances at the inception of the Fulbe jihad in what was to become the Emirate of Adamawa (straddling the northern border of contemporary Camerooon and Nigeria). The places they mention are, for the most part, those of the Fulbe lamidates founded in the wake of the jihad. The soldier Hutter (1902: 323) and businessman Esser (1898: 136) both attribute the 'Bali' (note: not Chamba) migrations to the pressure of 'Hausa' Muslims. More specifically, the cartographer Moisel (1908a: 117), drawing upon the knowledge of the missionaries Dorsch and Ernst (and probably Fonyonga's testimony to judge by his account of his visit, Moisel 1908b: 270) begins his version with the Bali being driven by the Fulbe from Koncha, having come there from a place unknown. The long-serving missionary Keller (1909a: 158–9) writes that the Bali were twice displaced by Fulbe pressure: from the vicinity of Garoua, in the first decade of the nineteenth century, and from Koncha or Takum, twenty or more years later. The consensus in these early German accounts is that the Bali were displaced southwards by muslim Fulbe or Hausa from places along the Faro-Deo river system: Garoua, Koncha, and Takum.

After this the order of events becomes rather scrambled: Keller implausibly has the Bali first allying with the BaTi and subsequently conquering the 'Dinschi' or 'Garindschi' (the contemporary Benue Chamba) whose language he seems to believe they learned only at this point (since he is told by German officers that Bali and Benue Chamba can still converse in it).[1] During the first two decades of German acquaintance with Bali, no connection was drawn with Chamba origins; the relationship between Bali and Chamba (as speakers of Chamba Leko) will subsequently be derived from the evidence of surveys of language distribution and significantly not from Bali testimony.[2] By the end of the twentieth century, Bali oral accounts about pre-diasporic times had become much more comprehensive than they were at the beginning of the century (a circumstance which encourages one to suppose that this more 'ancient' material may be of greater historiographic than historical interest). The circulation of texts about Bali history has accelerated this process.[3] However, my hunch would be that the absence of pre-diasporic traditions from the late nineteenth- and early twentieth-century sources is not accidental: local circumstances of particular migrations would have been sufficiently complex to have thoroughly disrupted the social categories (clans, chiefdoms and so forth) that structured recollection of previous historical narratives and gave them sense. Numerous groups, composed of what are quite different ethnic elements in today's terms, were set in simultaneous motion, clashing and combining opportunistically. Along with their dependants, these raiders established fortified camps from which they set about expropriating resources in different forms from the surrounding peoples. Frequently, they incorporated those among whom they settled. Presumably, such incorporation took place on terms dictated by the differential strengths of the parties and the overall logistics of their joint position. Only some of these sectional identities have persisted in the Bali kingdoms and have continued to provide organisational categories.

The earliest adherents of Bali Chamba raiding confederacies are nowadays recalled as Ndaga (or Ndagana), a term which might well be cognate with the sub-ethnic term Daka in use among contemporary Chamba (at least it does not appear to have derived from later historiographic influences). Ndaga themselves are subdivided into groups defined patrilineally: Sama, Nyema, Jaba. Patriclans with these names may still be found among Chamba Leko living north of the confluence between the Rivers Deo and Faro. The earliest allies of the Ndaga are recalled as Kaga and Peli. Kaga is the Chamba Leko term for Bata or Bachama, people who would have been their northern neighbours in the early nineteenth century. Peli or Pere, known to the Fulbe as Koutine, inhabit the Koncha area, and are neighbours immediately south of the Chamba. Both Bachama and Pere have ethnic-wide joking relations with their present-day Chamba neighbours. Thus the contemporary sectional identities in Bali provide a perfectly credible scenario for the inception of a raiding alliance consisting of localised Chamba patriclans and contingents of their neighbours: moreover, it is noteworthy that none of the ethnic terms current in the northern areas of present-day Cameroon and Nigeria (Chamba, Bachama, Koutine) features in these recollections, which corroborates an argument that these current ethnic terms crystallised only subsequently through a process involving both European outsiders and Hausa/Fulbe intermediaries.

The next allies were recruited in the vicinity of Ngaoundere, where contingents of Kefad or Kufad were picked up: people who nowadays would be related to Mbum. Further south still, Buti contingents were incorporated in the vicinity of Banyo, and Tikali or Tikari slightly further south of them. Immediately striking about this sequence of recruitment is the very close relation it bears to the progress of Fulbe state-building: initially near to Bata country (Gurin being capital of early Adamawa), then through a succession of sub-lamidates including Tchamba, Laro, Koncha, Ngaoundere, Banyo and Tibati. Apparently, the raiding bands drew their adherents from areas of Fulbe sub-lamidate building. The precise relations between the achievement of Fulbe ascendancy over several decades and the ongoing diaspora of Adamawan people in raiding bands happening at the same time are unclear, and likely to remain so, but what evidence we have reveals both that they were locally and temporally variable, and that they were not invariably based on simple antagonism.

Adamawa, named after its founder Adama, alternatively known as Fombina or the emirate of the south, was the open frontier of expansion of the Sokoto Caliphate and, as such, as little constrained by the niceties of jihadic war as anywhere. There is no indication of concerted Fulbe efforts to convert people to Islam, but abundant evidence of attempts to control trade, to either extract slaves or install them in slave villages, and to achieve regional dominance. Conflicts occurred between the Fulbe sub-lamidates almost as frequently as they did between Fulbe and non-Fulbe. On the ground, and at least during the early decades of the nineteenth century, the logistical challenges facing Fulbe and non-Fulbe aggressors were not very different: both needed to secure defensible positions for themselves, their dependants and their horses in order to provision themselves from a locality. All might require allies when facing competing local powers. The Fulbe armies, if we are to judge from later photographs such as that taken by Leo Frobenius's expedition in 1911, incorporated large numbers of non-Fulbe footsoldiery and possibly non-Fulbe cavalry as well (**Figure 28** 'Fulbe country. Tchamba on the River Faro: the great Salaam (Friday prayers)'). As well as using them as auxiliaries to their troops, Fulbe leaders also empowered clients to raid on their own behalf. For instance, there is a longstanding oral tradition of alliance between Modibbo Adama and the Chamba warrior Damashi. Damashi led his fighters directly west across the Shebshi Mountains, eventually implanting their chiefdoms among mixed populations in the northern edges of the mountains that consisted of Chamba Daka-speakers ethnically distinct from Damashi's followers, as well as various groups of Mumuye (Fardon 1988: 96–7). Some, admittedly confused, reports would have Damashi raiding down into Jukun country before doubling back to his Shebshi Mountain bases. Another group of raiders under Sama leadership (who would eventually found the chiefdom of Donga) allied with the Emir of Bauchi, receiving a flag from him (see Chapter 6). They had seceded from a raiding alliance that turned westwards after leaving Koncha and entered the plains below the River Benue, recruiting a cross-section of allies different from the Bali, but doing so on similar principles.

The Bali may not have been the vanguard of raiders moving into the Grassfields: groups recalled as Peli[4] and Daga preceded them (and Bali Nyonga conquest of Bali Konntan to occupy their present site may have represented a convergence of these waves of intrusion). Additional to these two, Russell has distinguished several Buti bands on the basis of Bali tradition (1980: 20). In the Grassfields – just as in Chambaland and below the Benue – raiding parties were numerous and their composition subject to rapid change. Oral traditions about nineteenth-century migrations, collected by the Donga chief Garbosa from the Benue regions, show that men (including Garbosa's own forebear) rose to leadership, as often as not, by defection from existing encampments. They took some followers with them and recruited others from whatever locale they currently exploited. It is likely that these were men without established chiefly pedigrees, so a period of resettlement and consolidation was needed before their descendants' claims to high office could be traditionalised. Typically, legitimacy would involve the provision of a dynastic pedigree predating the migrations that operated initially as a zero point of history. As Russell stresses, Ba'ni 'was a very loose confederacy' (1980: 20), if indeed it was a confederacy at all. The last group of allies picked up before entering the Grassfields consisted of BaTi from the Mbam Valley who were escaping the expansion of Bamum; they came to be known as Gawolbe's BaTi (Ti-Gawolbe) in contradistinction to a later group of BaTi who initially allied with Buti and joined Bali Nyonga only after Gawolbe's death: the BaNten or Lolo. Mungaka derives from the language of this second group (Russell 1980: 21–2).

Entering the Grassfields from the northeast, the Ba'ni raided across the plains towards the southwest over a period of perhaps a decade until defeated sometime in the 1830s at Kolm, near Bafu Fondong. Although it seems likely that Buti and Peli raiders were in the vanguard of several marauding waves, by Jeffreys' time it had become dogma that a single, united alliance split after Kolm: 'Present day Bali history does not accept that [Muti's Peli who went on to Takum] broke away in Gawolbe's day. It was the quarrels for chieftainship after Gawolbe's death that led to the break up of the Bali ...' (1962b: 178 Note 29). Since Jeffreys undertook his investigations during the period of rapprochement between the Bali Kingdoms in the aftermath of the Widekum riots (discussed below), the dogma of a once united alliance would have helped them present a united front. In the most formulaic of recollections, all these groupings would be represented as sons of Gawolbe. The course of events is likely to have been far more complicated than this, and any curious enquirer quickly learns alternative (though inconsistent) versions of the relations between the current Bali chiefdoms and the hero leader. However, the pattern of fracturing subsequent to the reverse of Kolm does not give the impression that the Ba'ni had been a unified alliance: each of the Bali chiefdoms is internally diverse, containing sections of the original allies, and this pattern of fracturing suggests that bases of support already crosscut ethnic or patrilineal descent-based identities.

One group, identified (apparently independently) as Muti's Peli in the Grassfields and as Mudi's Pyeri in the Benue Plains, failed in its attempts to settle in the Grassfields close to either Bafut or Mankon and eventually joined up with Chamba groups that had gone more directly to Takum. Zintgraff was to meet the leader of this group in Takum on his 1889 expedition (Chilver 1966: 16). A second Peli group, Bali Konntan, raided the Widekum before settling near the current site of Bali Nyonga into which they were eventually absorbed. The remaining five groups founded the extant five Bali chiefdoms, of which two are the most substantial.[5] Galabi led the most populous group and was soon to install his people on top of a mountain at Bali Kumbat dominating the Ndop Plain. He is held by some accounts to have been a war leader rather than a son of Gawolbe. Only towards the end of the nineteenth century would Fonyonga's Bali Nyonga overtake Bali Kumbat to become the most important Bali chiefdom. In this case too there is dispute whether Fonyonga was actually a son of Gawolbe; current Bali Nyonga orthodoxy is that Fonyonga was the child of Gawolbe's sister or daughter (thus *mundzad mfon*).[6] Fonyonga's Ba'ni sojourned on the borders of Bamum until driven away with a large and diverse contingent of people whom they call Ba'Nten and who are the majority in present-day Bali. Fonyonga I was to die at Kifom, near the present site of Bali, where he installed himself after defeating the Bali Konntan and their BaNtanka allies. It was his son, Galega I, who made the strategic move to the more defensible site of present-day Bali where Zintgraff encountered him.

By the time, in 1889, when Zintgraff met Galega I in Bali Nyonga, the Fon had probably been settled there for around fifteen years. As Russell describes it the early town was organised much like a military camp: with those longest allied living close to the Fon, and more recent allies settled in concentric circles around the palace, their relative proximity reflecting their closeness to the Fon as the centre of power.[7] The spatial arrangement of the camp, along the ridge of a hill with the palace at its centre and highest point (following Esser's 1896 description in Chilver & Röschenthaler 2001: 81) provided a more enduring image of differential incorporation than did Lela. However, such camps had lasted only a decade or so during previous phases of migration, hence even their permanence was relative.

Kaberry and Chilver's description of the 'traditional' political system of Bali Nyonga drew upon contemporary accounts as well as the memories of informants who were elderly in 1960 to reconstruct Bali organisation around the time of first contact in 1889. Galega I would, as they saw it, have had the advantage of the reputation of his Bali troops, but he also faced disadvantages in the enmity of many surrounding peoples, and in the need to hone a new form of warfare.

> At the heart of the settlement was the palace, *nted*, and its precincts where the Mfon's retainers and sons lived. Near by were clusters of compounds bearing the names of the contingents which made up Nyongpasi's army – Buti, Kefad, Tikali, Won, Nggiam, and so on. According to tradition Nyongpasi had bestowed on the leaders of these contingents the hereditary title of *Fonte* (chieflet). (Kaberry & Chilver 1961: 360–1)

A distinction was drawn, as Kaberry and Chilver elaborate, between *Fonte Ba'ni* and *Fonte BaNten*. Two of the five *Fonte Ba'ni* were drawn from Buti, and one each from Tikali, Ti-Gawolbe and Bali Konntan; additionally, nine BaNten leaders had their *Fonte* titles recognised.[8] The five *Fonte Ba'ni*, together with seven titled men drawn from the non-royal Ba'ni, known as the *Komfon* (in Mubako *Dama*), formed the war council.[9] Five of the dozen members of the war council were Buti, three Tikali, two Peli from Bali Konntan, and one each Kefad and Ti-Gawolbe: a distribution that presumably indicates the relative strengths of these Ba'ni contingents late in the nineteenth century.

Bali informants related that Gawolbe's original army had consisted of two sectors: *badmfon*, consisting of the Fon and his personal following, and *fonte*, the Ba'ni chieflets with their troops. One warrior took his title, *Tutuwan*, from the white flag he carried into battle; he was chosen from those handpicked warriors, *bagwe*, who acted as spies. By Galega I's time *badmfon* had become a bodyguard composed of retainers (who sport tall feathered headdresses in the Lela photographs from the time of his son Fonyonga II). Galega also established a palace lodge, Ndanji, of outstanding non-royal warriors under retainer leaders. The BaNten contingents were already grouped into military lodges (*manjong*) like those found among peoples to the east of Bali Nyonga. Galega had reorganised the military system when his two oldest sons came of age: the BaNten and royals (but not the Buti, Tikali, Ti-Gawolbe, Kefad and Bali Konntan who continued to fight under their own leaders) had been divided into two wings: Ndanjam under Tita Nji, and Manted under Tita Gwenjang or Mbo (the future Fonyonga II). Some of the other princes – with their maternal relatives and friends, so we are told – had named lodges within these wings. The previous distinction between mounted Ba'ni cavalry and BaNten footsoldiery had apparently lost its significance by this point. By the time Zintgraff arrived, the two wings of the army were the basis for the distribution of gunpowder, and the dual composition of the kingdom had also become the basis of military organisation: Ba'ni now aligned with Ndanjam under Tita Nji, and BaNten with Manted under Tita Mbo; Galega still maintained Ndanji as his own society.

Relations with non-Bali were mediated through *tadmanji*, whose exact powers depended upon the nature of the relationship they tended. Effectively they were absent overlords of subject peoples but intermediaries in relations with allies. Both Tita Sama (who looked after royal family affairs) and Tita Siköd (one of those who looked after running the palace and provisioning gatherings in the plaza) were *mundzad mfon*, or matrilateral relations of the Fon.

Although we lack direct evidence for the evolution of Lela during the nineteenth century, minimally we must imagine it functioning as a vehicle of incorporation and political ascendancy, changing as the initial core of neighbours (Chamba, Bachama and Pere) picked up increasingly foreign contingents. Eventually these contingents included Grassfield peoples who were still categorically distinguished from earlier adherents when Lela entered the historical record. Simultaneously, we need to imagine Lela changing from a military ceremony appropriate to mobile mounted warriors armed with bows and spears and supported by footsoldiery to something fitting what the Bali forces became after the Bafu Fondong reverse: larger scale military units armed with spears and muskets.

Using a series of comparisons, Chapters 5 and 6 capture a sense of these changes by constructing histories of particular elements within Lela. For reasons of method these comparisons are best presented in reverse chronology: beginning around the time of the 1908 Lela and proceeding into the more distant past as we peel away various accretions which have overlaid the earlier appearance of the ceremony. Widening the geographical scope of comparison potentially correlates, I shall argue, with chronological depth. The proviso 'potentially' is important here. I am not arguing a mechanical relation between range and depth; on the contrary, materials provided by comparison have to be interpreted in the light of familiarity with cultural repertoires local to different parts of the region. Before that, however, I want to return once more to Bali Nyonga to ask what particular features of Lela distinguished it from the general run of military ceremonial there. The installation of Fonyonga as a regional paramount provides an excellent case study of an occasion – other than Lela – of military ceremonial.

The Apogee of Germano–Bali Majesty: The 1905 Paramountcy

Robert O'Neil's account of the impact of Bali Nyonga 'German sub-imperialism' on Moghamo peoples, distinguishes three phases within German policy before our pivotal year of 1908 (1987: 94–6). The first runs from Zintgraff's arrival in Bali in 1889 to the death in 1901 of Galega, the chief with whom he established such cordial relations. The second, from 1902 to 1905, saw reestablishment of German military presence and a second highpoint in German–Bali relations. However, German metropolitan rethinking of colonial administration began to have an impact on Bali Nyonga's position almost from the moment of Fonyonga's installation as paramount chief in 1905, whereupon the means by which Bali fulfilled its role in German administration were subjected to scrutiny and found wanting. The deaths of Missionary Ernst and Hauptmann Glauning left Bali without the German allies on which its interests had leant so heavily (O'Neil 1987: 131–7; also Chilver & Röschenthaler 2001: 153–63).

The period 1889 to 1901 had seen the expansion of Bali hegemony, particularly following Leutnant Hutter's raising and training of the Balitruppe between 1891 and 1893, and the subsequent transition to labour recruitment for the plantations of the West-Afrikanische Pflanzungsgesellschaft Victoria from 1896. The men of Hutter's Balitruppe, now become Galega's Basoge or Bali irregulars, were put to service in the forced recruitment of labour. Between late 1901 and 1905, Galega's son and successor, Fonyonga II, had presided over the transition from a privateering to a more regular colonial relation between the Germans and the Bali. The Bali station was reopened by Leutnant Pavel's companies in late 1901 following military reprisal against Bafut and Mankon (Mzeka 1990: 72). The military headquarters moved in the following year to Bamenda. 1902 also saw: the official banning of slavery in February, Bali-supported German action against Nso in the course of which the palace was burned (Mzeka 1990: 73), as well as Fonyonga's enthusiastic reception for the first delegation from the Basel Mission led by Eugen Schuler in November (Schuler et al. 1903). In March 1903 the mission had been opened by

Ferdinand Ernst and the missionary-builder Rudolf Leimbacher, and by December of the same year a *Volksschule* was established, its royal patronage assured through the happy royal relationship with Ernst. Fonyonga staunchly supported the Germans during the revolts of 1904, making Bali irregulars available to German punitive operations in the south. Between 1904 and 1905, the extent of Bali suzerainty was recognised and raids carried out early in 1905 to 'pacify' recalcitrant communities, including the kingdom of Kom. Hauptmann Hans Glauning, the seasoned officer newly appointed as head of the Bamenda Station in 1905 – and still recalled as a great friend of the Bali – was much impressed by Bali military abilities. On 15 June 1905 he was present at the formal installation of Fonyonga as paramount chief of thirty-one tribes in the presence of forty-seven chiefs.

A month after this event, on 18 July 1905, Missionary Ernst wrote a description of the installation ceremony to his Committee in Basel that was extracted from his longer letter and, with slight editorial suppressions, published in *Evangelische Heidenbote* for January 1906. Ernst writes of the white Bali and red-white-black German flags flying side by side (although this may seem at variance with **Figure 30**). In addition to the forty-seven chiefs present, others had sent their delegations from places up to five days travel distant. Around midday the main drama took place. First, a speech by Hauptmann Glauning in Kru English (Pidgin), which most of the headmen apparently understood,[10] to say that the German Kaiser had recognised Fonyonga as their chief because of his loyalty to the German cause. Fonyonga then mounted the stone pile to announce that he would continue to support the Germans and to warn that any who failed to bring help to the station would be sent there for punishment. Ernst notes that the long faces of the listeners suggested his words had an impact. The full report from which this description was excerpted for *Evangelische Heidenbote* (reproduced in Merz 1997: 111–2) provided substance to their concerns, for it carried details of military operations both before and on the very day after the installation.[11]

Fonyonga's descent from the stone pile was accompanied by a cacophonous discharge of arms in salute: Ernst reckoned two thousand men were present, most of them armed. After distribution of some refreshments and cloth, storm clouds gathered, and rain put an untimely end to proceedings. At this point, the published version omits Ernst's reference to the fine palm wine served to 'us' (presumably the missionaries) in a Bavarian *Bierkruge* (clearly visible in **Figure 37**). The afternoon of the installation was curtailed by rain (and the photographs taken suggest an overcast day).

Hauptmann Glauning included mention of Fonyonga's investiture in his report for the *Deutsches Kolonialblatt* (1905: 667–8). He had arrived on 14 June bringing not only Leutnant von Putlitz but fifty soldiers, a hundred carriers and a machine gun, as well as Dr Handl and Unteroffizier Schriefer. Glauning notes that Fonyonga addressed the assembled chiefs at length from his 'holy' stones after Glauning himself had spoken, and that Fonyonga distributed cloth to them. A lot of powder was discharged in war dances; there were women dancing and plenty of palm wine to drink.

This defining drama of Fonyonga's early reign was evidently celebrated with all the pomp that a Germano–Bali ceremony could muster. We can follow some part of it through two photographic records: one, taken by Missionary Martin Göhring, consists of seven photographs, four of which (including one not in the Basel collection) entered the Linden-Museum Stuttgart from Leutnant von Putlitz in 1908 or 1909 (according to pencilled annotations). In Christraud Geary's opinion, which these photographs support, Göhring was a gifted photographer (Jenkins & Geary 1985: 61). In 1905 he was about to open the Basel Mission in the Bamum capital of Fumban from where he and his wife, along with Missionary Hohner, attended the installation and are pictured en route to Bali (BMA K 779/E-30.25.006, see also E-30.25.008).[12] Another four photographs – snapshots technically inferior in quality to Göhring's but of great evidential interest – entered the Linden-Museum via either Glauning's descendants or von Putlitz.

The photographic record depicts two sites on the palace plaza between which the ceremony was enacted. First, there is the fence of the palace compound, and particularly the entrance to the palace to the right of which from the orientation of the exiting Fon (therefore viewer's left) was placed the Fon's throne. Opposite the palace gate in the middle of the plaza was the stone pile which was a main focus of Lela and which the Fon mounted to address his people.

Quite what stage of the proceedings some photographs show is debatable. I shall treat three from which the Fon himself is absent as scene-setting shots, but they might as easily have been taken while the Fon had mounted the stone pile.

Figure 30 'Assembled sub-chiefs in Bali' (BMA K778/E-30.26.52; Linden-Museum Stuttgart: Westafrika II, Kam. 32 upper). Two flags fly over the entrance to Fonyonga's palace. One of them has an inscription of which only a few letters of the word 'Bali' are visible; it must be 'Fonjonge-Bali', one of a pair of flags – the other being for Sultan Njoya of Bamum – shipped from Germany in February 1905 for which Christraud Geary has located the invoice (1996: 191, Note 9). The same shipment contained green silk and red velvet; perhaps some of the latter found its way into Fonyonga's gown. The palace guards are apparent in their long feather headdresses. If this shot was taken prior to the enthronement of Fonyonga then its caption may refer to the assembly of sub-chiefs that Ernst tells us had convened by 11 a.m. Although it is very difficult to see without magnification, between and behind the first and second warriors on the left, it is just possible to make out the box of Fonyonga's foghorn resting on the ground, and one of the figures on his throne. The man in a chequered gown sitting on the floor just behind the left-most warrior appears in several other photographs.

Figure 31 'On the market place Bali gathered on the occasion of the proclamation, von Putlitz 1908' (Linden-Museum Stuttgart: Westafrika II, Kam. 33 upper – the date refers to the photographic donation not the event). The next photograph simply shows us what is happening left of the previous shot. Numerous men are sitting along the palace fence and out into the plaza around which they form an arc. They are heavily armed.

Figure 32 'Armchair throne in front of the house of the Bali chief, von Putlitz 1908' (Linden-Museum Stuttgart: Westafrika II, Kam. 32 lower; BMA K775/E-30.26.051 – again, the date refers to donation). This photograph shows the same stretch of palace fencing as the previous two. Three chiefs are seated on stools to the right (from their perspective) of Fonyonga's throne and foghorn. The stool of the chief sitting immediately right of the Fon has been placed on a leopard skin. He smokes a large pipe and wears a Bamum-style kilt. The chief seated to his right wears a Bali gown, and the chief to his right, who also appears standing in a later photograph (**Figure 36**), is naked to the waist clothed in a wrapper and cap. According to Geary, the man seated to the immediate right of the Fon's throne is Fomben Nguigong, king of the Pati (or BaTi) people who had been expelled from Bamum borders at same time as the future founders of Bali Nyonga and had remained their allies, seeking shelter within Bali Nyonga's borders from 1904 to 1911 (Geary 1990a: 432, 439 Note 38).[13] The men seated around their feet also appear at the extreme right of **Figure 31**. If all three of the men seated on stools were Bali Nyonga chiefs then it could be suggested (albeit speculatively) that the man in Bali dress was the chief of Bali Konntan; and the other figure with bared torso might be the Bawock (in earlier sources spelt Bawok) chief, Nana, except that the Bawock are thought by some commentators not to have moved their settlement to Bali before 1906.[14]

Figure 33 'Proclamation in Bali of King Fonyonga as paramount chief: 14 June 1905 [in fact 15 June], Keller, Ernst, Leutnant von Putlitz, Hauptmann Glauning, soldiers' (BMA K776/E-30.26.050; Linden-Museum: Westafrika II, Kam. 33 lower). Attention now switches from the palace fence (still visible to the right of this picture) to the stone pile opposite. Fonyonga has mounted this pyramid in the centre of the plaza and is receiving the salute of a group of warriors. Basel's copy of this photograph was sent with – and illustrated the version published in *Evangelische Heidenbote* of – the report contained in Ernst's letter of July 1905. Perhaps some of Göhring's other photographs of the event arrived at the same time. The copy in the Linden-Museum came via Leutnant von Putlitz. The collection of people in the photograph is fascinating. In the foreground are several African soldiers, probably Glauning's troops rather than Fonyonga's. To the left of the stone pile are at least three women, probably royal wives, and a young person dressed in white carrying the Fon's pipe. There are also three Europeans left of the stone pile: first, a figure in light-coloured hat, dark trousers and light jacket, from photographs of him probably Missionary Matthias Hohner who had been Göhring's travelling companion; then a tall man in a white flat cap, identified in Basel's archival notes as Missionary Jakob Keller; and next to him – closest to the Fon – in dark clothing and flat cap, the distinctive figure of Missionary Ferdinand Ernst. Just to the right of the stone pile are two figures in white dress uniforms with pith helmets; they may be Leutnant von Putlitz and another of the government party, either Hauptmann Glauning, or Unteroffizier Schriefer, or the doctor. A small group of Bali men in gowns is obscured from our view by the soldiers. They are probably playing *lela* flutes since they appear to be moving in a circle with their backs to the camera. All around are ranks of spectators, just as we saw in **Figure 30**.

This same scene, photographed from its right, appears in **Figure 34** (Linden-Museum S138 Glauning 1 147). Fonyonga, captured full face, is standing on the stone pile; and, although technically poor, the photograph clarifies details that were obscure in **Figure 33**. Fonyonga's European dress epaulettes are visible, as are other accoutrements that he either carries himself (such as the horse tail whisk) or has carried for him by attendants (an enormous pipe, a second whisk, perhaps carried by a favourite wife). The arm of one of the men in Bali dress seen in

Figure 33 occupies the extreme right of the photograph, reinforcing the impression that **Figures 33** and **34** were taken in swift succession.

Another photograph acquired by the Linden-Museum from Glauning shows the Fon returned to the palace gate and seated on his throne. This is the same location, but not the same moment, as **Figure 30**. **Figure 35** (Linden-Museum Stuttgart, S138 Glauning 2 151) is captioned 'Meeting of the Bali sub-chiefs in front of the Bali chief's palace, among the Europeans some missionaries as well as Leutnant von Putlitz and Chief Doctor Rauch, 15 June 1905'. The personnel are almost identical to those who stood beside the stone pile in **Figure 33**. Of the Europeans, the pair of men in white uniforms and sola topis (perhaps those named as Leutnant von Putlitz and Chief Doctor Rauch, although Glauning's report quoted earlier identified the doctor as Handl) still stand together, now to the left of Fonyonga's throne as we survey the scene.[15] The missionaries have also remained in a little knot consisting of, judging by other photographs of their dress, Leimbacher, Ernst, Hohner and Keller. As well as Göhring and Hohner visiting from Bamum, the mission-builder Leimbacher would still have been in Bali according to records of missionaries' movements (he was a burly figure from the description given by Isaac Fielding Pefok who learnt his trade from him, 1962: 82). Fonyonga's wives have taken their positions by the gate. A man standing to the left of the photograph leaning slightly forward, is immediately recognisable as the person on the extreme right edge of the group standing by the stone pile in **Figure 33**.

The same scene is shown in close-up in **Figure 36** (Linden-Museum Stuttgart, Westafrika II Kam. 42, lower right). This photograph came to the Linden-Museum via von Putlitz in 1909 and was accessioned with the caption 'Meeting of chiefs in Bali'. But it clearly belongs in the 1905 series. The bare-chested man who had been sitting third right of the throne in **Figure 32**, who is possibly the Bawock chief Nana, appears to have presented himself to Fonyonga with a slender spear in his left hand. His gesture may well have been the salute that, as we saw earlier, Bali call *lo'ti*. The two figures in the foreground with their backs towards the camera are those seen at the extreme left of **Figure 32**. The woman to Fonyonga's left is probably the favourite wife who appears in many royal portraits of this time. She remains by his side in **Figure 37** (Linden-Museum Stuttgart, S138 Glauning 2 149). To the Fon's right is the BaTi king, sitting in the same position as in **Figure 32**. Apart from the pipe bearer (whom we saw at the stone pile), another attendant carries a large *Bierkruge*, presumably that to which Ernst refers. The horned post at the palace entrance, where visitors are supposed to hang their weapons, is visible here as it was in the Lela photographs.

There is a strong likelihood that three photographs attributed to Göhring – one of them accessioned together with those of the 1905 event – depict the dancing which took place in the afternoon of the investiture. **Figure 38** (BMA K777=K1844/E-30.27.017) is of the Fon's wives, to judge by their elaborate costumes. The second wife from the right, pregnant in this photograph, is the woman photographed together with Fonyonga in 1903, apparently his favoured wife (see, BMA E-30.26.034 'Bali King with wife' G. Spellenberg). One of the other wives has fixed a hand mirror to her elaborate pubic cover or *ngwasi* (Baumann & Vajda 1959: 223).[16]

Figure 39 (BMA K1843/E-30.27.019) and **Figure 40** (BMA K1845/E-30.27.018) were probably taken sequentially (since their personnel overlap). I have reversed their accession numbers in presentation, because the seated woman of **Figure 39** is standing in **Figure 40**. And the dance itself appears to have moved across the plaza towards the palace fence, the corner of which – recognisable from other photographs of this occasion – is apparent in **Figure 40**.

The captioned photographs, taken together with the written record of the investiture, allow the ceremony to be reconstructed in vivid detail. The African chiefs, the missionaries, and the colonial officers appear as interacting clusters in the photographs, each concerned with its own affairs but in ways that articulate with those of the others. Fonyonga stands alone on his stone pyramid at the still centre of the storm of German-led attacks on, among others, Bafut, Mankon, Kom and Nso: the loyal ally, his own community thus far immunized against colonial violence by its Fon's loyalty to the incoming order. Although elements of the 1905 installation ceremony are familiar from Lela, at least so far as our sources on 1905 take us, we catch no echoes of the first day of Lela – when the auguries that led Striebel to describe the ceremony as an 'oracle' are carried out by the river. The elements that the installation shares with Lela include the gestures of fealty (*lo 'ti*), the outflow from the palace of victuals and gifts – particularly cloth – the dances and the salvos of arms, the display of wealth, and the Fon's speech from the stone pile. These, it might be suggested, are generic features of large-scale, durbar-style ceremonials involving the Fon and held in the plaza of his palace. The arrival of Max Esser with Zintgraff in 1896 precipitated a similar display of arms (Chilver & Röschenthaler 2001: 89–94). Ernst recorded that war games were staged in front of the house he and Leimbacher occupied after arriving in Bali (1903: 74–5). Göhring's letter, later also excerpted for publication in *Deutsches Kolonialblatt* (*Deutsches Kolonialblatt* 1906a: 353–4), suggested that Fonyonga routinely held a military display to welcome missionaries three days after their arrival. They would be seated to the right of the Fon's throne (the position given to allied chiefs in 1905) and watch the dancing, music making, military manoeuvres and salutes, while being served with warmed palm wine. All this was part of Bali's complex of martial ceremonial and quite appropriate as an adjunct to the war-related rituals of Lela. Later, I demonstrate how sharply these features of royal ritual contrast with the priests' Voma complex.

Notes

1. His informant may well have been Glauning who devotes some lines of his report on a 1905 tour (1906: 239) to the fact that the same language is spoken in Bali and by the 'Dinyi', demonstrating they are the same people (but not relating them to Chamba). Benue and Bali Chamba-speakers in fact are branches of the same emigration. Alternatively, or additionally, Keller may have read Zintgraff's account of his conversation with Sultan Yakubu of Takum in 1889 who claimed cousinhood between Galega's father and his own (Chilver 1966: 16).
2. The first to make this connection was probably Strümpell from his wordlists (Strümpell 1910).

3.   In the case of the Gara of Donga's book about the Benue Chamba (Garbosa n.d.), the account of a pre-diasporic Chamba origin from Sham (supposed to be in Syria) is literally pasted into the book. The Colonial Officer and anthropologist, M.D.W. Jeffreys' accounts of Bali history seem to have circulated quite widely. Unfortunately his interpretation of evidence is irresponsibly cavalier with sources: drawing upon Sultan Njoya's, then unpublished, *History of Bamum*, his 1957 paper argues that the Bali are 'the descendants of a defeated mercenary army of the Fulbe', but he then relates oral traditions from Bali Kumbat that do not support this assertion put so baldly. Among some interesting details of court cases and local traditions, Jeffreys' two 1962 articles contain a catalogue of errors. Jeffreys assumes that Fonyonga was seventy-five years of age in 1925, although witnesses twenty years earlier had put him in his forties; dating the battle of Bafu Fondong in relation to the birth of Fonyonga's mother on this basis puts it back a full decade (1962b: 170). Jeffreys next confuses Barth's reference to the Fulbe lamidate of Tchamba with the people Chamba and concludes that the Chamba were 'inveterate raiders and marauders' (1962b: 171). An implausible set of constructions is offered in interpreting the Donga regnal list; among these, simple errors of arithmetic add a quarter-century to the combined total of reigns (see Fardon 1980, Vol. 2: 210–1). Jeffreys cites Tita Nji, son of Galega, as the source of a Bali history transcribed by Isaac Fielding Pefok in 1933; however, Tita Nji died in 1896 according to Esser (Jeffreys 1962b: 173 Note 12, see also Pefok 1962: 89 Note 14, where Jeffreys treats the extended kinglist as fact and reiterates the mistaken identification of Tita Nji). This history added five chiefs before the Gawolbe who is accepted to have led the Ba'ni to the Grassfields. It was presented before the Fon's Council on 2 November 1960, which, Jeffreys reports, discussed the account at length without agreeing whether it should be accepted: two elderly title holders 'were intransigent in their refusal … [and] held that Bali tradition started five kings back and no more …' (Jeffreys 1962b: 192). Nonetheless, and contrary to the earliest sources, the extra kings and a pre-jihadic date for the departure of the instigators of the Ba'ni migrations have become accepted fact in Ndifontah B. Nyamndi's account (1988: 14–15), which prefers a longer to a more accurate, albeit briefer, history.

4.   On the basis of an unpublished manuscript by C.K. Meek (1928 Wukari District Office), Chilver has suggested that among the Takum inhabitants were Kpati (speaking a Grassfield language), Jidu (possibly speaking Buti), Tikari, and Chamba – as well as people from the Benue plains (Chilver 1964 Report No. 1). This would be entirely consistent with the Takum people having derived from a vanguard made up of Peli (Pyeri, Pere).

5.   Bali Gham, Bali Gashu and Bali Gangsin are smaller groupings each claiming descent from a son of Gawolbe.

6.   This version would be of a piece with the tendency at Bali Nyonga to divide matters into male and female sides.

7.   It is highly suggestive in this light that Fonyonga offered the missionaries a site in the heart of the town for their school – which he seems to have desired even more earnestly than their cultic protection from evil influences – on the upper side of the plaza on which his palace was situated (Ernst 1903: 75).

8.   Russell suggests that Fonyonga created the five Fonte Ba'ni titles in order to balance the Fonte titles that he had allowed the BaNten to retain (1980: 53).

9.   According to Kaberry and Chilver, the senior title, Tita Kuna, was vested in the Peli of Bali Konntan; the other titles – all of them prefixed by *Gwan* – were distributed three to Buti, two to Tikali and one to Kefad (1961: 361, and Note 2).

10.   Pidgin English remained the language of administration, trade and mission in much of Kamerun, a fact that led to all European languages other than German being banned from schools in 1910 (Gwanfogbe 1995: 52).

11.   Leutnant von Putlitz, who was present at the installation (see **Figures 33** and **35**) had personally shot the chief of Bawatju in 1904 (according to Missionary Keller's 1904 *Jahresbericht*, excerpted in Merz 1997: 75–7). In the immediate wake of the June

installation, a thousand Bali accompanied the Schutztruppe on a punitive expedition against Bameta from which they returned with skulls of the slain. These details were not vouchsafed to readers of *Evangelische Heidenbote*. According to Keller's report of the following year, Ernst remonstrated with Fonyonga about head-taking, but the only effect was that warriors returned from war that year openly displaying the penes of the slain as trophies (Keller 1906 *Jahresbericht*, excerpted in Merz 1997: 113). See O'Neil (1987: 124–9, 137) for details of Bali punitive raids on southern Moghamo villages in March and April 1905. For more general background, see *Deutsches Kolonialblatt* (1906b).

12.   Given that they have not previously been treated as such, it is necessary to demonstrate that Göhring's photographs are likely to belong to a series. **Figure 32** was accessioned as 'Reception for the Göhring couple' in Basel (originally K775, see also Geary 1986: 100, 1988a: 28, 1990a: 437). This probably resulted from misreading a letter in which Göhring is doing two things: responding to a request from Basel for a picture of the Fon's throne, and describing the reception that the Fon typically staged for newly arrived missionaries (with no implication that his photograph was of such an occasion) (11 December 1905, BMA E-220.390). The fact of a print from the same photograph entering the Stuttgart collection via a colonial officer demonstrates that it is of the 1905 installation. The next photograph accessioned in the Basel series (as K776) was **Figure 33**, showing the proclamation of Fonyonga; immediately after that, however, a photograph of elaborately attired, presumably royal, wives was accessioned (**Figure 38**; K777, another copy of same K1844). Presumably this was taken at the same occasion and, if so, then two further photographs of less elaborately dressed women dancing on a single occasion are likely to belong with it (**Figures 39** and **40**; K1843 and K1845). The next in the series (K778) shows the entrance to Fonyonga's palace (**Figure 30**); and after that comes the picture of Göhring, his wife and Hohner en route to Bali (K779). There must be a strong presumption that all these photographs were shot by Göhring around the same time. **Figure 31** from the collection of the Linden-Museum Stuttgart (which has not – or not yet – been found among the Basel photographs) surely must also be Göhring's work.

13.   Presumably this is the man who would almost lose his life when a keg of powder exploded at the 1907 Lela and burnt down his palace (Dorsch, *Jahresbericht* 1907, extracted in Merz 1997: 114).

14.   However, Sally Chilver tells me this dating is not entirely secure. Hans Knöpfli suggests Bawock were already present by 1905 (2002: 63).

15.   Glauning was dark-haired with enormous handle-bar moustaches. It is not clear whether he is one of the figures in white uniform. The taller figure in a topi in **Figure 33** appears to have a moustache, and accompanying notes suggest Glauning appears in the photograph. However, the same man in **Figure 35** is not identified as Glauning in the caption.

16.   Catherine Steinegger Nzie (1998: 15–24) offers a helpful summary of the literature on Bali women's clothing.

Illustrations

Translations of original captions are in inverted commas; in several cases these are amended in the text. All figures are copyrighted to the following institutions which have graciously permitted their reproduction:

BEM: © Staatliche Museen zu Berlin, Preußischer Kulturbesitz, Ethnologisches Museum (Berlin Ethnological Museum)

BMA: © Basel Mission Archive; K series are original 'Kamerun' accession numbers; E series are current catalogue numbers; QE series are engravings made for publication

L-M: © Linden-Museum Stuttgart, Staatliches Museum für Völkerkunde

FI: © Frobenius Institut an der Johann Wolfgang Goethe Universität, Frankfurt am Main

Copies of *Figures 30, 32, & 33* were donated to both BMA and L-M; reproductions here are from the BMA collection which are the better preserved.

Both the BMA photographs reproduced here, and others referred to by identifiers beginning with E-, may be accessed and magnified at <http:www.bmpix.org/>

Figure 1. 'Decorations on the outer wall of the King's compound in Bali' (BMA K 1535/E-30.27.003).

Figure 2. 'The Bali King's thrones' (BMA K 1569 probably/E-30.27.008).

Figure 3. '*King of Bali in dance costume in front of his house*' (BMA K 1536 lost/QE-30.010.page 30 no 3).

Figure 4. 'Two tu ntsubo' (BEM VIII A 5398).

Figure 5. 'Decorations on the outer wall of the King of Bali's compound' (BMA K 1537/E-30.27.002).

Figure 6. 'Post at the palace entrance' (BEM VIII A 5397).

Figure 7. 'The cairn on the market place in Bali' (BMA K 1538/E-30.27.004).

Figure 8. 'Wind musicians at the Lela festival' (BEM VIII A 6736).

Figure 9. 'Cairn on the market place, with the assembled people' (BMA K 1539/E-30.27.005).

Figure 10. 'Lela festival' (BEM VIII A 6737).

Figure 11. 'Parade (Aufmarsch) during the Lela festival' (BMA K 1540/E-30.27.011).

Figure 12. 'Two men fishing' (BEM VIII A 6744).

Figure 13. 'Lela festival' (BEM VIII A 6743).

Figure 14. 'Lela festival in Bali' (BMA K 1541c/E-30.27.013).

Figure 15. 'Lela festival in Bali' (BMA K 1541b/E-30.27.012).

Figure 16. 'King of Bali enquiring of the oracle' (BMA K 1541a/E-30.27.014/QE-K3410).

Figure 17. 'Interval during Lela dancing in Bali' (BMA K 1542/E-30.27.006).

Figure 18. 'Grassfields – the Bali or Banja area' (BMA E-30.27.007).

Figure 19. 'People leaving after Lela (Abmarsch der Leute vom Lela)' (BMA K 1543/E-30.27.009 & 010).

83

Figure 20. 'People at Lela festival' (BEM VIII A 5304).

Figure 21. 'People at Lela festival' (BEM VIII A 5305).

Figure 22. 'People at Lela festival' (BEM VIII A 5306).

Figure 23. 'People at Lela festival' (BEM VIII A 5307).

Figure 24. 'People at Lela festival' (BEM VIII A 5308).

Figure 25. '1907 portrait of Jonathan Striebel' (BMA QS-30.001.1243.01).

Figure 26. 'Letya' (BEM VIII A 6578).

Figure 27. 'Chief Galega II of Bali' (BMA E-30.85.213).

Figure 28. 'Fulbe country. Tchamba on the River Faro: the great Salaam (Friday prayers)' (1911, FI 5891).

Figure 29. 'Cavalry with flags on the parade ground of Dikoa, 29 February 1904' (L-M S 138 Glauning 1).

Figure 30. 'Assembled sub-chiefs in Bali' (BMA K 778/E-30.26.052); 'From von Putlitz 1908' (L-M Westafrika II, Kamerun, page 32 upper).

Figure 31. 'On the market place Bali gathered on the occasion of the proclamation, von Putlitz 1908' (L-M Westafrika II, Kamerun, page 33 upper).

Figure 32. 'Throne of the Bali King before the reception for the Göhrings in 1905' (BMA K 775/E-30.26.051); 'Armchair throne [Thronsessel] in front of the house of the Bali chief, von Putlitz 1908' (L-M Westafrika II, Kam. 32 lower).

Figure 33. 'Proclamation in Bali of King Fonyonga as paramount chief (Oberkönig): 14 [15] June 1905, Keller, Ernst, Leutnant von Putlitz, Hauptmann Glauning, soldiers' (BMA K 776/E-30.26.050); 'From von Putlitz 1908' (L-M Westafrika II, Kamerun, page 33 lower).

Figure 34. 'Fonjonge, chief of Bali, delivers a speech to his people from the King's stone' (L-M S138 Glauning 1 147).

Figure 35. 'Meeting of the Bali sub-chiefs in front of the Bali chief's palace, among the Europeans some missionaries as well as Leutnant von Putlitz and Chief Doctor Rauch, 15 June 1905' (L-M S138 Glauning 2 151).

Figure 36. **'Meeting of chiefs in Bali, von Putlitz 1909'** (L-M Westafrika II, Kamerun, page 42 lower right).

Figure 37. 'The Bali chief Fonjonge on his throne in front of the palace, 15 June 1905' (L-M S138 Glauning 2 149).

Figure 38. 'Chiefs' [Häuptlingsfrauen – so also chief's] wives dancing' (BMA K 777 = K 1844/E-30.27.017).

Figure 39. 'Bali women dancing' (BMA K 1843/E-30.27.019).

Figure 40. 'Wives of King dancing' (BMA K 1845/E-30.27.018).

Figure 41. (Ankermann's original photograph lost, reproduced from Stumpf 1911, illustration 3).

Figure 42. 'Musicians in Bali' (BMA E-30.27.022).

Figure 43. 'Grassfield Musicians' (BMA E-30.27.023).

Figure 44. 'Missionary Ernst and King Fo Nyonga at the school festival, April 1909' (BMA E-30.26.023).

CHAPTER 5

Lela in the Grassfields and the 'Graffi' in Lela: Or, More is More

The Importance of Origins

Where things came from mattered; but it mattered to different audiences in different ways. Bali Nyonga's eager adoptions of German, and other imported European signs of power and prestige – or simply fashionable adornment – were easily spotted by European outsiders. Entire army uniforms (or parts thereof: buttons, helmets, breastplates, epaulettes …), imported tapestries, decorated pottery, gramophone, foghorn, sunglasses, pith helmets, hand mirrors, boaters … these items and others impressed early observers forcibly, often eliciting their amused condescension in ways that the adoption of all-too-obviously practical breechloading rifles or European steel sabres did not. Yet, this concern with the more symbolic side of what later times would call 'colonial mimesis' between Africans and Europeans overlooked what was more significant to local observers than the mere matter of copying.

In Grassfield, or 'Graffi' political culture, prestige and public display were inseparable: royal prestige was made actual through an accumulation of treasures. Within two or three generations of entering the Grassfields, the newly arriving Bali had adopted this way of using the materials they sought out through gift and trade (in Bali Nyonga particularly, expectations about behaviour appropriate to leaders were presumably incorporated along with the Grassfield people who soon became the majority population). Hence, when Bali Nyonga Fons accumulated and displayed European manufactures they did do so in Graffi fashion, rather than in a way that somehow sprang unmediated from their own European encounter. It is not obviously the case that the distinction orienting their action was that between Africans and Europeans, rather than those between Bali and other Grassfield kingdoms.

The European encounter in the Grassfields was not the first occasion on which these raiders from what was to become Adamawa had adopted material expressions of the political cultures dominant in the places where they found themselves and added them to the self-consciously distinctive traces of their own previous past. To the Grassfielders among whom the Ba'ni settled, Adamawan traces may have seemed as worthy of remark as European traces but, lacking the requisite comparative knowledge, it would have been difficult for late nineteenth- and early twentieth-century European observers to discern them as such. Bali Nyonga strongly marked certain elements of their predominantly Grassfield cultural repertoire as exotic; and their neighbours recognised this by their acceptance of Bali proprietorship of ceremonies such as Lela or Voma, or by paying to adopt them, or by adopting them to indicate the existence of an alliance with those who owned them. Exotic resources were potential sources not only of distinction but also of wealth and alliance. Various items are still thought exogenous to the Grassfields by Bali themselves: some are reminders of their exotic origin such as seating mats woven in particular designs, or round rather than rectangular huts; others are involved with ritual practices, like the use of kaolin rather than camwood for reddening ritual objects, playing *lela* flutes and *voma* horns, and the consecration both of these wind instruments and of other paraphernalia with beer rather than the local alcoholic beverage of choice, palm wine. At an earlier time, these Adamawan materials were themselves differentiated to reference, or name-check, earlier incorporations outside the Grassfields of people whose rituals featured throwing knives or forked *lela* poles, and a memory of this remained at least until the time of Chilver and Kaberry's investigations. However, the fact of informants being able consistently to itemise more or less the same list of Ba'ni traits that were not of Grassfield origin serves to underline both how far the general run of Bali material culture became typical of its Grassfield setting, and how far assumed pre-Grassfield traits have been homogenised by classification as such. The Grassfields were home to one of the most prolific material cultures of sub-Saharan Africa in pre-colonial times; with a few exceptions (such as Mumuye wooden statuary, bronze casting, and certain types of mask) this cannot be said of pre-jihadic Adamawa. The Grassfields were increasingly incorporated into European trade circuits carrying diverse goods, whereas old Adamawa was relatively peripheral to northern trade circuits and received a restricted set of goods (Chilver 1961). The Grassfields must have seemed a land of abundance for those arriving from the north; while the Grassfielders hardly distinguished between waves of northern raiders, one of which became a permanent local feature when its members coalesced and then dispersed to settle in their own kingdoms. In this context, the opposition that mattered was that between people and things available locally (including European things) and people and things that came from the north. What came southwards from outside the Grassfields was identified with the Ba'ni irrespective of the particular people from which it originated. Hence, by the time they settled in the Grasssfields, things they had copied from the Fulbe, whose jihad had provoked the exodus of Adamawan raiders in the first place, had become included in the broad category of Ba'ni characteristics.

Bali material and performative culture thus drew on four types of source, but which was remarkable depended upon who was looking. Grassfield materials were relatively unmarked by their origin for Europeans, which allowed European imports to be clearly discernible to them as such. Some of the things and performances derived from non-Fulbe peoples of Adamawa were strongly marked

for Bali and their neighbours alike because they signalled the exotic northern
character of the most powerful elements of Bali Nyonga's hierarchy. However,
included amongst these in Lela were elements derived from the culture of Fulbe
warfare, particularly flags and, at one time, the durbar-style equestrian salute.
However, the source of these borrowings went unremarked, probably forgotten as
such. Their recollection would have required historical narratives different from
those Bali and non-Bali in the Grassfields generally told about one another.

More is More

In this chapter I want to concentrate on the Grassfield context of Bali performative
culture and on the organising contrast between things and practices acquired
before, and those acquired after, the Ba'ni entered the Grassfields. I start with
wood-carving about which I cannot do better than begin with the lesson Christraud
Geary drew from the evidence she marshalled.

> Figurative wood sculpture … was a major form of artistic expression and was an essen-
> tial part in the political and historical discourse in the Grassfields […] If the Bali-
> Nyonga were to be successful competitors in the region, they had to become conversant
> in this local idiom, just as they ultimately adopted a local language. (Geary 1988a: 18)

Transition to these Grassfield modes of material communication was facilitated by
the adherence of two populations with considerable sculptural expertise: the BaTi
(from 1904 to 1911) and the Bawock (from some time between 1905 and 1907
onwards).[1]

One of the most striking and obvious of changes in regalia occurred when
Fonyonga retired his father's stone throne and replaced it with a decorated sculpted
throne. According to Geary, Galega's stone throne (which we see in photographs
of Zintgraff's time outside and – for anyone exiting – to the right of the palace
entrance) was moved during Fonyonga's reign to a 'throne chamber' inside the
gates (effectively, a partitioned section of the veranda of an internal palace
building, see Northern 1973: 64, plate 56). A photograph taken by Ankermann
(BEM VIII A 5320; reproduced by both Geary 1988a: 26, plate 5, and Northern
1973: 65, plate 57) shows how, in its new position, the solid stone throne was
enclosed within a three-sided screen decorated with beads and a frieze of cowries,
and rows of ivory tusks were set lengthwise into the front edge of the circular
mound on which it stood. It was, in short, put into a Grassfield frame.

Albeit Chamba have sculptural traditions – as do other Adamawan peoples
whom they incorporated – so far as I am aware, and in contrast to the
contemporaneously founded Benue Chamba chiefdoms, no pieces in Adamawan
style have ever been collected from the Bali kingdoms (see Fardon & Stelzig
2005). On the face of it the implication is clear: the migrants lost any sculptural
traditions they might once have possessed and were forced to acquire these anew
in the Grassfields. It came as a grave disappointment to Ankermann to discover
that he had chosen as his field residence Bali, where there was a lively trade in
carvings but little production, rather than the Bamum capital, Fumban, where

there were active carvers. M.D.W. Jeffreys, when he had already been Senior District Officer for two years, and the long-serving Basel missionary Georg Tischhauser, were able to be definite when writing to the journal *Man* in 1938: Bali did not 'go in for wood carving' neither in 1938 nor in the past (Jeffreys 1938: No. 186, responding to Thomas 1938); this was true of both Bali Kumbat and of Bali Nyonga, with the single exception in the latter case of Batanwa'ni, an older brother to Tita Nji 'who understands to carve wood' as Tischhauser was told (Tischhauser 1938: No. 187). However, the record is not unanimous, and there have even been suggestions that the Bali Nyonga Fons themselves took up carving: a craft not incompatible with kingship for them, as it would have been in Adamawa, where carving tended to be associated with smithing. Tamara Northern recorded an accession entry in the Linden-Museum's *Hauptbuch* concerning a beaded stool (now lost) collected by Hauptmann Hirtler in 1904 from Bamenda:

> This stool comes without doubt from Bali, where it was used by the then reigning King FoNjonge. It was made by the old Garega himself just as the other beaded works (throne, half life-size figures, and the like) which always appeared in important ceremonies. On the occasion of the very interesting ceremonies in December 1902, Mr. Hirtler saw these objects himself [in Bali]. Bead decoration is occasionally used in Bali. FoNjonge was instructed [in beading] by his father Garega. FoNjonge is very attached to these heirlooms from Garega. (Quoted in English translation, with her insertions in square brackets, by Northern 1973: 66)

In Geary's opinion, based on wider knowledge of his reports, Hirtler was a reliable observer; and she notes plausibly that the ceremony Hirtler witnessed in December 1902 was likely to have been Lela. If this is the case, then there is a strong possibility that the sculptures in the regalia photographed at the 1908 Lela are the same as those seen six years earlier (**Figures 1** and **2**). In that case, however, they date from the end of Galega's reign rather than from the beginning of Fonyonga's. Galega's credentials as a carver do not go uncontested. In his survey of the region, Pierre Harter stated that the throne was the work of a Bawock carver on behalf of Fonyonga, and that the pair of standing figures was created by a Bali carver called Tanwani (1986: 231).[2] The figures were reported by him to have disappeared. Although the throne was allegedly still displayed among the palace treasures (Harter 1986: 230), Geary was unable to see it during the researches she conducted around the same time as his (Geary 1988a: 21). We know that Fonyonga's throne existed by 1905 because it appears in photographs of his installation as paramount; if Hirtler refers to the same throne in 1902, which is probable though not definite, then it is less likely to have been the work of Bawock carvers: they cannot have moved to Bali earlier than 1905 because the BaTi relatives who mediated their move themselves moved to Bali only in 1904.

The status of the throne is in fact more complicated than these commentators have allowed. An imitation of elaborate Bamum and Bamileke thrones, which it does not approach in sculptural authority,[3] it clearly consisted of two parts which are in different sculptural styles. Martin Göhring remarked, in a letter answering Basel queries about the throne (in 1905)[4] that the base was in one piece to which the figures serving as a backrest were attached; the bead decoration was in Bali style (BMA E-220.390). Because the base of the throne was only as wide as a large stool, the figures had to be attached by a single leg (at the cost of losing a foot) and they hang off the throne, hardly the strongest anchorage for a backrest, and an indication that the throne may have been cobbled together from pieces to hand. Perhaps this is what is meant by Galega making the throne: that he assembled and beaded the throne, or had these things done?[5] Base and figures are in distinct styles: the base is similar to other stools in the royal collection, while the figures are akin to the two freestanding regalia figures in execution. According to Northern, Babanki was the favoured supplier of carvings to Bali during the early twentieth century (1973: 62), and it may be significant in this context that Babanki was among the Grassfield chiefdoms that adopted the Lela ceremonial from the Bali. Hans Knöpfli, from long experience of carving styles around Bamenda, concurs that the throne figures were in Babanki style but that the stool at the throne's base must have been made by BaTi or Bamileke (personal communication, May 2001). In asking for (or being given) four Babanki statues to add to the royal regalia, perhaps the Bali Fon was introducing a practice that we also find in the Bafut Lela in the mid-twentieth century (see below). The exact course of mutual influence involved is difficult to trace, but the effect is clearly to bring Bali Nyonga – and the Lela ceremony – into line with Grassfield practices, and the upshot is that both Bafut and Bali once had a pair of anthropomorphic statues in the regalia they exhibited at Lela (albeit the Bali statues later disappeared from the scene).

Grassfield artworks in general carried a very high degree of embellishment in various media: carving, beading, embroidery. For Grassfielders it seems that more usually was more: ornamentation of particular objects went hand in hand with the accumulation and display of aggregates of objects. At first sight, the treasure display at Lela fits comfortably within this aesthetic. However, closer inspection suggests a distinction between what is likely to be the longstanding apparatus – the *lela* flutes, iron spears and spear bundles, and forked *lela* poles – which has remained relatively unadorned, and display elements that are hardly involved in the auguries carried out on Lela's first day. Aside from the royal stools and statues (and the collection of beaded calabashes kept by the flags, of which we lack photographs in Bali, but are documented from Bafut), two pairs of poles which caught Ankermann's eye are elaborately beaded.

One pair of posts with prongs stood to what would be the left side of the palace entrance for the exiting Fon (**Figures 5** and **6**). Redecorated for Lela, the posts stood bare for the remainder of the year. Fonyonga, as we already learnt, told Ankermann that their routine function was as a stand for weapons belonging to men visiting the palace for palavers. Harter records that clan chiefs possessed similar poles on which to hang knives or lean spears during solemn occasions (1986: 230). If my supposition that the palace entrance was oriented with respect to the exiting Fon has substance, we could motivate the everyday arrangement of throne to the right, and weapon stand to the left, which Bali Nyonga shared with Bali Kumbat (Baumann & Vajda 1959: 300) in terms of common associations between more and less auspicious sides. However, once decorated for Lela, the weapon stands must have had a more representative function: displaying the range of Bali weaponry and Lela insignia (as well as enemy skulls in Hutter's time). The main trunk of the decorated poles of 1908 featured lizards on a red background, while the horns were patterned in blue and white lozenges. Knöpfli lists several characteristics of lizards as apposite royal images, not least that they were among the creatures into which Fons were capable of transforming (1999: 55–9). Explanations of the number of prongs on the posts have been subjected to frequent revision: most recently the posts (as well as the flags and Y-shaped *letya*) have been motivated as male and female and, in accordance with common sub-Saharan African reckoning, claimed to have three and four prongs on this account (Russell 1980: 61–2). The late twentieth-century scholar-missionary and founder of the Bali artisanat, Hans Knöpfli, heard what is probably a created tradition convenient to Bali Nyonga's hegemonic interests: that the two posts had seven points in sum in order to represent the seven components into which the Bali split after their defeat at Kolm. As noted earlier, in Mungaka these posts are called *tu ngangeid*: *tu* simply means wood or something made of wood; and I speculated, following Tischhauser's dictionary definition of *ngangyed* as bow, that a 'wooden pole for bows' might fit with the idea of weapon stands for a people who entered the Grassfields initially as mounted bowmen.

Another pair of decorated posts, the *tu ntsubo* – erected as gateposts to the palace entrance, photographed by Ankermann in 1908 (**Figure 4**) – apparently served a straightforward display function: given the Fon's identification with the leopard and the scale of royal polygyny, the symbolism of the poles' leopard finials surmounting four female figures atop each other seems to require no esoteric exegesis. According to the Tischhauser's Mungaka dictionary, the translation of *tu ntsubo* is entirely prosaic: wooden pole at the yard entrance.

Since Lela celebrated the achievements of warriors, it is no surprise that the fighting men of Bali were tricked out in their finery as, in a quite different way, were the women. The 'traditional' Bali men's costume, now typical of the Grassfields as a whole, derives from a synthesis of northern and Grassfield aesthetics that the Bali catalysed.[6] As Gardi has shown, the garment has evolved over at least a century that we are able to document while remaining similar in conception: the gown is T-shaped (consisting of a body and two wide sleeves); two types of material are used (the neck and the extremities of both the body and the sleeves are in a dark cloth, the mid-body and upper sleeves are in patterned cloth); there is always dense embroidery around the neck, but this may extend – with increasing expense – to much of the garment. The garment evolved rapidly alongside newly available materials. The Bali entered the Grassfields, so oral recollections have consistently recounted, as horsemen who wore gowns and chewed kola. Presumably these northern gowns were trade items. The contemporary Bali gown more resembles a tunic with arms than the flowing ceremonial robe of the north; presumably it evolved from the northern war tunic, since it is generally shorter than a dressy northern gown and has closer fitting sleeves. The patterned sections of the oldest gowns were probably made from blue cloth with white patterns that was imported predominantly from the Jukun town of Wukari (Rubin 1969: 55). White patterns were produced by sewing strips of raffia through designs sketched in charcoal so as to resist subsequent immersion in indigo. This cloth was so valued in the Benue region that Warnier suggests it mostly passed as gifts between chiefs rather than in open market (Warnier 1985: 112). However, the importation of European cotton was to displace African materials: Warnier's information suggests that during the nineteenth century plain black cloth was first imported to the Grassfields and used to make Bali gowns in combination with decorative panels from the Benue; later a checked cloth became available as a cheaper alternative for the patterned sections of the gown (Warnier 1985: 166–7). As well as embroidery, crocheting was encouraged by the importation of brightly coloured yarns, so that the Bali gown and cap both became increasingly colourful and distinctive. The men's undergarment, meanwhile, retained its Adamawan form: rather than pantaloons, Bali men wore – and wear – kilts under their gowns made of two panels: longer at the back and shorter at the front. In Adamawa these kilts were made predominantly from narrow loomed cloth; however, the most expensive of them would have a larger central back panel of resist-dyed cloth. This makes one wonder whether the Bali gown, with its decorated central patterns framed by a plain border, does not preserve an overall conception and aesthetic characteristic of men's ceremonial clothing in Adamawa. According to Hans-Joachim Koloss's investigations in Oku, Grassfielders claim the use of cloth was once restricted to masquerades (2000: 239). Whether or not this was literally the case, it indicates the very high value once commanded by cloth. Men's everyday dress was bark cloth, and woven cotton cloth was reserved for the most special occasions. Galega's 1896 comment, reported by Esser – that 'dresses were not healthy for women and cloths existed only to adorn men in war and at the celebration of a victory' (Chilver & Röschenthaler 2001: 90) – suggests that the Bali were responsible for associating the use of cloth with the violence of making war or celebrating warfare, turning the adorned body of the warrior into a masquerade-like object of menacing power. By Keller's time there was a fashion for men's ceremonial kilts to trail some metres of cloth on the ground behind them, a conspicuously heedless use of a commodity recently so scarce and still so costly (Keller 1919: 116).

The most lavish evidence for Bali Nyonga's adoption of Grassfield standards of competitive material display is architectural. Photographs of Bali town at the turn of the nineteenth century and for a few years thereafter reveal a very unshowy style of architecture. However, Fonyonga had a large and ornate meeting house erected just before the First World War to replace the plain building seen to the observer's right of the palace entrance in earlier photographs.[7] Geary has observed that the building of this statement about Bali power, encrusted with carvings of Bali warriors, coincided with the erosion of Bali's actual power under successive German reassessments and the competition between it and Bamum for German favour (1988a: 33). One might add that the building process also coincided with the marked deterioration in relations between the palace and the Basel Mission that followed Ernst's death and the realisation that the missionaries were powerless to halt Bali's declining importance to German administration (Steinegger Nzie 1998: 34–35 Note 42). It seems that Fonyonga reused some of the sculptures in a new clubhouse when his palace reception room was rebuilt, and these were subsequently dispersed when that building fell into disuse.

Lela Adopted in the Grassfields

It was not only in the field of material culture that the Adamawan core of the Bali chiefdoms adapted to a Grassfield context. Cultural, performative and organisational repertoires were affected more generally. For instance, Bali Nyonga adopted military and regulatory societies of Grassfield origin; or, more accurately, these organisations may have come to Bali together with Grassfield populations incorporated into the kingdom. To do more than note such developments would take us far from our main theme, but they provide a context in which to appreciate a traffic in public culture that appears on the surface to have taken place in the opposite direction: sources consistently, but probably not independently, mention three places as having adopted the Lela solemnities: Bafut, Mankon and Babanki/Kijem Kegu (e.g. Harter 1986: 230; Russell 1980: 36). All three kingdoms lie between, and to the north of, Bali Nyonga and Bali Kumbat, so either of the bigger Bali kingdoms might have given them their Lela ceremonies. Bali Nyonga's relations with both Mankon and Bafut were poor. Before reaching Bali Nyonga, Nyongpasi's Bali had camped at Bafreng for some time, probably during the 1840s, and allied with them; this alliance in turn may have provoked Bafut and Bali Kumbat to ally against the new arrivals exchanging both gifts and institutions (Chilver & Kaberry 1963: 6). Bafut and Mankon emerged as the leading local states from these disruptions and, on the arrival of Zintgraff, they too made common cause in their enmity to Bali Nyonga.

Chilver and Kaberry's Bafut informant on Lela in 1960 was an aged senior councillor of *kwifon* named Che (Lord) Bina (who is directly quoted on other matters in Chilver & Kaberry 1963: 21–2). Their account concurs closely with those by Robert and Pat Ritzenthaler (1962: 126–30) and Pat Ritzenthaler (1966: 186–90); however, all could well have come from the same local sources. In a chapter she calls 'A dance for the Fon', on the grounds that this is considered the more correct name for the event, Pat Ritzenthaler states that once Lela had been borrowed from Bali Kumbat it was combined in Bafut with sacrificial ceremonies called Ebin. The fourth day of each week honoured the Fon, and every fourth week on this day sacrifices were made at pools where it was supposed the royal dead lived. Once a year, at a time that usually fell around the third week in December, the elders of *kwifon* sacrificed a goat at a pool six or eight miles outside Bafut as a preamble to Lela.

According to Bina's testimony to Chilver and Kaberry, the alliance between Bali Kumbat and Bafut was sealed by sacrifice, after which the Bafut saw Lela and copied it, making their own flag which they called *chetuwara* (after the Bali *tutuwan*). This tradition concurs with 'Bali traditions [that] Bafut acquired *lela* from Bali-Kumbad in the reign of the fourth *Ga*, Galabi II, on the occasion of the renewal of the non-aggression treaty first made in the reign of the second *Ga*' (Chilver & Kaberry 1968: 66). Like its Bali equivalents, the Bafut Lela involves decoration of the royal compound with Jukun or Ndop cloth and the exhibition of treasures (including imported pottery), flag-washing, tributes from sub-chiefs (Ritzenthaler & Ritzenthaler 1962: 128), displays of loyalty by *manjong* military lodges, and the use of *ati lela* or forked poles equivalent to *letya*, flutes, and a royal spear. Pat Ritzenthaler (1966: 188) describes how the forked *lela* poles were cut on the first day of the festival and stripped of their bark. A goat (in earlier times a human) was sacrificed at their base, after which a bull's eye design of concentric circles was burned and carved at the fork of the pole and a mouth-like lateral cut made in the stem (Ritzenthaler & Ritzenthaler 1962: 128, plate 63). Two near life-sized wooden figures also formed part of the paraphernalia: their bodies were beaded, and the male figure, clothed in a cap and patterned wrapper, carried a drinking horn; the female figure wore a necklace and waistband of cowries and, upright on her left palm supported by her right hand, she carried a gourd, presumably for palm wine, as if prepared to pour. These figures called *maanfo'ti* were an ancestral royal couple who received offerings of palm wine (Ritzenthaler & Ritzenthaler 1962: 127 Plate 62, 129 Plate 64; Knöpfli 1999: 49).

Chilver and Kaberry's informant explained that *manjong* (the military society) was formerly sent to capture a 'slave' for sacrifice at the *ati lela*. Nowadays a goat is used instead; but the goat, as formerly the man, should still be killed by the Fon (recall that Ankermann had been told by Ernst that the Fon of Bali himself made sacrifice in 1907, although we have no record of his doing so subsequently). The sacrifice is apparently buried in a large hole by the forked poles. None of the sources on Bali Nyonga reveal what was buried at the foot of the *lela* poles, although Chilver and Kaberry were given the names of two pots that were somehow involved. However, we know from Hutter that human victims were captured and executed in preparation for the 1891 Lela, and we might speculate that the forked *lela* poles may relate to grave markers: Fonyonga told Ankermann that a new Fon had to make new *letya* or risk his father's curse (Baumann & Vajda 1959: 244). Forked poles might well have evoked bovine horns, as they do among Dowayo (Seignobos 1998, and below), and could have fused with evocations of the dead to condense the dangers of both the bush and the underworld.

Bafut's Lela may well have features of Adamawan provenance, but just as pertinent to our present interests are those Grassfield features it also shares with the Bali Nyonga. The magnificent pair of ancestral sculptures brought out during Bafut's Lela are both larger and better executed than the figures displayed among Bali Nyonga's Lela treasures prior to the First World War. Bali Nyonga's figures may have been ancestralised in conception, like their Bafut counterparts – their placement alongside the royal throne makes this possible – but we lack any explicit indication of what the presence of the statues in **Figures 1** and **2** may have meant to Bali people in 1908. A notion present in Bafut's Lela, but absent from Adamawan ceremony, is that previous Fons inhabit pools. Such an idea of ancestral presence was entertained by at least some in Bali, but to my knowledge it lacks Chamba precedents. Chamba make offerings to their dead relatives on their graves, or on their skulls, or in small beer pots, but deep water is generally reckoned the abode of dangerous and maleficent genies. In the context of Chamba rituals, 'washing' usually meant a metaphorical cleansing rather than literal immersion in water. The speculation – on the basis of no more evidence than I have given here – is that Bali Chamba have literalised the sense of 'washing' in their rituals by taking on some of the associations that Grassfielders like Bafut make between deep water and ancestors/chiefs. This literalisation has subsequently been christianised through the parallels that Basel exegesists, and local commentators influenced by their teaching, made between Old Testament rituals of purification and some elements of Lela.

For all its musketry and marching, however, the Bafut Lela apparently was not an augury of military success in the sense that so struck Striebel of Bali's Lela. Pat Ritzenthaler writes that Lela was strictly the name of only the last two days of Bafut's four-day ceremony, the time when dancing and saluting took place in more or less identical fashion to Bali. One gains the impression that for Bali, on the contrary, the serious part of Lela was what happened during the first two days, to which the other days were a festive coda as well as an occasion to demonstrate loyalty.

Chilver (in a written comment on a transcription of the interview she and Kaberry carried out on 26 June 1960) has noted that Nkwen (or Bafreng), Bafut's neighbour, also had a Lela ceremony involving flag washing. There is no information when, or from whom, Nkwen adopted Lela; however, there was an alliance between Aze'fo II of Nkwen and the Bali leader Nyongpasi which might well have been the occasion for such a transfer: Nkwen remained an ally throughout the German period (Chilver & Kaberry 1968: 61). In Nkwen, as in Bafut, Lela was assimilated with the pre-existing ceremony of *aben* (1968: 62). Given that Bafut allied with Bali Kumbat rather than Bali Nyonga, it may be more plausible to imagine Bali Nyonga's Lela ceremony initially adopting its particular Grassfields features from Nkwen rather than Bafut. For its part, we know that Big Babanki was a major supplier of carvings to Bali Nyonga, so it seems likely it adopted Lela via this relation rather than from Bali Kumbat.[8]

About the circumstances of Mankon's adoption of Lela we know relatively little. What we do know – both about Mankon's alliances and the nature of its Lela festival – point towards a relation with Bafut and/or Bali Kumbat (rather than Bali Nyonga) as the source of the festival. The Mankon royal lineage maintains a war lodge – under the name of 'Nda' or house of 'Lale' – which holds an annual dance around December. Called the 'dance of the Fon', it features two Y-shaped poles, erected in front of a podium on which the Fon is seated, as well as four *lela* flutes and a flag. Jean-Pierre Warnier, to whose personal communication I owe this information (17 November 1999), feels that the complex of Lela features is most likely to have been imported during the nineteenth century. The close relations between Mankon and Bafut during their alliance against the combined forces of Galega and Zintgraff, might have provided one occasion for the transfer of Lela. Celebrations following their victory over the German–Bali alliance apparently continued for weeks until there was no more palm wine to be had (Ritzenthaler 1966: 38, 42–3, referring to Mankon as Bande). Alternatively, alliance between Mankon and Bali Kumbat, and consequent transfer of Lela, might date to Bali Nyonga's initial disruption of the status quo when displacing Bali Konntan in the mid-nineteenth century. The overall likelihood is that we are dealing with a wider uptake of Lela in the context of hostilities between Bali Kumbat and Bali Nyonga: the longer-established of the two Balis extended Lela to Bafut and Mankon, both of which shared its antipathy to Bali Nyonga; the latter shared Lela with its ally Nkwen and client Big Babanki. The outcome of these transactions was not only the export of the Adamawan elements of Lela, but the importation of Grassfield elements into Lela.

Lela and Voma in the Bali Kingdoms

Among central Chamba, where my intensive researches have been largely confined, Lela and Voma are contrasted terms. The contrast is multivalent, but its most straightforward implications might begin with their respective performative cultures: Lela is performed publicly with tuned sets of bamboo flutes; the sets of calabash horns on which Voma is played are not seen other than by initiates. Voma is also the generic term for a profusion of named cult groupings, each entered by initiation and payment, each controlling its own paraphernalia, procedures and distinctive performance, and each capable of averting ills and/or bringing about well-being. Beyond these shared characteristics the variety of particular Voma is wide: from highly restrictive and dangerous cults deploying the threat of dread disease, to cults virtually free from contagion which perform harvest dances shielded from the sight of women and children only by a matting fence. Voma is both the totality of such cults and each of them individually. In Chamba chiefdoms the contrast between Lela and Voma corresponds ideally to the distinction between the powers of chiefs and those of their priests who control the most important cults of the land, and deal with the bodies of dead chiefs, installing their successors.

Something akin to this division of responsibilities survives in Bali Kumbat and Bali Gham; Stuart Russell calls it the Ba'ni system on the assumption that it preserves organisational categories that mattered to the united Ba'ni alliance before their defeat at, and dispersal after, Kolm (1980: 36). The Fon (known by the Chamba Leko title *Ga*) appoints two sister's sons on his enthronement to serve as Do Kuna, his deputy, and Do Nyagang, his military leader: both titles which, shorn of the honorific 'Do', are in wide usage in Chamba chiefdoms. There is a division of labour such that members of the royal patriclan, Sama, prepare the Lela celebration, while certain among the Ndagana, the kingdom's population of non-royal origin, succeed to hereditary priestships (*ba-ngwana* or *-nwana*) the duties of which include organisation of Voma. All these terms (Sama, Daka, *nwana*), like the office titles (Gara, Kuna, Nyagang), are Chamba Leko in immediate origin (though not confined to Chamba in their northern range).

Bali Nyonga's organisation is less clear-cut than this pattern, which Bali Kumbat and Bali Gham created for themselves with strong Chamba precedents. As Chilver and Kaberry demonstrated, power was concentrated in the hands of a succession of able and long-reigning Bali Nyonga monarchs to an unprecedented degree. Even where there was an expectation that a title would remain within a family line, title holders were subject to appointment by the Fon. Thanks, presumably, to the Fon exercising his right to select office-holders as he saw fit, both the Sama office-holders and the *ngwana* are diverse in their origins. The powers that Voma wields in other Bali chiefdoms passed in Bali Nyonga to the Grassfields regulatory society of *nggumba* (*kwifon*) as well as to appointed *nkom* who act as 'magistrates' (Russell 1980: 36). Bali Nyonga is alleged to have lost its Voma organisation entirely prior to the late nineteenth century when it was reintroduced by a sister's son of the then Fon, Galega I, upon whom the title Tita Gwanvoma was conferred. However, Galega gave custody of Voma to one of his senior Sama, and also appointed other Sama to be *ba-ngwana*, including his senior standard bearer at Lela, Tita Nyagang (Russell 1980: 59). By doing so, he effectively fudged the contrast between Lela and Voma officials typical of the other Bali kingdoms and of Chamba chiefdoms. We do not know whether he did this consciously, or indeed quite what might have been his motives for acquiring so markedly Ba'ni a piece of custom at so late a date. One might speculate that fences were being mended with Bali Kumbat, and there were also reasons for Ba'ni interests in Bali Nyonga to wish to distinguish themselves from the non-Ba'ni who outnumbered them. Reclaiming Gawolbe's skull and weapons from Bafu Fondong – where they are alleged to have been kept following the defeat of the Ba'ni at Kolm – occurred around the same time and suggests an attempt by Bali Nyonga to be recognised as the senior of the Bali kingdoms (Jeffreys 1962b: 182). It is typical of the Bali Fons that they should simultaneously be pursuing cultural policies of competition with Grassfield rivals in terms of Grassfield norms, modernisation in alliance with the German commercial, political and religious-cum-educational interests, and a retraditionalisation of ceremonial to emphasise their northern origins.

Written descriptions of Voma among Bali Chamba are scanty in comparison to those of Lela, and the photographic record of Voma is slight. Because Lela was, among other things, a show of arms and allegiance, it had to be public by its very nature. Insulation from unfettered public gaze was just as intrinsic to the character of Voma as publicity was to Lela. I have seen only three photographs of Voma performers dating from the German colonial period: a published photograph taken by Ankermann, the original of which is now lost, **Figure 41** (Stumpf 1911, illustration 3), and two photographs in the Basel Mission collection. One of these was taken by Missionary Martin Göhring (archived as taken between 1902 and 1912, but probably dating from 1905 or 1906 when he was based in Bali); the other was submitted to the archive by Missionary Johannes Ittmann (between 1911 and 1913) and filed as 'musicians': **Figure 42** (BMA E-30.27.022), **Figure 43** (BMA E-30.27.023). All three photographs show sets of horns, graded in size and thus pitch, each made of interlocking sections of calabash, a design typical of Adamawan cults; rhythmic accompaniment was supplied by drumming but also by more esoteric instruments: sack rattles that players of the larger horns in the Voma band shook in their left hands. Not every Chamba cult possessed a full set of horns and rattles, or indeed any horns at all, in its paraphernalia. The horns and rattles accompanied singing and dancing, and they were associated most closely with the cults that appeared at harvest festivals and during funerary wakes. Being the most public, and relatively unthreatening, of cultic performances, these were among the more immediate references of Voma for non-initiates. But specific Voma were also known as agencies capable of 'catching' any who broke their rules concerning non-revelation, or who breached rights – for instance of property – over which Voma had been set as protective devices.

Understandably, such descriptions as we have of Voma predominantly concern the more public aspects of the cults. None of these descriptions derives from missionary eye-witnesses, which suggests that Voma represented a paganism beyond the pale in ways that Lela did not. The same story is retold by Russell, who states it concerns Lydia Keller, wife of the missionary Jakob (1980: 74 Note 35), and by Malcolm Green, who tells it of an unnamed German woman (1982: 22). This woman is claimed deliberately to have witnessed Voma when pregnant sometime between 1910 and 1914 and to have gone into labour for two weeks until her husband paid seven goats to Voma (as well as seven fowls and money in Green's version). The Voma then 'cried' around the health centre and the child was born and named Na-voma. The chain of events – infraction, the cult 'catching' according to its type, reparation, performance, and rectification – would have been entirely familiar in the Chamba homelands from which the forebears of the Ba'ni originated. But the events which inspired the story might well have occurred a little earlier than these versions suggest, during the period in the aftermath of the 1905 installation when palace–mission relations were becoming more competitive. Jakob Keller's annual report for 1906 (*Jahresbericht* 1907: 103) may shed light on the events that gave rise to the recollection: he concludes his report, 'Voma lost plenty of its respect and reputation this year, because Frau Keller witnessed the whole affair and in spite of the requests of the Voma people did not remove herself.' The following year Jakob Keller had to accompany his wife home when she became sick. The story would appear to have associated the facts of witnessing and sickness, and drawn a connexion between them. Its pertinence could have been underlined in 1908 when Frau Ankermann also witnessed Voma; Bernhard Ankermann recorded being approached by a young man who spoke English and asked that his wife buy an egg so that the proprietor of the performance could give her an *ntan* ('excuse', according to Tischhauser's Mungaka Dictionary). Whether or not she complied goes unrecorded (Baumann & Vajda 1959: 269), but we do know that Frau Ankermann was in ill health during her time in Kamerun.

Such insights into Voma are few. On 31 January 1908, the occasion on which Frau Ankermann witnessed Voma, Ankermann's diary describes his coming accidentally upon a Voma ceremony (Baumann & Vajda 1959: 267–9). The Fon sat on his stool by the palace entrance to witness a performance unfolding in the vicinity of a tree and small hut on his plaza. Ankermann's description is without exegesis: he saw eight gourd horns graded in size, basket rattles, four throwing knives decorated with red, white and black stripes, bullroarers, spears and staves, one of them hung with five long iron clappers.[9] After a musical performance circling the tree, the cult practitioners set off through the town, unobserved by women. Were this performance held in Chambaland, so comprehensive a range of cult equipment would be assembled only if several individual Voma cults had been combined to drive evil forces out of the town. However, there are indications from Bali Gham (see below) as well as Bali Nyonga that Bali may have collapsed a range of Chamba cults into a single society, conceived on the lines of a Grassfield regulatory society.

The major Voma ceremony of 1908 had occurred, almost a month late, from 17 to 23 October. The eight horns (which Ankermann describes as 'mother voma' and her 'children', see also Russell 1980: 74 Note 35) performed to the accompaniment of drums. Women came later to dance, turning their backs to the instruments to avoid seeing them. Dancing continued throughout the ceremony, during the entirety of which the four throwing knives (which Ankermann calls 'lam', compare Chamba *lama*) were fixed at the palace entrance. As was his custom on such occasions,

Ankermann turned to the missionaries for clarification. Vielhauer's long letter to Ankermann, solicited after the latter's return to Berlin, notes that in Bali Kumbat women do see Voma (a custom still remarked upon by Bali informants as an oddity in the 1980s). Vielhauer's informant tells him that Bali men must pay nine goats for entrance to Voma and then a further seven fowls if they want to handle the bullroarers ('vom lanngu', compare Chamba *langa*). The bullroarers are swung to announce the beginning of the harvest, and guinea corn is taken from farms on which it was still grown (apparently only that of the Fon) for later dedication to the forebears of compound heads.

In Chambaland too harvest-time dances led by the cult horns permit the new guinea corn to be harvested and eaten; each priest (*vom-nwana*) has an insigne called *lama*, although this is usually a sickle with a lightning point rather than a throwing knife (see Wente-Lukas 1977: 81);[10] metal bullroarers called *langa* form part of the cult apparatus, although these are not usually sounded as part of the harvest rituals; horns and basketry rattles are virtually identical to their Bali counterparts and, if the musicians had played from within a matting enclosure, Ankermann's description of dancers circling the horn players would be accurate of dances I witnessed often in Chambaland.

Quite how or why Bali Kumbat came to allow its women to witness Voma has not, to my knowledge, been recorded. Because Bali Nyonga reconstituted its Voma organisation by importing it from Bali Gham, where women are prohibited from seeing Voma, its regulations also derive from that source.[11] Bali Gham had maintained its Voma organisation after the break-up of the Bali alliance, perhaps because the Voma officiants remained within this section. Chilver and Kaberry were told how Voma in Bali Nyonga was revived with help from Bali Gham (Chilver & Kaberry 1968: 69); the names of some Ndagana clans in Bali Gham can be traced back to clans and localities in Chambaland (Fardon 1988: 247). The smaller Bali chiefdoms may well have retained more Chamba features in their Voma cults. According to sources with whom I spoke in Bali Gangsin in 1984, membership of Voma was permitted to princes, but the chief had to renounce membership on accession. He was permitted to enter the house and 'see' Voma, but had to sit on the ground and be treated as an ordinary Bali man. Bali Gham informants told me that Voma consisted of a number of named elements secreted by the priests in the bags they bring to meetings. In Bali Gashu some of these elements could be named and attributed specific effects: *langa* which affects the eyes, *ja luga* which causes madness, *noga* which causes stomach pains, *sela* which causes swellings, *ngöri* which 'cries the deaths' of king's children (*ga yebba*), and *gbana* the conical raffia mask. Not only are *langa*, *ja ləəg*, *noga* and *səəra* Chamba cults, but Chamba associate them with identical symptoms. *Gbana*, the conical mask, is restricted, so far as I know, to eastern Chamba who speak Chamba Leko, the language Bali Chamba call Mubako, which is still spoken in all the Bali chiefdoms other than Bali Nyonga. Only *ngöri*, of Tikari origin, is unlikely to have come from Adamawa; this might have been incorporated along with Tikari or Buti adherents outside the Grassfields, or else via Bamum (Ian Fowler, personal communication).[12]

Voma's range of functions was virtually identical to that in Chambaland: it might be used as a threat to extract confessions from adulterous women. It possessed a medicine (*gaan*) which was applied to the forehead or drunk in drafts; itching was auspicious in the first case but not in the second, which suggests that the medicine might consist in part of the onionlike bulb known to Chamba as 'female medicine' (an amaryllidae species), which would be capable of producing this effect.

Chilver and Kaberry briefly describe the two major Voma festivals (1968: 67): at the planting Voma (*vom naba*), the gourd horns are played and the *lama*, throwing knives decorated with red and white stripes, are waved. Before harvest, at *vom yed do'mba*,[13] the first heads of guinea corn are picked and placed at the gates of officials belonging to Voma and Lela by men wielding bullroarers (*langa*). Both rites are explained to ward off malign influences that might otherwise affect the crop. Russell adds some more general features,

> As part of its priestly function Voma has a peace-keeping and reconciliation role. The power can be used to catch a thief, and only in the central Voma shrine (*dola*) can a man be cleansed of leopard killing or manslaughter. Voma is believed able to control lightning and rain for the benefit of the community. Voma is not a masked society, nor do the *bangwana* hide from the public. Voma was concerned with male circumcision, and the ritual removal of the two top incisors in women, but both practices fell into disuse, along with the demise of age sets, in the 1940s. (Russell 1980: 57–8)

Again, this range of activities would be wholly recognisable to Leko-speakers within Chambaland (where women's tooth evulsion also went out of fashion). In summary, other than in Bali Nyonga, our information suggests that the Bali chiefdoms retained unbroken transmission of their Voma cults, and the cults retained most of the functions they had played prior to leaving Chambaland. However, there has been conflation of distinct cults, and weakening of the contrastive relations between royal Lela and priestly Voma (especially in Bali Nyonga) as well as between men's control over and women's exclusion from Voma (especially in Bali Kumbat). Women's cults have also been maintained in the Bali chiefdoms (*vom keena*, cult female), although there is little information beyond this bare fact. Even in Bali Nyonga, Voma has not entirely lost its association with the enforcement of discipline, since the regulatory society *nggumba* or *kwifon* is called *vomjana* in Mubako (Kaberry & Chilver 1961: 366).

As I noted at the outset of this chapter, Europeans were especially struck by the contrast between African and European cultures in the Grassfields, tending to interpret the latter as a dilution of the former. To Grassfielders, I am suggesting, the situation may have looked rather different. The organising distinction of greatest relevance concerned things susceptible to accumulation, Graffi-style, within the Grassfields (whether or not they were European in origin) and what came from the north. The Ba'ni were marked as powerful intruders by virtue of what they brought with them. That Ba'ni were internally differentiated by this northern patrimony was of less interest to outsiders. In any case, particularly in Bali Nyonga, the origins of different parts of the northern patrimony were of dwindling significance; overridingly important social and political distinctions concerned relations between the palace, the Ba'ni, and the earlier and later

Grassfield adherents. Hence, most of what befell the Ba'ni between leaving the confluences of the Rivers Benue, Faro and Deo, and arriving in the Grassfields lost relevance to the social charter and faded from memory by the late nineteenth century. We can best recuperate some of the forgotten history of Ba'ni ceremonies through comparison, which we do in the next chapter. In the next but one chapter, we shall see how Bali themselves began to reconstruct what befell them before the Grassfields when those events became relevant to the politics of identity of the mid-twentieth century.

Notes

1. The substantial contingent of Pati or Bati or BaTi (three thousand of them) who moved to Bali Nyonga to escape hostility in Bansoa, were soon to move out again in the wake of the crisis in relations between the Bali palace, mission and administration that occurred between 1909 and 1911. The Bawock chief, Nana, had come to Bali Nyonga under the auspices of the BaTi chief, to whom his sister had been married. Resenting the way the BaTi chief 'interposed himself between [himself] and Fonyonga, the Basel Mission ... and the military station at Bamenda', Nana succeeded in returning to Bali after being taken 'as a kind of hostage' by the departing BaTi (Chilver 1964: 121).

2. Without the pre-fixed 'Ba-', Harter's 'Tanwani' is presumably the same name as 'Batanwa'ni', the brother to Tita Nji about whom Tischhauser (1938), quoted above, was told.

3. Of numerous such thrones, see, for instance, the Bamum and Bansoa thrones in Geary (1988b: 48, 51), Northern (1984: 39, 101, 102) and Preston Blier (1998: 164, 167). The evidence of Knöpfli's older informants would suggest human throne figures are likely to represent slaves (1999: 45–6).

4. Efforts in the Basel archive to trace the queries to which he was responding have been unavailing.

5. Ian Fowler informs me that the senior man who finishes a craft piece in Babungo is considered to have made or authored it, which would support this construal of the evidence.

6. Bernhard Gardi's dubbing this the Bamileke 'boubou' or gown (2000: 86) speaks to its range rather than origins. Since the late 1970s, the Chamba Cultural Association of Nigeria has promoted the introduction of this innovative Cameroonian form as Chamba 'traditional' dress, worn on appropriate occasions by both men and women.

7. Even this apparently utilitarian building, according to Schuler's account of his first visit to Bali, may have been built in coastal style so as to be suitable to receive visitors (Merz 1997: 123).

8. Ian Fowler cautions that there might be an alternative route: to Big Babanki via Small Babanki's almost symbiotic relation with Bali Kumbat (personal communication).

9. Note that this is not the type of rattle-topped spear used at Lela – and documented in photographs of the augury in 1908 – which is associated in Chambaland with overt violence. Baumann and Vajda's (1959) selection of Ankermann's sketches from the Grassfields does not include a spear answering this description, so we have only the rather vague verbal description to go by. As Ian Fowler advises me, this might easily apply to the sacra of the Grassfield 'Ngumba' society. However, iron spears hung with clappers are also a common element of Chamba cults and chiefly regalia (Leo Frobenius's artist recorded just such a cult object in Chambaland in 1911, see Frobenius 1913: 'Heiliges Gerät der Dakka' no.2).

10. I met a priest in Mapeo whose main constituency was amongst the neighbouring Koma; he had inherited a throwing knife as his *lama*. However, this was exceptional. Elsewhere, Frobenius illustrated a throwing knife from the southern Chamba Daka-

speaking chiefdom of Kiri (Frobenius 1913: 242). Chilver was told by one of their custodians that the Bali incorporated ceremonial throwing knives along with their Kufad (Mbum) contingents relatively early in their southward migrations.

11. Russell claims that Bali Nyonga's Voma was reintroduced from Bali Kumbat, but this may be erroneous (1980: 59).

12. Aletum Tabuwe and Fisiy take issue with Paul Mzeka's view that 'ngiri' was introduced to Nso at an early period and attribute responsibility for this to a clan still found in Nso that acquired this princely society from Bamum (1989: 57).

13. No translation is given, but the first two words are Voma (i.e. cult) and guinea corn. The third word may be the verb to greet or salute: this would yield, 'Voma greets the guinea corn'.

CHAPTER 6

Lela Precedents: Beyond and Before the Grassfields

Cautiously interpreted, the variation between the ceremonies of the five surviving Bali chiefdoms within the Grassfields yields indications of the organisational and performative repertoires the Ba'ni shared during the decade or more they spent in the Grassfields before defeat at the hands of the Bamileke. So far as most Grassfield observers have been concerned, cultural repertoire not acquired locally is accounted for sufficiently by assuming it came with the Ba'ni. However, comparison of Chamba communities outside the Grassfields can provide us with a fuller conjectural history of the changes the raiders are likely to have undergone in the years spent between leaving Adamawa and entering the Grassfields. The best place to begin is with the other main thrust of Adamawan raiders who turned to the south-west rather than continuing south towards the Grassfields.

'Spear Washing' in the Benue Chamba Chiefdoms: Flags, Gowns and Horses

Most of the Chamba founders of chiefdoms in the plains below the River Benue (including those of Donga, the largest of them) claim to have arrived there as members of an alliance called Den Bakwa and led by Loya Garbosa of the Sama. There are close parallels between Garbosa and his Den Bakwa, and Gawolbe and his Ba'ni. In both cases, the name of the leader includes the Chamba Leko term for chief (*gara*); each leader's name is invariably associated with the collective term for those he led; and the leader's death and the break-up of the alliance are narratively related.[1] According to traditions collected by one of his successors, Mallam Bitemya Sambo Garbosa, Loya Garbosa's Chamba left a home they call Dindin and regrouped just south of the future Fulbe lamidate of Koncha. From there they struck westwards (whereas the Ba'ni had continued south), establishing a warcamp at Gildu (close to the Beli Hills); Loya Garbosa drowned during a river crossing as the group moved westward; his followers then established a longer-lived settlement at Gankwe. Garbosa's successor, Garkola, fell out with his predecessor's son who left the alliance and, under the chiefly title Garkiye, raided south towards Takum and the River Katsin Ala. His raiders clashed in these parts with another Chamba group (the Daka under Gyando's successor Kumboshi), and were made to move north once again. By the mid-nineteenth century, Garkiye had become elderly and his warriors occupied a stockaded encampment on the River Benue. His son, Nubumga Donzomga, fought on behalf of Ibrahim, the Fulbe Lamido of Bauchi, receiving a flag, thirty horses and a group of Jafun warriors on this account. C.K. Meek later recorded that,

> [t]he present chief of Donga claims to have this flag in his possession at the present time, and produced it. It is a white flag of European manufacture attached to a bamboo pole, 11 feet long. The head of the pole is surmounted with ostrich feathers, and lower down the pole are two red streamers. Further down still there is a leather case containing charms written in Arabic. At the top of the flag there is an Arabic inscription, written in ink, as follows: 'This flag is of the Leader of the Believers (i.e. of the Sarkin Musulmi of Sokoto). Whosoever waits on his decisions shall not be ashamed. Allah is with those who wait patiently on him. By patience men shall overcome the host of unbelievers; and the unbelievers themselves shall repent afterwards.' This flag may have been the identical flag conferred on Nubunga (if any flag was indeed conferred), but the cloth of the flag displayed did not have the appearance of being over seventy years old, and I could not help feeling considerable doubts both as to the genuineness of the flag and also of the story by which it was said to have been conferred. (Meek 1931b I: 331–2)

Meek does not explain why the Donga Chamba might have wanted to fabricate (as opposed to renovate) such a flag by the 1920s; I do not myself find this story *prima facie* implausible given the motley alliances that pursued wealth and power under the guise of jihad on the fringes of the Caliphate. In his work on the Jukun, Meek himself described the Chamba raiders as 'trained in the Fulani method of warfare', and he cites several occasions when Fulbe chiefs faced one another along with non-Fulbe allies (Meek 1931a: 57). Whatever the case, and with or without his flag, Nubumga Donzomga went on to found the town of Donga after displacing another group of Chamba who had defected from Gankwe under the leadership of Garbanyi. This displaced group, having failed in its attempts to regain the site of Donga, eventually settled at Suntai (nurturing ill-will towards Donga).

The Gankwe camp is likely to have been in existence around the time Gawolbe led his Ba'ni into the Grassfields. Loya Garbosa and Gawolbe would therefore be rough contemporaries. Their successors (Garkiye and Nyongpasi) were old men by the early years of the second half of the nineteenth century, and it was their sons (Nubumga Donzomga and Galega I) who would found Donga and Bali Nyonga in their contemporary sites. Put in other terms, two full generations (over half a century) elapsed between the displacement of the early Chamba alliances from Adamawa and the foundation of the contemporary settlements. Neither Bali Nyonga nor Donga was the first group of emigrant raiders to occupy its present site (they respectively incorporated the Bali Konntan, and displaced the founders of Suntai). The populations of both Bali Nyonga and Donga had become highly diverse by the time they settled; in both cases, Chamba Leko became a restricted court language and more local languages (forms of BaTi and Jukun) became the everyday languages. As a final convergence, at least for the time being, both Donga and Bali Nyonga were established nearby competitor chiefdoms which had maintained their Chamba language: Suntai and Bali Kumbat.

Assuming we can place some faith in the broad strokes of oral traditions (which, after all, began to be collected only a half-century after the latest events they portray), the Benue Chamba chiefdoms and their Grassfield counterparts developed independently of one another after the first quarter of the nineteenth century. The performative and organisational repertoires they shared by the early twentieth century must either pre-date their parting, or else represent convergent processes of change. The ethnographic record from the Benue Chamba chiefdoms is relatively thin, for instance we have almost no reports on the cultural repertoires of people in Suntai or Takum. Yet, thanks to the interrelated efforts of the colonial government anthropologist C.K. Meek who spent time in Donga in 1927 (1931b I: 346–72), and his then research assistant, Mallam Bitemya Sambo who became Garbosa II of Donga (Garbosa, n.d.), we do have some useable materials on Donga. However, we cannot assume that Bali Nyonga and Donga shared wholly identical patrimonies prior to their separation. Various types of evidence (oral traditions, certain cultural traits and dialectal characteristics) together suggest the likelihood that the Donga Chamba were drawn predominantly from an area of Chambaland slightly south of the Bali Chamba, and this may have been reflected in the Chamba cultural baggage with which they set out.

Our evidence will suggest that Donga retained a wider repertoire of Chamba ceremonies than did Bali Nyonga. This is hardly surprising, since the Donga Chamba did not enter a cultural environment so radically different from their homelands as that encountered by their Bali counterparts in the Grassfields. By the early twentieth century, and despite a century spent in an increasingly islamised environment, Donga retained more in the way of esoteric Chamba ritual than Bali Nyonga. The similarities between the two repertoires are nonetheless striking: Bali might lack the skull/relic (*vara*) cult of the dead that persisted in Donga, but both Donga and Bali have Voma for men and Vomkeena for women, and there are close resemblances between Lela in Bali and the martial rites of Donga.

A brief description of the *vara* cult illustrates the greater Chamba retentions in Donga (and might provoke a reader from one of the Balis to enlarge upon the slight indications we have from the Grassfields that some kind of royal skull cult survived there). Although Meek takes the primary sense of *vara* to be skull, his further comments suggest a complex of senses like that found in Chambaland. Each clan had a *vara* shrine which received periodic sacrifice when the head of the clan was able to brew beer (1931b I: 347), the shrines contained 'pots which symbolise the cult of *vara*' (1931b I: 370). *Vara* also remains the term for the wooden-headed, theranthropic (animal-human) fusion mask with fibre costume that comes to mourn the death of a clan member. Comparing Meek's rough, outline sketch of this mask (1931b I: 347) with Rubin's photographic evidence from the mid-1960s (Rubin 1978: 57, Figure 13; McNaughton 1991: 43) and with the Donga mask collected by Leo Frobenius in 1912 that is now in the Linden-Museum Stuttgart, I have suggested that the Donga *vara* mask might be a Jukun reinterpretation of Chamba masquerade conventions (Fardon 2006: in press). Notwithstanding some atypical features, this remains recognisably the Chamba mask, something which is entirely absent from the Grassfields. Suntai's *vara* mask resembles its Chamba counterparts even more closely (Rubin 1978: 57, Figure 14; Fardon 2006: in press).

Meek is not entirely clear whose skulls were kept (although this is also true of other Chamba communities). Skull retention was a Chamba religious practice especially susceptible to abandonment in the face of world religions. In 1927, Meek was told that only the skulls of chiefs were preserved, and that these were removed ten to fourteen days after death (1931b I: 365). The new chief took part in a rite during which libations of beer were offered to the skulls of his predecessors; participation confirmed him in office as well as assuring the welfare of the whole town. Before 1918, according to the accounts Meek heard, not only the chief's skull but the skulls of all members of the royal patriclan were preserved. However, Meek's further statement that the *vara* rites of the chief were performed in secrecy lest the people see '… that his special cult differed little from their own' (1931b I: 366), sheds some doubt on the abandonment of skull retention other than in the case of chiefs, and suggests he suspected that skull-taking was practised in all Donga patriclans. For chiefs and clan heads, secondary funeral rites were performed at the crossroads where beer lees were scattered and a small spider, like the skull called *vara*, was caught. The spider seems to have been transferred to the pot shrine where a chicken was sacrificed, and all those taking part in the rite were smeared on the forehead with corn paste (Meek 1931b I: 370). (There is a virtually identical ritual in Yeli, southern Chambaland, see Fardon 1991: Chapter 5.) The only indication of a skull cult I have come across in the Bali chiefdoms concerned a small round hut called the 'skull hut' (*vad-wudla*) in Bali Gham where the royals carried out unspecified esoteric rituals around the time of Lela; Chilver and Kaberry refer to this as the 'royal grave-hut' (1968: 70).

Donga Chamba maintained cult institutions, known generically as Voma the men's cult and 'Vonkima' (*voom-keena*) the women's cult, under individual names, some of which are familiar from both Chambaland and the Bali Chamba chiefdoms. As in Bali Nyonga, the major observances of Voma had become attenuated to a single institution under the control of one of the chief's officials called 'vompobiya' (a title likely to be composed of *vom(a)* and the root of the verb to supplicate, *pob-*, which we encountered already in the Bali phrase *pob lela*, the rite inaugurating the Lela festival). The paraphernalia of Voma included sets of calabash horns (illustrated in sketched outline by both Garbosa n.d.: 83 and Meek 1931b I: 348) and basketry rattles. However, judging by Meek's account, Voma had lost its associations with causation of disease to become simply a rain cult.[2] He describes at some length how, in the event of drought, the chief sent two pots of beer and a calabash of beer lees to the Voma priest.

> The priest places the horns in a row at the door of his hut, and deposits a little of the beerlees on the outside of each instrument. Then, holding a calabash of water in his right hand and a calabash of beer in his left hand, he squats down and says: 'You my (deceased) elder brother, from whom I received this cult, come here and take your stand. If what I now do is a thing of my invention, then do you repudiate me. But if aforetime you also did as I am about to do, then grant that the rain may come to refresh our crops.' He then calls on his elder brother's father, his father's sister (the Mala), and his grand-father, to bless the rite with their presence. After the prayer he pours a little water on the ground in front of the horns and then a little beer. This is done three times. The priest drinks up the remainder of the beer left in the calabash. The attendant horn-blowers are also given beer; and when they have drunk, the priest hands to each one of the calabash

horns. A little water is run through the horn in order to improve the tone. All then proceed to the chief's palace and there the horns are vigorously blown and a dance is held, the hornplayers using also bellshaped rattles made of plaited grass, with a piece of wood at the base, and pebbles inside. On the conclusion of the dance the horns are deposited in the palace, and every morning, until the rain comes, the horn-blowers arrive and blow the horns. After the first fall of rain the chief presents some corn and a sheep to the priest. The corn is made into beer which, with pieces of mutton, is divided up between the priest and the hornblowers. (Meek 1931b I: 3489)

This lengthy description proposes that the Voma paraphernalia was physically under the control of the palace in Donga, as it is in Bali Nyonga. Such an arrangement subverts the contrast between chiefs and priests which is important in Chambaland chiefdoms. However, various interpretations would fit the facts: for instance, that kingly control came to be exercised over cults wherever Chamba led ethnically diverse alliances or, alternatively, that kingly control of cults predated the departure of Loya Garbosa and Gawolbe's raiders. Other than this, Meek's informants have really vouchsafed little to him: anointing the gourd horns with paste outside and water inside recalls similar actions upon the *lela* flutes in the Bali chiefdoms, and indeed are standard gestures. Meek's description of the Voma rattles suggests they were identical objects to those used in Bali (and in Chambaland), which is confirmed by the sketched outlines of these sack rattles in Garbosa's and Ankermann's accounts (Garbosa n.d.: 79; Baumann & Vajda 1959: 311, Figure 34).[3]

The women's cults ('Vonkima') are known under the same generic name as in Chambaland (*voom-keena*, cult-female) and employ the same hoe-blade percussion instruments. Meek describes how women accompanied their songs by beating together small iron hoe-blades. Although there are references to the existence of women's cults in the Bali chiefdoms, these do not provide the evidence we would need to extend detailed comparison. However, Donga women's cults are apparently close counterparts of those in Chambaland: the cults are said to be owned by each patriclan, although related clans may share them (1931b I: 340), and they may be propitiated to cure cases of male impotence that they are divined to have caused (1931b I: 347). The persistence of women's cults as agents of misfortune suggests that men's cults, which tend to be more esoteric than women's, would also have retained earlier characteristics that Meek failed to detect.

In addition to 'Voma' and 'Vonkima', Meek identified two other cults as 'Tsera' and 'Mwa Lebsa'. The latter term, for a lightning cult, corresponds to no term I know of in Chambaland, where the lightning cult is called *vo*. Meek's 'Tsera' could be the *sɔɔra* of Chambaland, possibly equivalent to *sela* in Bali Gashu. The *sɔɔra* cult is the sole prerogative of a Chamba clan (Yam in Chamba Daka; Jeng in Chamba Leko) renowned in Chambaland for its war-like activities: especially those involved in the foundation of western Chamba chiefdoms. A clan named Jeng is also recalled to have formed part of the initial Bali Chamba alliance.

A third ceremonial complex described by Meek and Garbosa invites direct comparison with Lela. Donga Chamba performed two ceremonies designed to enhance their success in arms: *ding sugnbia* and 'Purma'. According to Meek, every Donga patriclan had a 'talisman' or spear called 'Disakuna' which was used in a ceremony that Donga informants told me was called *ding sugnbia* (Meek

1931b I: 340). My Donga informants (in 1977 at the palace) knew of only four such spears belonging to the clans of the chief, of two subordinate chiefs, and of the Pere (equivalent to Peli in Bali), the earliest allies of the Chamba drawn from their southern neighbours. They called such spears *ding sa kuna*, 'the spear which looks out for the clan'. In Chamba Leko, the verb *sugnbia* means to wash, so the ceremony of *ding sugnbia* is 'washing the spear'. After harvest, the spears were taken outside the town and a cockerel was beheaded before each of them; if the cockerel ran around headless this was considered a favourable omen, the bird was caught the third time it fell and its blood dripped into a shallow trench in front of the spear. If the bird fell over stone dead, discussions would have to take place to account for the poor omen. A small cup at the top of each spear was filled with 'medicine' which the senior *mala* (father's sister) of the patriclan daubed on the forehead, right arm and over the heart of every warrior. In turn each warrior took a spear and ran off to aim an imaginary thrust, before returning to face the *ding sa kuna* and salute it by waving his own spear (Meek 1931b I: 340–1). Donga's 'spear washing', while not literally a washing in water, bears very close resemblance to the events of the first day of Bali Nyonga's Lela involving the washing of military regalia in the river, and the ensuing sacrifice-cum-oracle. The gestures warriors made with their spears are reminiscent of what Bali would call *lo'ti*. Although no Bali Nyonga woman plays so prominent a ritual role at the public ceremonial as the Donga *mala*, saluting the Bali Nyonga monarch's official mother and sister may represent a different development of some previously more important female role in the ritual itself. While Donga's 'spear washing' much resembled the first day of Bali Nyonga's Lela celebration, its military units were patriclans (rather than lodges or wards) and, in this respect, it remained within Chamba organisational resources.

'Purma' (Meek 1931b I: 349–54; Garbosa n.d.: 91–3) was a far larger ceremony held in October when, as Meek put it, 'the grain on the stalk of the guinea corn first begins to burst forth'. Meek believed its name might derive from that of the Jukun harvest festival of 'Puje'. However, since Puje is said to mean 'booths of menstruation' (Meek 1931a: 145) and, later, to be the place where such booths are erected outside the capital for the duration of the ceremonial (Meek 1931a: 146), except that both are ceremonies lasting some days that took place around harvest time, it is difficult to see a close resemblance between Puje and Purma. Meek and Garbosa liken Purma both to a form of military training and to a ceremony of allegiance to the chief. As with Lela, the time of Purma is announced so that beer brewing may be put in hand. Purma is organised around a series of military displays and salutes to the chief by the *gangum* or war-chief in the field (who was a subordinate of the *nyaa* or war official (Meek 1931b I: 334); as demonstrated already, some variant of *nyaa-gang* was the usual title for a warleader in Bali and among Chamba elsewhere. On the opening day, the warriors clear a site for the display 'treading down the grass and cutting off twigs of trees and plants as though they were cutting off the heads of enemies'; they salute the chief in the early evening and later that evening the oliphants summon all armed men to the palace where they salute the palace officials (Meek 1931b I: 350). The next day is the principal day of the festival when the chief distributes gowns or horses to the men of his family. The chief departs to the prepared site of the war games and is installed in a hut from where he receives 'salutations of the people' and watches the warriors' manoeuvres. Under the charge of *gangum*, the leaders oversaw a display by the younger warriors as well as a dance called *daya*, performed to the accompaniment of small, hour-glass shaped, tension drums wedged under the player's left arm (so that drum-pitch varies with the pressure that the drummer exerts on thongs which run from the drum's head to its base). Such drums would be considered in Chambaland to be of Fulbe origin. The troops danced according to their age groups, which had developed as the basis of Donga military organisation (Garbosa n.d.: 91–3). That afternoon the warriors raid a neighbouring farm, overturn the protective charms there and pillage the crops. Then all ride back to town in ceremonial order, and more salutes occur at the palace in the presence of the royal gongs. Food and then beer are distributed by the chief, and that evening he may ask for the royal *lera* flutes to be played for dancing. As in Bali, the second day seems to be more relaxed: the senior Mala holds her court and supplies beer and food to her visitors; and the chief attends dancing in the afternoon clothed in his royal robes; he may occasionally beat a drum or blow a horn himself. The ceremony, Meek writes, continues spasmodically for seven days and must have represented a great drain on the chief's resources by the 1920s when gifts to him of corn had diminished (Meek 1931b I: 354).

The similarities between the different stages of the Bali Lela and the two Donga festivals of 'spear washing' and 'Purma' are too striking to be accidental. Common elements include the idiom of 'spear washing' itself, affirmations of loyalty to the chief by military units, ordeals of fowl decapitation to divine the success of the forthcoming military campaign, and the licence allowed warriors for petty theft. In both cases, expensive gifts, as well as food and drink, flow out from the palace against a return of salutes from warrior lodges or age regiments. The multiplication of minute duties and perquisites for officials – reflected in the different versions of the ceremony they give from the vantage of their own participation in it – offered scope for all involved to express their self-importance in running the annual festival.

It is likely that the emergent Fulbe Emirates offered a model of military power to the earliest adherents of the groups that were to found Bali and Donga. Damashi, the most famous leader of Chamba raiders in western Chambaland, is claimed to have received leave to carry out his activities on behalf of Modibbo Adama, founder of the Emirate of Fombina. The Chamba leader is reported to have received a flag and Koran from Adama in exchange for a bow and arrows (Fardon 1988: 96–7). Donga Chamba, as we have already learnt, were later to claim to have received their own standard from the Emir of Bauchi. Although there is no record of formal endorsement by Fulbe of the Bali Chamba, their adoption of flags (called *tutuwan*, derived from the Fulfulde *tutuwal*) suggests similar circumstances. According to Bali Gham traditions collected by Pius Bejeng Soh, the flags replaced a spear with a bunch of leaves attached to it (Soh 1975: 47); and, according to the same source, the cotton tassel containing medicines from the bark of trees, rather than the flag itself, was still considered the most significant part of the assemblage (Soh 1975: 89). The general form of salute, waving spear or musket at the chief, may have begun in imitation of the durbars at muslim capitals. Robed horsemen who chewed kola and came from the north would probably have been distinguished with difficulty by those upon whom they preyed.

Such indications of the specific relations between the Chamba raiding bands at their inception and the emergent Fulbe Emirates would have been controversial throughout the colonial period because they potentially constituted grounds to sanction indirect administration through Fulbe chiefs. It is unlikely that further details will come to light through oral traditions at this late moment when relations between ethnic groups in the Benue plains have hardly become less contested. However, we may imagine that the organisational problems facing the various raiding alliances setting out from the old Chamba Leko homelands were largely dictated by their marauding activities. They needed to incorporate non-Chamba and sustain a reasonable raiding strength (strong enough to deal with the villages in their path, but not so large as to be impossible to provision), while undergoing constant fissioning. Given that the Chamba elements, with their oldest allies, managed to retain overall leadership of the multiethnic alliances, the means they adopted to this end must have been adequate. The elements of Chamba culture retained in the two cases are not identical: Donga Chamba retained patriclan organisation, the skull cult of *vara*, the special position of the father's sister (*mala*), women's cults, the wooden-headed Chamba mask, and a number of features which appear to be absent among the Bali Chamba. However, the martial festivals in the two areas are close counterparts. Military manoeuvres, the assessment of fighting strength, and pledges of loyalty were more than ornamental; and the fowl ordeal, common to Donga and Bali Nyonga, suggests that the success of raiding was not a foregone conclusion. In all Chamba conquest chiefdoms, the significance of patriclanship was enhanced while matriclanship receded in importance; and channels of power, including ritual, became increasingly subject to royal control. In their outline of Bali Nyonga political organisation, Kaberry and Chilver (1961) emphasise that this high degree of centralisation was unusual in comparative Grassfield terms. It was not, however, a 'Chamba' feature in any essential sense, centralisation of power in the person of the leader was rather a response to the exigencies of raiding as a mode of livelihood and to the fissiparous tendencies of the raiding bands. It appears to have occurred in Donga as well as in Bali (Meek 1931b I: 334).

Adamawan Elements in Lela: Death, Killing and Commemoration

I have assumed that widening the spatial scope of comparison allows us to deduce the stage of separation before which particular features of public culture must have entered the Bali Nyonga repertoire. Hence, we have traced features common to Germano–Bali ceremonial, and to the five Bali kingdoms of the Grassfields. We have seen the reciprocal influences between Bali and other Grassfield societies. In the last section, we looked for features common both to the Ba'ni raiders who entered the Grassfields and to raiders of similar origins whose trajectories led them to the plains below the River Benue. Logically, this comparative exercise must conclude by asking what, if any, features of Lela in the Bali chiefdoms may be claimed as plausible retentions from the Adamawan (that is eastern middle-belt) contingents present among the earliest adherents of the raiding alliances two centuries ago? Surprisingly, perhaps, quite a number of such features persist, amounting to most of the core observances. We need to approach this question from two ends: first by identifying a residue of Bali practices the origins of which we have been unable to explain in terms of later sources closer to the Grassfields, and second by asking whether anything similar occurs among contemporary Adamawan populations. As before, material culture will provide our starting point.

There can be no doubt that the *lela* flutes, as well as the *voma* horns and rattles, were carried from the earliest inception of the raiding bands to eventual resettlement in Bali Nyonga and Donga. Not only materials and design, but even nomenclature correspond to those in Chambaland. The ceremonial spears which represent contingents during the military festivals may also derive from Chamba precedents. We have to exercise more caution in this case, since similar forms of ironwork are distributed widely in West Africa,[4] but it is nonetheless the case that types of ceremonial spear illustrated or described in sources on Bali Nyonga also exist in Chambaland. Two forms are especially striking. The rattle-topped staff – that I refer to as a 'spear' only because Chamba call it such – has no offensive potential as a thrusting tool. This spear appears in several of the photographs from the 1908 augury by the river, but it is seen best as the left hand of two spears stuck into the ground in **Figure 13**. Ankermann also sketched the iron feature at the head of the spear (Baumann & Vajda 1959: 311, Figure 33a), which is best described as a rattle, similar in design to iron ankle bracelets Chamba women wear for dancing. The rattling is produced by a small pellet in a metal casing (like a single iron pea too large in diameter to escape from a split iron pea pod). This is not an unusual piece of ironwork, however very similar 'spears' are found in Chambaland; there, they are normally made entirely of metal and the rattle feature is less flattened; otherwise they are the same. I saw such spears most often in the regalia of Daka-speaking Chamba chiefdoms where they were called *səəm saken*. *Səəm* simply means spear (equivalent to *dinga* in Chamba Leko); those informants, prompted by me, who had any idea what *saken* might mean derived it from *sogen* because it could be 'stuck into the ground'. This always seemed unconvincing, and I now wonder whether *səəm saken* might be related to *ding saa kun*, the name Donga Chamba give spears owned by patriclans there.[5] Terms and snippets from Chamba Leko are quite often imported without translation into Chamba Daka where a ritual observance has come from the east (and there are less frequent instances of traffic in the other direction). In the Chamba Leko-speaking chiefdom of Yeli such spears were used in annual royal funerary rites. I was told that only killers who had 'seized a stone' (added a stone to their clan shrine having killed a man or dangerous animal) could handle such spears; they were called *yaa dinga*, or horse spear, and assumed once to have formed part of the paraphernalia of a cavalry.

The only part of Chambaland where – so far as I know – spears were themselves the objects of ceremonial (rather than just being used in ceremonies) was the northern foothills of the Shebshi Mountains where annual ceremonies called *səəm simi* (Chamba Daka) or 'spear beer' were reported around harvest time: the same time of year as martial ceremonies in the Bali chiefdoms and Donga.[6] The dominant clans of this area were various sections of Yambu, as well as Bata (Kambu in Chamba Daka). They had settled among local sections of Chamba Daka who were culturally distinct from themselves, as well as Mumuye, and ceased to speak their previous language which they believed to have been Chamba Leko. This is the region associated with the Chamba warrior Damashi who, as noted earlier, is reputed to have received permission to raid west of the Shebshi Mountains from Modibbo Adama, founder of the Adamawa Emirate, when Gurin was the capital of Fombina. Although I was not present when they took place, I was assured that festivals of 'spear beer' involved sacrifices at the graves or skull shrines of chiefs, the anointing of spears, and dancing with *lera* flutes. In the Bata-founded chiefdom of Mbulo, I find from my notes that a dispute over leadership was phrased as two contenders each wanting their own *səəm saken*, and it was also in Mbulo that I was told such spears should be made from captured metal. There was a striking illustration of the ritual character of such spears in Tolla where the reputed grave of Damashi is tended. Damashi's 'spear' consisted of a stick about two feet long which had been inserted through a hollow, spherical brass ornament. This was a 'spear' in name only, but planted in the ground at the time of an attack, it was supposed to assure success in battle.

The set of offices typical of the northern Shebshi chiefdoms is also reminiscent of that reconstructed by Chilver and Kaberry for the Ba'ni: the chief's assistants were titled Gban and Kuni (in Chamba Leko the latter would be Kuna); and the leader of the warriors, Nyagang (a pervasive title in the area), was often a royal relative. The priests responsible for installing the chief and for maintaining the most important cults of the land belonged to families distinct from that of the chief.

Other than the flutes, two types of object are associated with Lela in Bali by name: the *letya* or Y-shaped poles, and the *wolela* or stone pile in the middle of the palace plaza. These items are not easily inventoried by origin: they do not seem to be Grassfield traits, but neither do they correspond exactly to any contemporary Chamba items; finally (with the possible exception of a reference to sacred stones outside the palace gate, Meek 1931b I: 335), they do not turn up in recorded observations at Donga. Can we offer any plausible conjectures?

To start with the forked, or Y-shaped poles: the derivation of the term for them, *letya*, differs from that of the other two pairs of pole we see in photographs of Lela performance: *le-* derives from Lela,[7] but there are two grounds for believing that *-tya* does not derive from *tu*, meaning tree or post, such as we found in compound terms for the horned posts on which weapons were hung (*tu-nganged*) and the ornate posts which decorate high status entrances such as that to the palace (*tu-ntsubo*). Both these post types are known by Mungaka compound terms; and in both case the word for 'wood' or 'post' is in initial rather than final position. Because the forked posts are made and known as *le-tya* in all the Bali chiefdoms, regardless of language, the term must be Mubako (that is the Grassfield dialect of Chamba Leko). *Le-tya* is likely to be no more than a variant pronunciation or transcription of *le-teea*, Chamba Leko for '*lela* pole'. Lela poles have not (or not yet) been recorded from contemporary Chamba,[8] however if such poles were known by a Chamba term it would suggest either that the Bali chiefdoms have retained a feature of Chamba material culture that Chamba themselves have lost, or that the poles were brought to the Ba'ni alliance before it broke up, while Chamba Leko was still its *lingua franca*.

Tall, decorated, forked poles – virtually identical to *letya* – were an important material element of Dowayo ritual (people living just east of the Chamba). The Dowayo groups studied by Nigel Barley erected such poles on three sorts of occasions: during the skull festival, and during the purification rites of killers of outsiders or of leopards (Barley 1983: 43). In some areas, the bulky, bundled corpses of men of substance, wrapped in cow skins, were stood against these Y-shaped poles to produce a theranthropic fusion formally identical to that achieved by Chamba through their masquerade (Gardi 1965, 1995; Fardon 2006: in press; Krüger 2003: 41 reports a Dowayo variant of such practices). Nowadays because Chamba have masquerades, while Dowayo have funerary bundles and forked sticks, these differences appear as ethnic characteristics. However, Chamba and Dowayo would not have been so clearly distinct before the disturbances of the nineteenth century cleared settlements from the plains between the hill ranges in which they respectively sought refuge. The eighteenth-century situation destroyed by later predation is difficult to reconstruct, but it also involved a different economy and ecology: characterised by the presence of dwarf, humpless cattle and ponies. Free settlements of non-Fulbe were not confined to the hills and mountains – or places in easy reach of these – as they would be by the time late nineteenth-century travellers recorded their impressions. Entire chiefdoms, the names of which had been handed down to elderly informants to whom I spoke in the 1970s, had ceased to exist when their populations had to choose between becoming raiders, or refugees, or subordinated to Fulbe states. It would be an anachronism, therefore, to suppose that forked funerary poles were an ethnic feature at the turn of the eighteenth into the nineteenth century: present ethnic identities had not gelled, and the distribution of population around the Faro-Benue-Deo river confluences was quite different from what it would be by the turn of the nineteenth into the twentieth century. The mapped discontinuities in the distribution of present-day ethnic groups result from nineteenth-century movements. Earlier settlements were likely to have interpenetrated, and so the forked poles would have been a local rather than ethnic trait. My hunch (not a lot more than that) would be that *lela* poles were already a feature in the local performative culture of the region east of the River Deo before the Chamba who were to reach Bali quit that region.

Different Dowayo groups call the forked poles that are erected in the public space *dongriyo* (Seignobos 1998: 96) or *donre* (Barley 1983). Although the Dowayo studied by Barley, erected a *donre* for their skull-festival, or for the slaying an outsider or leopard (1983: 43), in practice these events shaded one into another: Barley's older informants told him that in times past the erection of a *donre* for the skull festival of a prominent man involved killing an outsider whose head would be removed and smashed to pieces (Barley 1983: 61–2). Once erected, the *donre* might subsequently be used in rituals to remove the pollution of killing a man or a leopard, 'the *donre* emphasises man as killer' (Barley 1983: 44, 63), just like Chamba stone shrines.

Seignobos (1998: 98–9) – writing of Dowayo living slightly further north – also records that a forked pole was erected by the son of a big man. Made from the most durable of woods, the poles were of two types: predominantly either theriomorphic or anthropomorphic. The oldest posts resembled the heads of dwarf cattle, although the design at their fork was similar to the scarifications Dowayo carved on their own faces from the corner of the mouth to the ears. Anthropomorphic poles often had a pronounced navel carved at their fork as well as genitalia. The forked horns of theriomorphic poles, or forked upraised arms of anthropomorphic poles, were usually sculpted at their ends and reddened with ochre. Judging from both Barley's and Seignobos's descriptions, it sounds as if all forked poles could be read either in human or bovid terms. Barley remarks that young Dowayo Christians reinterpreted the arms of the forked pole as a site of crucifixion (Barley 1983: 61; see also Krüger 2003: 42). Although no such practice existed, they are right to associate the *donre* with the memorialisation of deaths in several senses: insiders' skulls are associated with the *donre*, outsiders' skulls are destroyed at the *donre*, and killers of people or human-like creatures bring heads to the *donre* in order to avert the consequences of killing.

The northerly Dowayo, to whom Seignobos's description refers, believed their own use of forked poles had been adopted from people to their north who in turn had copied them from the Bata living by the River Benue. To the Bata these were chiefs' poles: newly carved on a grand scale, it was here that a deceased chief's body was placed before it was fumigated prior to skull-taking. A successor would have to be placed alongside the forked pole before his installation, in other words, in the same position as Dowayo placed the corpses of big men. A collection of such poles make up a sacred site consecrated to former chiefs.

These indications resonate with things we have learnt about the *lela* poles in Bali: we know that Fonyonga told Ankermann he had to renew the *letya* on the occasion of his father's death; Hutter witnessed foreign victims being hunted and killed before Lela began, and their skulls hung from the poles used for Lela; and we hear from the Ritzenthalers that the version of Lela adopted by Bafut from Bali Kumbat required a human sacrifice to be buried at its base. From Bali Gham, we have indications that a skull house received offerings at the inception of Lela. Chilver and Kaberry recorded the use of forked sticks both as biers and grave markers in Bali Nyonga: a dead Fon is buried in effigy just before his successor is installed, and this effigy consists of a forked stick which is planted by his 'grave' (1968: 72).[9] When princes or princesses, priests or priestesses die, a bier is cut with three or four arms (depending upon the deceased's gender) and, once the grave is closed, 'the bier is then cut to form a forked stick like a male *letya*, with the left arm shorter than the right' (1968: 74–5). As in Adamawa, the *lela* poles in the Bali kingdoms associate strongly with the deaths of important men (here royals and especially Fons),[10] with the installation of their successors, with skulls, with power and with killing. Forked poles may have featured in a variety of rituals more or less common to people once settled below the Benue; clearly their capacity to fuse anthropomorphic and theriomorphic forms means they can be interpreted very variously; any attempt to fix some essential meaning would be misplaced. On the grounds of both their form and Mubako name, I would incline strongly to believe that *lela* poles were brought from the north as part of the clan patrimonies of the raiders; but of which clans?

We know two things that may help: names purporting to be those of the original adherents of the raiding alliances are recalled both in the Bali kingdoms and in Donga; Bali kingdoms have *lela* poles which Donga lacks; however, Donga and Suntai (and perhaps Benue Chamba more widely) have masquerades which are absent from Bali. In the contemporary Bali chiefdoms, commoners belong to one of four categories (Nyamndi 1988: 167). Aside from the royals, or Sama, there are Ngadan-bila (plural of Ndagana) who are putatively non-royal Chamba, Ba'ni who are adherents not of Grassfield origin (and therefore include Ndagan-bila), BaNten or Grassfield allies, and finally the recent allies who fit none of these categories (such as the immigrant Bawock in Bali Nyonga). The small chiefdoms of Bali Gangsin and Bali Gashu are entirely composed of Ndagan-bila and other Ba'ni. Bali Nyonga and Bali Kumbat have the largest and most diverse populations. Taking all the Bali chiefdoms together, however, only five patrilineal descent groups make up the Ndagan-bila, those believed to constitute the non-royal Chamba core of the Ba'ni. Most widely distributed are the Djab-nebba who occur in all five chiefdoms. Kaga/Kag-nebba and Peli/Ped-nebba are each found in four chiefdoms, Nyem-nebba in three, and Gbadi-nebba (whom I shall not discuss) only in Bali Kumbat.[11] Two of these five are nowadays ethnic terms in the area from which the raiders departed: Kaga is Chamba Leko for the Bata or Bachama who lived to their north, and Pere (Peli in Bali, Pyeri in the Benue) is the preferred self-designation of the people living south of the Chamba Leko, around Koncha, known to the Fulbe as Koutine.[12] Both Kaga and Pere have ethnic-wide joking relations with Chamba Leko nowadays. Djab-kola is the Chamba Leko term for a place that appears on maps of the eastern face of the Alantika Mountains as Lowol. Hence, people of Djaba would be Djab-nebba. In Bali Gham, I was told that the idiom 'to climb Djab-kola' still means to achieve something difficult, albeit none there had seen Djab-kola. The priests (*nwana* sing.) of Djab-kola are Nyem-nebba who moved from the plains under Fulbe pressure. The chiefly clan of the Alantika Mountains at Saptou are the Sama who left communities east of the River Deo where their neighbours were Bata and Pere. When the annual exchange of guinea corn for salt with the Fulbe became an exaction, and Hamman Sambo began a war on the other side of the Deo, the Sama say they moved from the plain to find refuge in caves on the Alantika Mountains. At harvest they claim to hold a celebration called '*lela* beer' so that the chief will be able to eat the new season's guinea corn. Soon afterwards, at the festival of 'grave beer', when the tombs of the chiefs are repaired after harvest has been completed, only four of the six *lela* flutes are played (and four is the number of flutes in the Bali set).

The associations in play here look very promising when compared with the residue of Bali culture we have deduced to be of Adamawan origin. In the late eighteenth century, the plains south of the River Benue and east of the Alantika Mountains may have been populated by speakers of Bata/Bachama, Chamba Leko, Dowayo and Pere. People probably lived under chiefdoms in the plains and less centralised forms of government in the hills. Ponies and dwarf cattle were kept, and guinea corn and bambara groundnuts grown. Trade routes traversed the area, bringing salt in particular; local smiths produced iron implements for both mundane and ceremonial purposes and there was a developed tradition of brass casting of prestige objects among the Verre (and perhaps among others, like Koma, too). Deterioration in this environment may have been linked to the expansion of the Atlantic slave trade fed by this hinterland and had been exacerbated by drought and pestilences. The original Ba'ni (although it is unlikely this was yet what they called themselves) may have departed under Sama leadership, picking up Nyema priests, people from Djaba Mountain and contingents of both Bata and Pere. Since their language became the *lingua franca* of the allies, presumably Chamba Leko predominated in these bands. The *lela* and *voma* musical instruments were in their original patrimony, so were forked sticks which featured in the death rites of kings whose skulls were preserved. Chilver and Kaberry were told that in Bali Gham that the carving of the *letya* sticks somehow commemorated the original adherence of the Djaba with the 'Ndagam' or Ndagan-bila (Chilver 1964 Report 2: 7). Festivals at the beginning and end of the harvest honoured the *gara*, chief, and his ancestors, and these were also the occasion for the clan sections of warriors to renew their loyalty. A flag was either copied from the Fulbe, or else actually received from one of the lamidates. We know that raiding occurred virtually on commission from the Fulbe lamidos, and the flag signified a licensed raider as much as a jihadist in any stricter sense. The associations between forked sticks, the use of four *lela* flutes, and a royal skull cult would all seem to derive from Adamawa. Can the same be said for the stone pile that the Bali Fon mounts at his installation and again at Lela?

Possible precedents for the stone pile, or *wo-lela*, are numerous but insufficiently precise to inspire confidence (see Knöpfli 2001: 109, for an illustration of the stone pile in 1972). This applies to the compound term itself: *wo-lela*, the prefix of which, *wo-*, is probably not in Mubako. *Le-* is invariably prefixed to Mubako compound terms for Lela apparatus that we have come across: as in *le-tya* meaning *lela* pole, or in the individual names of the *lela* flutes. None of the descriptions of Lela I have read provides an etymology of *wo-lela*, however Tischhauser's Mungaka dictionary translation of *wo* is simply 'stone'. In both Chamba languages, 'stone' is also the term for hunting or killing shrines (Leko *vaga*, Daka *van*) which consist of stones, each deposited to represent the skull of a dangerous animal or human kill. The actual skulls are hung from branches by the killing shrine. Stones are durable stand-ins for skulls throughout the area from which the Ba'ni alliance set off (e.g. Barley 1983: 62 for Dowayo; Meek 1931b I: 45 for Bachama). Could this have anything to do with the stone pile in the Bali Nyonga palace plaza? The cartographer Max Moisel was told by Ernst and Dorsch that Fonyonga's stone pile represented the peoples he had conquered (Moisel 1908b: 270). Perhaps this could be interpreted as a scaled-up version of the stones representing individual kills in Chamba shrines? Lela does fall at the time of the year – the beginning of dry season – when hunting rites involving the refurbishment of stone shrines take place among Chamba. An ordeal involving decapitation of a fowl may be carried out to see whether there are impediments to success in the hunt, and this ordeal, as the reader may recall, also found its way to Donga. However, that is as far as analogy between the Bali stone pile and Chamba killing shrine takes us. In order to argue that the stone pile as a physical object was of Chamba origin, we would additionally need to propose that, like Lela, it was subsequently diffused within the Grassfields: for when Zintgraff attacked Bande (Mankon) they clearly had a stone pile since the Bali briefly managed to erect a German Imperial flag in it (Chilver 1966: 27). It seems more likely that the stone pile is a Grassfield feature that Bali Nyonga and perhaps remotivated.

An alternative, or complementary, argument might instead begin with the Chamba idiom 'to sit him on the stone', meaning to make someone king. We know that Galega I kept a stone throne by his palace entrance rather than the wooden stool favoured by his son Fonyonga II who moved the stone throne onto the veranda of his father's old living quarters. We know, furthermore, that Bali Fons are installed when they mount the *wolela* and that they also make public speeches at Lela time from the stone pile. Could this 'Lela stone' draw upon the symbolisms both of the stone killing-shrine and the stone throne? Again, this is conceivable but not demonstrable. Perhaps the stone pile might represent a convergence of pre-existing Grassfield and Adamawan material objects and motivations? But this remains speculation.

Thus far we have failed to specify any particular contribution that Pere (Peli in the Grassfields, or Pyeri below the River Benue) made to collective Ba'ni culture. This may be because a majority of Pere were not early adherents of the Ba'ni but rather moved ahead of them. An alliance in Adamawa between Kaga, Djaba and Nyema would most likely have been forged nearby the confluence of the Rivers Faro and Deo; but Pere raiders would have set out some way south of this, near to Koncha. Grassfield traditions consistently indicate the Pere to have been the vanguard of raiding. One section of 'Pyeri', it may be recalled, altogether left the orbit of the Grassfields to raid into the Benue Valley and settled in Takum; another section of 'Peli' (Bali Konntan) was first to reach the current site of Bali Nyonga where it was defeated and absorbed. Other sections of Peli were absorbed into the Bali kingdoms (sometimes following defection from Bali Nyonga, as at Bali Gham). The evidence that Peli, and probably Buti, preceded the Ba'ni as raiders is slight but consistent. The ethnographer of Adamawan Pere, Charles-Henry Pradelles de Latour, was able to meet the Pere chief of the Bali Konntan in Bali Nyonga. He confirmed to Pradelles that *gerem*, which is the Pere equivalent to the Chamba *voma*, persisted under that name in Bali. However, the cult had lost all its apparatus and retained only the sympathetic action of compressing a sacrificed chicken until its colon extruded from its anus: as would that of anyone breaking the cult's taboos (1995: 86). Pradelles de Latour was struck by just how little of Pere culture remained, even *gerem* had been reduced to the most esoteric of its rites.

So far as Bali are concerned, Djaba and Nyema, Pere and Kaga are all Ndagan-bila. The first of the non-Ndagan-bila people to have been picked up would have been the Kufad from around Ngaoundere. Their slight impact on Bali culture, despite a presence in the four larger chiefdoms, suggests they may not have joined on strong terms. Kaberry and Chilver's informant, himself a *voma* priest, proposed that throwing knives were their contribution to Voma (Chilver personal communication); however, throwing knives, although rare, are not entirely unknown to Chamba (as noted above, Frobenius illustrates one from his 1911 visit to the Chamba chiefdom of Kiri, 1913: 242). These insignia of the Voma priests, or *nwana*, became known by the term (*lama*) applied to the sickle-shaped insigne with lightning point most commonly used by Chamba priests.[13]

Remarkably, we may conclude, the majority of the paraphernalia crucial to Lela (flutes and drums, rattle spears, *lela* poles, and possibly the stone pile) and Voma (calabash horns and sack rattles, bullroarers and throwing knives, iron spears hung with clappers) probably has specifiable Adamawan origins. What of the performance itself? Even in Bali Nyonga where the language became restricted to the palace, *lela* songs are in Mubako. It would be interesting to learn whether any of the songs were recognisable for Chamba in Chambaland.[14] The literal-minded washing of military paraphernalia is absent from Donga ritual, which must heighten suspicion that this is a Grassfield innovation. However, the ordeal of beheading a fowl is shared between Bali Nyonga and Donga, and Chamba also have rituals in which the beheaded fowl must 'fight' to demonstrate that procedures have been successful. My surmise would be that the events of 'spear washing' in Donga and the first day of Lela in Bali Nyonga derive their shared features from ceremonies practised in some Chamba chiefdoms prior to the inception of the raiding alliances. The subsequent days of Lela in Bali Nyonga, and the military manoeuvres of Purma in Donga, seem apposite to the life of the raiding encampments and probably derive some of their characteristics from festivals of arms in the Fulbe lamidates. Hence, the impression that the contemporary Lela ceremonial is a composite of different observances is likely to be historically well-founded.

Notes

1. This association between the names of leaders and the names of the alliances they led is general. Damashi's Yambu raided across the Shebshi Mountains entering the sub-Benue plains well north of Garbosa's band; Mudi's Pyeri of Benue traditions (presumably the same people recalled as Muti's Peli in the Grassfields) headed back up from the Bamenda Grassfields towards Takum and Kashimbila; like the Pyeri, Gyando's Daka are recalled to have been in the vanguard of Adamawan raiding. They still provided a ruling family in Takum in the early twentieth century. I find it plausible that groups of marauders during these violent times would have cohered only under strong leadership.

2. Assessing information on Chamba cults is complicated by the fact of the collectivity of cults conventionally being spoken about in the singular; moreover, public discussion is likely to be confined to rain and harvest cults, which perform in public spaces. Hence, the casual enquirer is unlikely to come away with extensive accounts of esoteric cult matters.

3. Chamba construct the base of such rattles from a half calabash (in convex position) rather than from wood. One wonders whether Meek observed Donga rattles closely enough to assure himself this was not also the case there.

4. Knöpfli notes that the rattles now made only in Babungo in the Grassfields were previously made throughout the region (2002: 49).

5.   However, Donga spears, as illustrated by Meek, are not reminiscent of ironwork I know from Chambaland (Meek 1931b I: 340). Meek himself remarks that these resemble Hausa designs.

6.   My experience of this area is restricted to group interviews carried out during my researches between 1976 and 1978, and particularly during March 1977 when I visited the chiefdoms of the area consecutively.

7.   The individual names of the members of the set of *lela* flutes are similarly prefixed by *le-* rather than *lela-*.

8.   However, I did see smaller forked poles at Danubi, the place in Gurum through which Bachama are said to believe their dead pass (Stevens 1976). A chiefly cult in the Chamba-speaking chiefdom of Mbulo, which has a ruling patriclan universally conceded to be of Bachama or Bata origin, is reported to have a horned pole amongst its apparatus.

9.   Sally Chilver's collected notes (2001) on the subject demonstrate the contradictory statements made about royal burials which are shrouded in secrecy in Bali Nyonga. The persistence of a royal skull cult in other Bali kingdoms seems likely.

10.   Although I have seen nothing to corroborate this reading, one wonders whether the forked branch is able also to evoke the crossroads which is so important a site of Chamba funerary ritual (and West African rituals more generally).

11.   Differences of pronunciation and transcription, as well as optional forms, tend to obscure similarities. Suffixes like *-nebba* (people) or *-bila/-bira* (plural) are optional, hence Kaga, Kag-nebba, and Kag-bira are equivalent. Chamba Leko dialectal variation between [r] and [l] is common: so, like *lera* and *lela,* Pere and Pele/Peli are the same word, and both become Ped-nebba if the suffix for people is added. Chamba patriclans are usually named after a place, ethnicity, ancestor or office holder. Gbadi-nebba might possibly include the title *gban*, chief's assistant, which crops up in a lot of patriclan names. However, I know of no resources to pursue (or discount) this possibility.

12.   In northerly Chamba Leko dialects Pere are termed Pele. 'Pere people' contracts to Ped-nebba (see Note 11).

13.   *A lama* is usually a sickle with zigzag lightning point but is not forcibly such: I earlier mentioned one priest whom I met operating out of Mapeo among the Koma whose *lama* was a throwing knife; Yeli priests (*nwana* sing.) used *lama* made of a single wooden crook terminating in beak-like parallel planes that are wholly without iron components.

14.   Ankermann's wax cylinder recordings of *lela* musicians in Bali Nyonga (preserved in Berlin's Ethnological Museum) include a rendition of a *lela* song by Fonyonga himself.

CHAPTER 7

Fast Forward: From Adamawa to Late Post-Colonial Cameroon

By dint of a series of comparisons we have arrived at a reasoned appreciation of the stages by which, over the preceding century, Lela took the Kamerunian form documented in the decade before the First World War by Basel missionaries and the ethnologist Bernhard Ankermann. So far we have reconstructed these stages backwards. In conclusion, I want to rerun our reconstruction fast forward, noting its distinctive characteristics and continuing the story beyond the demise of German Kamerun to discuss the British Cameroons under Mandate and Trusteeship, and the post-independence history of Lela in Cameroon.

I have been arguing that the contemporary Lela ceremony contains traces of its entire history, and that it is not paradoxical to suggest that Lela has always been simultaneously, at least in some senses of these terms, both traditionalising and modernising. The durable core of the ceremony is composed of practices and materials belonging to the area around the confluences of the Benue, Faro and Deo rivers. By the mid-eighteenth century, recurrent famine and an intensifying regional slave trade had provoked increasing militarisation of communities speaking languages that today would be identified with Bata and Bachama, Chamba Leko and Pere people, as well as others to their south, notably Buti. Annual ceremonies evolved, or perhaps only increased in importance, which were concerned with the martial strength of the patriclans of chiefdoms, and of their chiefs and his officials. I argued in earlier work that these changes in the nature of chiefdoms were effected by increasing the salience of patriclan organisation at the expense of matriclan organisation, and by enhancing chiefly control over the ritual regulation of the community at the expense of the countervailing powers of his priests (Fardon 1988). Transition to an intermittently predatory mode of livelihood prior to their dispersion is suggested by the common core of the 'spear washing' ceremony being shared by the Chamba raiders who subsequently dispersed. The trigger to this dispersal was the Fulbe jihad of the first decade of the nineteenth century. Relations between Chamba-led freebooters and Fulbe lamidate builders were far too volatile for us ever to reconstruct them all in detail. But we have reports which suggest Chamba raiders operating almost on commission, and adopting flags into durbar-style spear-washing ceremonies to display the fact, and we also know that the trajectory of the raiding bands southwards and south-westwards was in part due to the menace posed by Fulbe state-building. As they dispersed, squabbled, split, incorporated new adherents, and pursued their raids from camps established for a few years, new elements were brought into the raiders' annual celebrations of the spoils of warfare and their auguries for the coming season's campaign. Leaders of the more powerful new adherents were able to retain titles to office, and elements of their ceremonial culture were incorporated into the annual cycle of rituals. The extended and additive character of martial ceremony in particular, meant that there were opportunities concurrently to display the distinguishing origins and identities of the raiding alliances' particular components, as well as to parade the most desirable treasures newly available in whatever area had been opened up to exploitation. Hence, the ceremonies looked forward and backwards in both the immediate and longer terms. In the immediate term, this meant forward to assess the alliance's current fighting strength and loyalties in the coming campaign, and back to what had transpired over the past year. In the longer term, it meant back to the distinctive origins and identities of an alliance's components, and forward to its eventual resettlement by carving out a new kingdom.

The ceremonial repertoire was always composite: initially because Chamba speakers were themselves highly varied, then because they allied with other non-Fulbe peoples of what was fast becoming the Adamawa Emirate, and subsequently because acquisition of accoutrements, both material treasures and ritual performances, whether of Fulbe, Grassfield or European origin, was one of the objectives and part of the logic of the lifestyle of raiders in exotic lands. In the Ba'ni case, this meant embracing a Graffi aesthetic of ornamentation and accumulation (as well as lots of Graffi people). Thanks to its twin imperatives – to incorporate people and novel materials, while simultaneously differentiating among categories of the kingdom's subjects and between those subjects and all others by reference to origins – Bali Nyonga could seem at once open to the influence of its surroundings and retentive of its own traditions. This may have contributed to the missionaries' sense of Bali's decline and loss: an empire lost, and religious observances become empty shells. In fact, Bali was accommodating itself to the changing requirements of early German colonialism with remarkable acumen: its techniques of war had been overhauled as it became Zintgraff and Hutter's ally in the conquest of the Grassfields. Hutter's Balitruppe had subsequently become the Fon's Basoge and assisted Zintgraff and Esser's plans to recruit plantation labour for the coast. When German colonial administration of the Grassfields was resumed in the early twentieth century, Bali proved a loyal ally and initially was rewarded with paramountcy on an unprecedented scale. At the same time, the Basel Mission's delegation was received hospitably, assisted to build a mission station and to inaugurate both schooling and its Mungaka scriptural translation project. The mission had military aspects of its own: an astounded Max Moisel – the visiting cartographer – recorded that Missionary Ernst (who had undertaken military service himself) drilled his schoolboys to Prussian commands (1908b: 270). Evidently Bali Nyonga, or rather its Fon and his advisers, felt that they served their own best interests by embracing change, however the more interesting observation is not that they acted from perceived self-interest but how they calculated that self-interest: as people who mastered new environments, the Bali ostensibly judged external challenges to the established order as opportunities rather than threats. Support for education, promotion of Mungaka as a regional language, interest in a new foreign religious cult … an encompassing and accommodative strategy served Bali Nyonga, particularly the palace, and its German allies well until around the time of the 1908 Lela when Bali's mediation of German relations in the Grassfields began to be reassessed as part of the problem rather than the solution.

There seems no reason to believe that Ba'ni, or indeed other raiding alliances, would have behaved differently towards the Fulbe than they did towards the Germans. Presumably they adopted what attracted them about their clothing, ceremonials and military technology: in this case robes, durbars and arab horses, rather than army uniforms, military drill and breechloading rifles. The trajectory of the Chamba/Ba'ni/Bali would be not just southwards in geographic terms but also towards ever more exotic incorporations of personnel and culture: initially from their neighbours, then from cognate Adamawan peoples, the Fulbe, Grassfielders, and finally Europeans for whom houses and roads were built, and to whom food was supplied and prestige goods like robes, skin bags, and ivory tusks were given as gifts (see Jenkins 1996).

By the early twentieth century most of the elements of contemporary Lela ceremonies were already present. It remained for them to be standardised and their exegeses stabilised by a new generation of western-educated intelligentsia. This took place during the British Mandate and Trusteeship and, subsequently, post-colonial government.

Bali Nyonga is not as well documented during the early years of the British Cameroons Mandate as it had been for the era of German Kamerun. By 1912, the Germans had removed most of the villages they had so recently placed under Bali sub-imperialism. As we saw, when the Germans retreated in 1915, Fonyonga locked the new Basel Mission Church and took the key to Bamenda, threatening imprisonment to any who preached (O'Neil 1987: 163). He appears to have been as pragmatically welcoming to the British as he was to the Germans: a leopard stool gifted by Fonyonga to George V in 1916 is currently loaned by his grand-daughter, Queen Elizabeth II, to the Liverpool Museum (Accession no. 7.3.1925.1). A memorandum by the Lieutenant Governor of the Southern Cameroons in 1921 directed that the Bali Fon 'be treated with utmost consideration and liberality' (Public Record Office, London, CO 750/4 Register of Correspondence, 15 November 1921).

The Basel missionaries did not return until 1925, when Adolf Vielhauer (who had first come to Bali in 1906) reopened the mission. After trying to force Meta and Moghamo villages back under Bali, the British had reassessed Bali's paramountcy – partly in the light of an improving knowledge of the later years of German colonialism – and gradually restricted it (Chilver 1963: 98–104).

There is no suggestion that the succession of Lela ceremonies was interrupted during this period. By the time of Wilhelm Zürcher's photographic record of Lela (from the 1930s), Bali ceremonial dress had settled into its present form, that adopted throughout the Grassfields; the four-day ceremony had been normalised; and various pieces of apparatus had assumed their current significance. However, as I showed earlier, general interest in Lela reached a low ebb during a period when modernisation was a compelling concern. Vielhauer's (1930) *Jahresbericht* for 1929 (BMA E-5–2.4, 51) notes that attendance at Lela was poor and such youngsters as attended showed no appetite for war games. Bali, particularly Bali militarism, did not enjoy the importance under the British Mandate and Trusteeship that it had under German pioneer colonialism, and this also may have diminished the enthusiasm to invest resources so heavily in the old martial ceremony. However, this was to change in the protracted run-up to the Southern Cameroons Trusteeship joining an independent Cameroon.

The immediate catalysts of Bali concern were the late-colonial Widekum riots of 1952 which claimed several lives and caused considerable destruction of property. The resort to violence by Widekum (or Meta) people was an unsuccessful attempt to wrest control over land which had been ceded to Bali as long ago as the 1905 paramountcy settlement. An enquiry which delved into the history of landholding found for the Bali, and the Widekum had to pay £10,000 in compensation. However, the Bali were left feeling isolated within the Grassfields (see Chilver 1963: 135–6; Fardon 1996: 43 Note 8). Closer relations between the Bali chiefdoms and a more focused attention to history were two of the reactions that ensued. As noted earlier, as late as 1910, when he published his report on his researches in Kamerun, Ankermann was apparently unaware of the relation between Mubako and Chamba Leko; the closest relation he could trace was with Verre – courtesy of a communication from the linguist B. Struck (Ankermann 1910a: 309, Note 1). Glauning (1906: 239) reported that 'Dinji' (that is Benue Chamba) and Bali shared a language, but did not trace this to a common origin in Chambaland. Jakob Keller (1909a: 162) deduced that Bali must have spoken Mubako in the days before they left Garoua, which he learns was one of their original homes; however, he makes no connexion with Chamba. So far as I am aware, there is no evidence of Bali themselves articulating an historical relation with Chamba before the First World War.

Knowledge that Mubako and Chamba Leko were in fact the same language was to become common only after the war, thanks to consultation of wordlists collected by colonial officers (particularly Strümpell 1910), and the ethnographic researches of Frobenius and Meek. Yet, as late as 1931, a history written down by Adelheid Hummel, albeit from the eighty-year-old Fotikali,[1] traced Bali Nyonga origins only from as far north as Banyo and attempted to derive the ethnic term, Banyonge, from this place-name (BMA E-5–2.7, 2). The third volume of Leo Frobenius's *Und Afrika Sprach*, which contains rich chapters on Chamba Leko and Chamba Daka, is a rare book, still not translated into English and, given its publication in 1913, was unlikely to have circulated in colonial Kamerun before war broke out. Even Frobenius, a German investigator, failed explicitly to link his accounts of Chambaland with the emigrants to the Grassfields, both of which populations were then in Kamerun, although he did recognise this origin for the Nigerian Chamba of Bakundi, Donga and Suntai (1913: 250). The published account of the British colonial government anthropologist, C.K. Meek, which particularly concentrated on Donga (1931b), might have circulated among literate Bali soon after its publication, but Meek also drew no links between the Nigerian Chamba in Donga and the Bali Chamba by then in British Cameroons. This is a strange oversight since the common origin of both Benue and Bali Chamba from Adamawa was known to British officials by Meek's time; W.E. Hunt's 'Assessment of the Bali clan' in 1925 asserted that the Bali 'clan belong to the Chamba-Leko tribe'. How quickly this also became conventional knowledge among Bali themselves is unclear, but thirty years later, the earliest of M.D.W. Jeffreys' published reports on Bali history – largely derived from Bali Kumbat – claimed the Bali to be of 'Chamba stock' (1957: 108). It looks as if knowledge of the relationship between Mubako in the Grassfields, the Chamba language retained by some of the Nigerian Benue Chamba, and Chamba Leko was gradually spreading from a small circle of German scholars and administrators at the tail end of the Kamerun colony, through the British mandate administration and into Bali consciousness.

Bali themselves appear not to have known about their ancestors' origin from Chambaland, at least not in those ethnic terms, although origination from the north was explicit in their identity; instead, Europeans deduced this ethnic relationship from the evidence of language distribution. The potential significance of this specific shared origin seems to have dawned slowly on the Bali. Coming so soon after the Widekum riots, the visit of the Gara of Donga from Nigeria in 1954 was an important event in this process. The Gara, as we have seen, was himself a keen student of Chamba history and the author of an account (n.d.) of his own and other Benue Chamba groups. M.D.W. Jeffreys (1962b: 172) had a translation from the Hausa made of the shorter of Garbosa's two works concerned with the chiefs of Donga, *Salsalar sarakunan Donga*, by a member of the veterinary department. Since Jeffreys served as District Officer for Bamenda between 1935 and 1946, and later wrote up his materials as a Senior Lecturer in Social Anthropology at the University of Witwatersrand in Johannesburg, presumably he gained access to Garbosa's work at some time during that decade. I have no idea in what form it may have circulated then: perhaps cyclostyled or such-like; and so far as I know, no copy of this English translation survives. Garbosa's final book underwent several drafts and consisted of two parts: as well as the account of the chiefs of Donga about which Jeffreys knew, there was also Garbosa's Chamba history, the first and longer part of the book (*Labarun Chambawa da al'amurransu*), which was referenced by Sally Chilver as a typescript dated 1956 in the University of Ibadan Library (Chilver 1967: 479 Note 2). The two texts were privately published together sometime later (I was given copies in 1976 which did not look new but unfortunately carried no publication date). This final version included details of Garbosa's 1954 trip to Bali (I have not seen the version in Ibadan to see whether this is also true of the earlier copy). In the absence of evidence for his texts circulating in Bali, I would assume Garbosa's presence made a greater impact than had his writings. The first published account of the impression Garbosa made on the Bali chiefs was given to the District Officer, M.D.W. Jeffreys, by Isaac Pefok Fielding. Jeffreys quoted Fielding's recollection of Garbosa's lecture as a caution against accepting revised accounts of Chamba origins that were circulating: in this case, Garbosa proposed a Syrian origin for Chamba (Jeffreys

1962b: 313). As an insert in his later published book reveals, Garbosa reasoned that Chamba had come from Sham in Syria simply on the basis of a similarity between names; much later Chamba were displaced by the Hausa and forced by this into a life of raiding. While drawing upon Jeffreys, Ndifontah B. Nyamndi, interprets this visit differently. According to him, Garbosa II visited Bali Nyonga to give Galega II 'moral support' in the wake of the Widekum riots; there he

> ... delivered a lecture (in Mubako!) and invited the Bali to treat their own history with greater interest, as a source of pride and a factor of unity. He also travelled to the other Balis to renew acquaintances with them, and he urged the Bali leaders to constitute themselves with the other Chamba leaders of Nigeria into some sort of permanent pan-Chamba affiliation. (Nyamndi 1988: 155)

The Chambas National Union – with membership apparently limited to the Bali communities and their diasporas – was founded, 'perhaps in answer to this call', in Bali Gham in 1958 (Nyamndi 1988: 155). However, the Union was short lived, and its major achievement appears to have been the production of a 1961 'Chambas National Almanac' consisting of a calendar and illustrated with photographs of the five Bali Fons, as well as photographs of inaugural meetings of branches of the Chambas National Union that were held in 1958 and 1959. Interest in Chamba history was renewed during the same period: Jeffreys learned – apparently on the basis of a revisit in 1960 – that a Bali Historical Society was in existence (1962b: 310); and it was through this body – over which the Fon himself presided – that Kaberry and Chilver carried out their initial research in Bali Nyonga in 1960 (Kaberry & Chilver 1961: 355). Sally Chilver's detailed findings were submitted as two substantial reports to the historical society in 1964 and, Stuart Russell reports, she was later 'quite distressed ... that some of her writings had become accepted as "official accounts"' (Russell 1980: 350). An intermittent tradition of local publication became established around this time: the Cameroon Protestant College acting as catalyst with a series of cyclostyled publications beginning in 1962 under the title *"It's like this ..." Essays on Traditional and Church History, Social Structure, and Other Aspects of Life in Various Tribes in East and West Cameroon*. The short essays, edited by Gilbert Gordon,[2] identified in the publications only as GEG, had been written by fourth-year students as a requirement of their English Language course. Unsurprisingly, a substantial proportion of the students were from Bali. The first issue carried essays written in 1961 on the 'Traditional history of Bali', 'Traditional history of the Chamba tribe', 'Traditional Chamba history'. Each of these essays was framed by concern with the relatively recent Widekum riots, began with an account of migration from the north impelled by famine and Fulbe attacks, and devoted some attention to Lela, as a national festival, along the way (CPC 1962). The 1962 students may have been set slightly different topics: two essays focus on social structure, and two others on Church history and titles respectively (CPC 1964). Aside from a well-informed piece on the Church, these essays tended to be set more firmly in a timeless ethnographic present and lack the contemporary referents of the previous year. GEG himself weighed in with a cyclostyled volume called *Bali History* in 1965 (revised 1971). This drew heavily on Jeffreys' published articles (1957, 1962a,

1962b), and Sally Chilver's first report to the Bali Historical Society (1964), as well as draft sections she had written with Phyllis Kaberry of what would be published in Cameroon in 1968 as *Traditional Bamenda*. For a generation of educated youngsters, GEG's *Bali History* propagated what became the conventional view of Bali history. Significantly, GEG's account of Lela makes reference to no diminution of interest in or enthusiasm for the ceremony, as had been the common theme of previous accounts. The recent Widekum riots had apparently reawakened popular appetite for an opportunity, such as Lela provided, to demonstrate Bali's military past; Lela sutured northern origins with a Grassfield identity through the re-enactment of might and wealth.

The stream of local writings on Bali history may well have been relatively uninterrupted from the 1960s. However, not all the sources circulated widely so, to judge only from those I have come across, there seems to have been another revival of interest in Bali history during the mid-1970s. A couple of academic dissertations appeared then: Pius Bejeng Soh tendered *A Study of Lela, a Bali State Cult of the North-West Grassfields of Cameroon* for examination in sociology at the University of Yaoundé in 1975; while in 1978 Henri Buma-Foncham Fomuso submitted an account of *Sacrifice among the Bali-Nyonga in Mezam Division N.W. Province of Cameroon* for a Licence en Théologie to the same University's Faculty of Protestant Theology. A series under the title *The Living Culture of Bali-Nyonga* – largely edited by Elias Nwana and Augustine Ndangam – was inaugurated, also in 1978, with an account of the Lela festival. An LP of Bali music (including Lela music) issued in France in 1979 was counted a second publication in this series; and this was followed in December 1981 by a pamphlet listing Bali names along with an illustrated inventory of some traditional material culture; that same month, the authors devoted a publication to *A Portrait of their Royal Highnesses*, the Fons of Bali. After a gap of a few years, two book-length volumes of locally authored history appeared in 1988: Titanji et al. *An Introduction to the Study of Bali-Nyonga*, a substantial collection of essays assembled as a tribute to Galega II who had died in 1985, and Ndifontah B. Nyamndi's *The Bali Chamba of Cameroon: A Political History* to which I referred earlier. From the mid-1970s to late 1980s there is demonstrably a continuous stream of publications concerned with Bali history, many of which give prominent place to consideration of Lela. Together these show a consistent formalisation of what – earlier in the century – had seemed a somewhat sprawling event. Each day was named and allocated a particular content and significance; the paraphernalia of the ceremony was remotivated consistently; the accounts became increasingly similar as a canonical Lela took shape (at least textually).

Stuart Russell's description, based on research during the 1970s, is more extensive than any of the local publications but echoes what are presumably the terms of elite conversation at that time. His introductory words could have come from any contemporary source: 'Lela is the most important Bali festival. While it has significant religious aspects, it is primarily military and political in character' (1980: 60). The first day of Lela, 'Sufu' or 'washing off', culminates in the representatives of the descendants of Nyongpasi's allies demonstrating their allegiance. On the second day, 'Loti', a 'mock campaign to the market and return to the central square symbolize defense against the Widekum and the gathering of Bali from every corner and farm area to defend the town against attack' (1980: 63). The military societies perform manoeuvres and the population salutes the Fon according to descent group. 'The third day is the people's day' (1980: 63), when the Fon feeds his people and announces new appointments to title. The fourth day 'Dsonikang' involves ritual washing by the Sama in a sacred stream below the compound of Fomofosing, whose Mubako title is 'Doh vuneb'. Russell translates this title as 'grandfather of the gods', presumably following local exegesis.[3] The Samas' ritual is believed to 'drive away evil influences'. The day culminates in the Fon's speech, made through an intermediary, exhorting his people to live in peace. Flags are taken in at dusk when the Fon's custom is 'to receive distinguished foreigners and visitors on his veranda after the dancing ends' (Russell 1980: 62–3).

The persistence of specific reference to defence of the town against the Widekum in Lela of the 1970s, demonstrates both that Lela continued to ceremonialise the most recent conflicts in the minds of those taking party, and that disputed claims to land continued to sour community relations. Stuart Russell noted several changes to Lela's symbolism apparently unaware, or not made aware by his informants, they were such: 'Male and female sides of Bali are carefully represented at Lela' (1980: 6). This had not, to judge by our records, always been so; the consistent gendering of pairs of Lela equipment, carefully recorded by Russell, replaced earlier motivations.[4] By the 1970s the flags, *tutuwan*, were said to be male and female (the latter with a red band at its top, see Russell 1980: 60). This reading was already current by the 1960s (see GEG 1971: 8), but we know that during the late nineteenth and early twentieth centuries, the paired flags were a German tricolour and an all-white Bali standard; realising this Fomuso explains that the male and female flags are historically derived from Bali and German flags (1976: 17). Prior to that, it seems likely that each raiding confederacy had only a single flag (copied, I have suggested, from Fulbe precedent or Fulbe mandate); some Bali sources claim that Bali Nyonga, uniquely among the Bali, had a pair of flags because Bali Konntan was allowed to keep its flag when it agreed to submit to Bali Nyonga.[5] Jeffreys (1962b: 194–5) quotes Sama Fokum of Bali Nyonga giving evidence before the District Officer in 1941, during the 'Intertribal Boundaries Settlement Ordinance', to the effect that Bali Nyonga captured Bali Konntan's flag, after which the two groups had 'become merged'. By the 1960s, the Y-shaped poles, *letya*, were also considered male and female (GEG 1971: 8). *Tu nganget*, the horned pillars ostensibly for storing the weapons of visitors, are likewise claimed to be gendered female or male and accordingly have either four or three prongs (GEG 1971: 8; Russell 1980: 62). Fonyonga had told Ankermann, it may be recalled, that the number and size of prongs on such poles simply reflected the number of palavers a man was likely to hear, and hence the prestige of their owner: the Fon's being greatest. An alternative to the gendered explanation of the number of prongs, also recent, is that they represent the seven components into which the Ba'ni split. We know from photographs that the posts did not perforce have a combined total of seven prongs in the early twentieth century; however, motivation by gender, or by sevens, seem to have become default settings for Bali symbolism. Not just the flags and *tu nganget* but the *letya* and the pair of spears that, with the flags and spear bundles, compose the *kong* have also become gendered pairs; not only are there historically, for preference, seven Bali sections, certain offices are described as having been seven in number (for instance the *nkom*) although there are many times this number of officials lately, and there has been no period when there demonstrably were seven office-holders.

Nwana and Ndangam introduced their subject not dissimilarly to Russell as an annual festival 'which has become one of the most cherished and admired institutions not only by the Citizens of Bali but also by many other Cameroonians and tourists alike' (1978: 1).

Bali Nyonga monarchs, they explain, are descendants of Nyonga, the daughter of Gawolbe, and this is the 'origin of the "Dual Sovereignty" which is represented by two flags (Tutuwan) in Bali-Nyonga. Nyongpasi became the first monarch of Bali-Nyonga and was called Fon-Nyonga I while Nyonga his mother became the first "queen mother" (ka).' (1978: 3). Perhaps this semi-official acceptance of Nyongpasi as *mundzad mfon* (or matrilateral relation) to Gawolbe, the hero leader of the united Ba'ni raiders, is of a piece with the consistent motivating of paired items by gender.

Four 'phases' of Lela are distinguished by Nwana and Ndangam even more rigorously than they were by Russell's informants: religious, military, political and 'the festivity itself'. Lela's inception is fixed as the night of the fifth weekday (in the eight-day week) following the appearance of the December moon. Six days later, the standards and spears are taken for 'cleansing' at the 'lela shrine' by the river two miles outside town. 'Nowadays' people are allowed to watch the descent into the river. The authors note a parallel between eating the sacrificial goat at Lela and the eating of a ram at the 'Feast of the Passover in the Old Testament' (1978: 11). The description passes over without comment the fact that Fon attends Lela on horseback, which was not the case in the early twentieth century, and probably had not been so in the second half of the nineteenth century either. That night each of the original Ba'ni groups is called by name in Mubako and renews allegiance to the Fon in the course of a solemn beer drink.

On the second day the procession goes to the weekly market place and back to perform *lo 'ti* salutations to the Fon. They stop at the residence of the queen (royal sister). Unlike Russell, no reference is made here to the conflagration of relations with the Widekum in the early 1950s, but a show of arms follows on immediately.

THE CLIMAX: The following event is generally acknowledged as the climax of the entire festival. The huge crowd of both participants and spectators, the stirring rhythm of the lela orchestra, the amount and scale of the gun shots in which the men affirm their qualities of manliness and bravery! The men pour out in groups, run with raised guns to the Fon in traditional military salute (lo'ti); then they turn and rush outward either pounding their chests in manly assertions or brandishing their guns as if to charge an imaginary enemy; then they sweep back to the Fon in another salute before they turn to firing. The most moving event of the show comes when the Fon himself, and alone, rushes out to take his turn in firing! He is accompanied by his umbrella carrier but the latter usually finds it difficult to run apace with him. Sometimes the Fon races in excite-ment round the entire dance ground firing amongst earbreaking cheers and yelling from the women folk. The whole scene is as moving and as captivating as the climax of a great national event can be! (Nwana, Ndangam & Nti 1978: 14)

The third day involves dancing without gunfire, when dancers may exchange admiration gifts. The remark-worthy features of the fourth day (the third is not specified further) include the Fon's speech to his Koms (roughly, magistrates): 'The speech usually includes something on increased economic and agricultural productivity' (1978: 14). Honours, if any, are announced.[6] On a fifth day, there is a brief procession to various compounds (including those of the queen and queen mother). The description ends with a list of projects for improving the Lela:

PROJECT NO. 1 :   Levelling the lela dance ground with possible extension of the dance ground.

PROJECT NO. 2 :   Construction of toilet facilities. Both pit (for general use) and water system for V.I.P.'s and guests.

PROJECT NO. 3 :   Construction of a grandstand.

PROJECT NO. 4 :   Construction of a stone wall between the gate into nka'nted and beyond the palace gate i.e. site of old court. This will give the palace enclosure a permanent structure.

PROJECT NO. 5 :   Construction of an arch at the lela shrine.

PROJECT NO. 6 :   Construction of a properly designed enclosure for the lela standards when it is out.

PROJECT NO. 7 :   Filming the whole festival to keep for future generations.

PROJECT NO. 8 :   Lighting the lela ground.

(Nwana, Ndangam & Nti 1978: 16)

While the authors' suggested improvements seen in one light appear innovatory, looked at another way they simply continue the project of incorporating signs of the most attractive, and latterly modern, innovations (whether people or material culture or motivating ideas) while retaining a capacity to differentiate its participants by reference to the past.

Nwana and Ndangam's description of Lela footnotes, and apparently draws upon, the slightly earlier work that Fomuso had completed for his 'Licence en Théologie' in 1976. Fomuso is concerned to highlight the way that Bali conceptions of a High God, *Nyikob* in Mungaka, and especially their ancestors as intermediaries to him, connect with their practices of sacrifice. It is because the ancestors' closeness to God allows them to foretell the future that, according to Fomuso, they receive sacrifice at Lela (1976: 9). Apparently without *direct* recourse to the earlier Basel missionaries' accounts of Lela, Fomuso draws many of the same parallels with sacrificial customs reported in the Pentateuch. Sacrifice involves 'preparation of the body and making oneself free of all moral uncleanliness', which Fomuso says is the sense of the Mungaka term *chuhtimbum* (1976: 13). The theme of purification is followed through in the name of the stream in which Lela paraphernalia is washed: *Ntsi suhfuh* or 'stream of purification' (1976: 13). The initial (restricted) stages of Lela are treated by Fomuso both as a way for the Sama to surround the ceremony with solemnity and as a practical deterrent to 'the efforts of evil persons who may wish to disturb the smooth running of Lela' (1976: 17). After the palace has been prepared the *lela* musicians begin to play the '*Loti*'.

> This *Loti* is a sign given, and a preparation made before a gun is fired during religious and social celebrations. In *Loti*, the person or persons firing the gun have before them an imaginary enemy just as if they were at war. They hold their guns ready to shoot, run ahead slowly a bit, then run backwards at the same pace, as if they were trying to take a good aim at the supposed enemy. (Fomuso 1976: 3)

The Fon delegates his powers to Tita Nyagang, who will oversee the sacrifice by the stream. Before washing the flags in the stream, Tita Nyagang is reported to call the names of the past Bali Fons. The 'immolation' comes next as the 'officiating priest' cuts the head off the sacrificial cockerel; if it dies well (after struggling and not lying on its right wing) this signals that 'the ontological balance which should exist between the people and their ancestors as well as with Nyikob, is there' (1976: 19). Fomuso's description recounts the procession back to the palace, stopping at the compound of the Fon's mother, while the different *manjong* societies take their places on the plaza. The *lo'ti* is played and the Fon salutes the palace entrance before receiving the 'reinforced *Kong*' (the Mungaka term literally meaning spear, but here signifying the assemblage of spears and flags taken to the river) (Fomuso 1976: 17, 21). The Fon then declares the Lela open and dancing takes place around the *wolela* (stone pile) 'on which the musicians stand to play' (Fomuso 1976: 21).

The ensuing days are described in familiar terms: the second day is largely made up of '*Loti*' in the marketplace. 'In recent years, those who once served in the colonial army put on their ex-servicemen's uniforms' (Fomuso 1976: 21). The Fon leads his warriors home and makes a state visit to the 'king of women', a royal sister enthroned with him.

> The third day is 'basically a dancing day' when the people are dressed in their most beautiful gowns. The dance on this day is performed slowly and honourably with the wives of the Fon all dancing together in a particular place using the jinglers [iron leg rattles] to add to the beauty of the music. At a certain time, the Fon dressed in his most magnificent traditional gown, joins the crowd and dances in great splendour. One of his attendants carries a large multicoloured umbrella over his head while another follows very closely behind him with an elephant tusk which he blows from time to time. Each time the tusk is blown, the women yell in excitement pronouncing as many attributive names of their Fon as possible. As soon as the Fon joins in the dance, the women no longer dance upright as the men do. They dance bowing down as a sign of respect for the ruler of the land. (Fomuso 1976: 21)

The fourth and final day is one of 'benediction'. The Fon makes a 'state speech' after which the *kong* (collection of flags and spears) is returned to the palace. This action is 'accompanied by the sending away of evil spirits and the spirits of all evil persons' (Fomuso 1976: 22), words that might have been music to the ears of Galega I who had shared his worries about maleficent influences with Esser eighty years earlier. Fomuso concludes his account of the major Lela by noting how the ceremony has been transformed from what was 'essentially a military sacrifice' into a predominantly religious celebration in which 'the people ask for blessings on the chiefdom so that no evil should befall the land'. Later he concludes his dissertation with the thought that Lela is really a rite of regeneration, 'In effect, when the Bali-Nyonga wash the flags, when they purify the *Tutuwan*, it is an attempt to wash away every evil that is of the old year' (Fomuso 1976: 38). As such, Fomuso seems to claim, albeit rather indirectly, that Lela resembles some of the early practices of the judaic world which judaeo-christian thought transcended by introducing a more complex view of man's position in the world that took time and history into account. In making this argument, Fomuso is again – whether or not he realises it – echoing analyses that the Basel missionaries had proposed in the early part of the twentieth century.

*   *   *

It would have been possible to write an account of Lela's development over two centuries that emphasised the cultural disjunctions between epochs – Chambaland before the jihad, the Adamawa Emirate, German colonial Kamerun, the British Cameroons Mandate and Trusteeship, post-colonial Cameroon – each seen as providing a culture within which to contextualise Lela. This periodisation has provided an irreplaceable scaffolding to our history, but the continuity of Lela would be obscured by an over-emphasis on contextual change. In many respects, the context that mattered to Lela has remained similar. Thanks to its capacity to absorb practices, Lela became a baroque ceremonial, made up of numerous parts. This has allowed it to be motivated in different ways that are not mutually exclusive: as a ceremony that is religious (in some respects both traditional and christian), military, political, diplomatic and simply festive. Throughout it has been able to achieve what might seem contrary aims: it has acted as a time capsule of past practices and yet been at the cutting edge of Chamba, Ba'ni and Bali adaptation to changing times; undergoing constant change, it has nonetheless always seemed to be a piece (more accurately, several pieces) of patrimony. Lela has both integrated diverse elements within the Bali population and differentiated between them. Its additive composition has allowed it to be many things to many people, becoming, at the last, explicitly various in the idea of its having religious, military, social and political days. As I have been able to show, the stated motivation of elements of Lela changed demonstrably over the twentieth century in the course of intriguing and detailed substitutions of things and ideas. But, like the most enduring of traditions everywhere, Lela has adapted to changing times with a timeless air.

Although Lela is not atypical in these respects among the ceremonies of West Africa, it may be an extreme case. Its passage with a migrant people increased the variety of its elements. It derived from pre-jihadic Adamawan cultures, and was then changed by the conjuncture of muslim jihad in the north and European slave trade in the south, and by its insertion into the environment of the western Grassfields. The ceremony began to crystallise in alliance with German colonialism and christian mission, and it continued to be adapted under later British administration and during post-colonial times when the history of the Bali, and its relation to Bali's power, continued to be sources of controversy. For Bali migrants both within and outside Cameroon, as well as for tourists armed with guide books, Lela has become a compulsory engagement in the Cameroonian year.[7]

Notes

1. Presumably he was the chief of the Tikali (Tikari) section of Bali Nyonga as his name suggests.
2. Gilbert Gordon, a pastor in the North American Baptist Missionary Society, taught Literature and Religious Knowledge at the Cameroon Protestant College Bali during the 1960s. Later he worked as a teacher in the Baptist College and then Baptist Seminary in Ndu (Mathew Gwanfogbe, personal communication, September 2005).
3. *Veneb* (a dialectal variant of 'Vuneb') has also been used in Chambaland to designate the christian high God; however, it was not traditionally the term for the high creator God (who was identitified with the sun), rather it is the singular form of the term for the dead.
4. This balancing of male and female sides seems to correlate with the immense significance that mother's kin have for the life chances of the numerous children of large-scale polygynists. Fathers typically cannot usually afford to educate all their children if they are numerous, so those with rich matrikin will have a better chance to prosper, and hence eventually succeed to their father. Several well-placed examples of this were pointed out to me during my brief visit in 2004.
5. Nyamndi (1988: 61) sees the simultaneous presence of the two *tutuwan* of Bali Nyonga and Bali Konntan as evidence of their unity rather than of conquest. Lela is performed with a single flag in Bali Kumbat (from photographic evidence) and in Bali Gangsin (where I witnessed an enactment).
6. In Bali, as in chiefdoms elsewhere, the bestowal of a title is a useful (and economical) way to associate distinguished emigrants, as well as useful foreign residents, with the aspirations of the palace and community.
7. I should add, 'at least in those years when it takes place'. Unfortunately my own 2004 visit took place in a year when there was no Lela. Palace sources attributed this to the expense of palace refurbishment which competed for resources with Lela. Outside the palace, it was rumoured that the support of the Fon for the Cameroonian ruling party, while the populace largely voted for the opposition party, meant that Lela risked providing an opportunity for dissension rather than an occasion for the celebration of unity.

References

Published References

Aletum Tabwe, Michael & Cyprian Fonyuy Fisiy, 1989, *Socio-Political Integration and Nso Institutions, Cameroon*, Yaoundé: Sopecam.

Ankermann, Bernhard, 1910a, 'Bericht über eine ethnograpische Forschungsreise ins Grasland von Kamerun', *Zeitschrift für Ethnologie* 42: 288–310.

———1910b, 'Über die Religion der Graslandbewohner Nordwest-Kameruns', *Korrespondenz-Blatt der Deutschen Gesellschaft für Anthropologie, Ethnologie und Urgeschichte* XLI 9/12: 1–2.

Ankermann, Bernhard & Felix von Luschan, 1914, *Anleitung zum ethnologischen Beobachten und Sammeln*, Berlin: Museen.

Anon, 1908, 'Hauptmann Glauning gefallen', *Deutsche Kolonialzeitung* 28 March 28(13): 215.

Apter, Andrew, 2005, *The Pan-African Nation: Oil and the Spectacle of Culture in Nigeria*, Chicago and London: Chicago University Press.

Barley, Nigel, 1983, *Symbolic Structures: An Exploration of the Culture of the Dowayos*, Cambridge and Paris: Cambridge University Press and Maison des Sciences de l'Homme.

Baumann, Hermann & László Vajda, 1959, 'Bernhard Ankermanns völkerkundliche Aufzeichnungen im Grasland von Kamerun 1907–09', *BaesslerArchiv* NF 7(2): 217–317 (including letter from Adolf Vielhauer to Ankermann of 22 November 1910, pp. 271–76).

Chilver, E.M.,1961, 'Nineteenth century trade in the Bamenda Grassfields, Southern Cameroons', *Afrika und Übersee* 44(4): 233–58.

———1963, 'Native administration in the West Central Cameroons, 1902–1954', in Kenneth Robinson & Frederick Madden (eds) *Essays in Imperial Government*, Oxford: Basil Blackwell.

———1964, 'A Bamileke community in Bali-Nyonga: a note on the Bawok', *African Studies* 23(3–4): 121–27.

———1966, *Zintgraff's Explorations in Bamenda, Adamawa and the Benue Lands 1889–1892*, Buea: Ministry of Primary Education and Social Welfare and West Cameroon Antiquities Commission.

———1967, 'Paramountcy and protection in the Cameroons: the Bali and the Germans, 1889–1913', in Prosser Gifford & Wm. Roger Louis (eds) *Britain and Germany in Africa*, New Haven and London: Yale University Press.

Chilver, E.M. & P.M. Kaberry, 1963, 'Traditional government in Bafut, West Cameroon', *The Nigerian Field* XXVIII(1): 4–30.

——1968, *Traditional Bamenda. The Pre-Colonial History and Ethnography of the Bamenda Grassfields*, Ministry of Primary Education and Social Welfare and West Cameroon Antiquities Commission, Buea: Government Printer.

Chilver, E.M. & Ute Röschenthaler (eds), 2001, *Cameroon's Tycoon. Max Esser's Expedition and its Consequences*, Cameroon Studies, Volume 3, Oxford and New York: Berghahn.

CPC (Cameroon Protestant College), 1962, *'It's Like this ...' Essays on Traditional and Church History, Social Structure, and Other Aspects of Life in Various Tribes in East and West Cameroon*, Volume 1, *Bali*, Bamenda: Cameroon Protestant College.

——1964, *'It's Like this ...' Essays on Traditional and Church History, Social Structure, and Other Aspects of Life in Various Tribes in East and West Cameroon*, Volume 2, Part 1, *Bali Area and South*, Bamenda: Cameroon Protestant College.

Dah, Jonas N., 1995, *Chieftaincy, Widowhood and Ngambi in Cameroon*, Pforzheim-Hohenwart.

Deutsches Kolonialblatt, 1906a, 'Aus dem Bereiche der Missionen und der Antisklaverei-Bewegung. Missionspioniere im Grasland von Nordwest-kamerun', *DKB* 17: 353–55.

——1906b, 'Kamerun. Zu den Unruhen in Kamerun', *DKB* 17: 516.

Edwards, Elizabeth, 2001, *Raw Histories: Photographs, Anthropology and Museums*, Oxford and New York: Berg.

Ernst, Ferdinand, 1903, 'Die ersten Erfahrungen unserer Brüder in Bali. Bericht von Br. F. Ernst, dat. Bali, den 27 Juni 1903', *Der Evangelische Heidenbote*, Parts 1–4 October 1903: 73–75; Part 5 November 1903: 86–87.

——1906, 'Eine Thronrede in Bali', *Der Evangelische Heidenbote*, January 1906: Parts 2 and 3 (illustration).

Esser, Max, 1898, *An der Westküste Afrikas*, Berlin, Köln and Leipzig: Alfred Ahn.

Fardon, Richard, 1988, *Raiders and Refugees. Trends in Chamba Political Development 1750–1950*, Washington: Smithsonian Series in Ethnographic Inquiry.

——1991, *Between God, the Dead and the Wild: Chamba Interpretations of Ritual and Religion*, Edinburgh: Edinburgh University Press for the International African Institute.

——1996, 'Ethnicity, the person and the problem of "identity" in West Africa', in I. Fowler & D. Zeitlyn (eds), *African Crossroads: Intersections between History and Anthropology in Cameroon*, Cameroon Studies, Volume 2, Oxford: Berghahn.

——2004, 'The ethnologist and the missionaries: recording the 1908 Lela in Bali Nyonga', in Michael Albrecht, Veit Arlt, Barbara Müller & Jürg Schneider (eds) *Getting Pictures Right: Context and Interpretation*, Köln: Rüdiger Köppe Verlag.

———2005, 'Tiger in an African palace', in David Mills & Wendy James (eds) *The Qualities of Time*, ASA Monographs in Social Anthropology 41, Oxford: Berg.

———2006: in press, *Fusions: Masquerades and Thought Style East of the Niger–Benue Confluence*, Chamba Arts in Context, Volume 2, London: Saffron, Afriscopes.

Fardon, Richard & Christine Stelzig, 2005, *Column to Volume: Formal Innovation in Chamba Statuary*, Chamba Arts in Context Volume 1, London: Saffron, Afriscopes.

Fohtung, Maxwell Gabana, 1992, 'Self-portrait of a Cameroonian, taken down by Peter Kalle Njie and edited by E.M. Chilver', *Paideuma* 38: 219–48.

Fritsch, Gustav, 1906, 'Praktische Gesichtspunkte für die Verwendung zweier dem Reisenden wichtigen technischen Hülfsmittel: Das Mikroskop und der photographische Apparat', in Georg von Neumayer (ed.) *Anleitung zu wissenschaftlichen Beobachtungen auf Reisen*, Hannover: Max Jänecke.

Frobenius, Leo, 1913, *Und Afrika Sprach*, Volume 3, Berlin: Vita Deutsches Verlagshaus.

Garbosa II, M.S. (Gara of Donga) (n.d.; completed circa 1956), *Labarun Chambawa da al'amurransu* and *Salsalar sarakunan Donga*, Nigeria: privately published as a single volume.

Gardi, Bernhard, 2000, *Le Boubou – c'est chic. Les boubous du Mali et d'autres pays de l'Afrique de l'Ouest*, Basel: Museum der Kulturen and Editions Christoph Merian.

Gardi, René, 1965, 'Über den Totenkult bei den Doayo in Nordkamerun. Beobachtungen und Tagebuchnotizen', in Carl A. Schmitz & Robert Wildhaber (eds) *Festschrift Alfred Bühler, Basler Beiträge zur Geographie und Ethnologie, Ethnologische Reihe* 2: 117–26.

———1995, *Momente des Alltags: Fotodokumente aus Nordkamerun 1950–85 (Tchadsee, Mandara, Alantika)*, Basel: Museum of Ethnology and Swiss Museum of European Folklife.

Geary, Christraud M, 1986, 'Photographs as materials for African history: some methodological considerations', *History in Africa* 13: 89–116.

———1988a, 'Art and political process in the kingdoms of Bali-Nyonga and Bamum (Cameroon Grassfields)' *Canadian Journal of African Studies* 22(1): 11–41.

———1988b, *Images from Bamum: German Colonial Photography at the Court of King Njoya, Cameroun, West Africa, 1902–15*, Washington: National Museum of African Art, Smithsonian Institute.

———1990a, 'Text und Kontext: zur Fragen der Methodik beider quellenkritischen Auswertung historischer Photographien aus Afrika', *Zeitschrift für Kulturaustauch* 40(3) Teil 1: 426–39.

———1990b, 'Impressions of the African past: interpreting ethnographic photographs from Cameroon', *Visual Anthropology* 3: 289–315.

———1990c, 'Photographie als kunsthistorische Quelle. Das *nja*-Fest der Bamum (Kamerun) im späten 19. und frühen 20. Jahrhundert', in Miklós Szalay (ed.)

Der Sinn des Schönen: Aesthetik, Soziologie und Geschichte der Afrikanischen Kunst, Munich: Trickster.

―――1994, *The Voyage of King Njoya's Gift: A Beaded Sculpture from the Bamum Kingdom, Cameroon, in the National Museum of African Art*, Washington: Smithsonian Museum.

―――1995, 'Art, politics, and the transformation of meaning: Bamum art in the twentieth century', in Mary Jo Arnoldi, C.M. Geary & Kris L. Hardin (eds) *African Material Culture*, Bloomington and Indianapolis: Indiana University Press.

―――1996, 'Political dress: German-style military attire and colonial politics in Bamum', in Ian Fowler & David Zeitlyn (eds) *African Crossroads: Intersections between History and Anthropology in Cameroon*, Cameroon Studies, Volume 2, Oxford: Berghahn.

GEG (Gilbert Gordon) 1965, revised 1971, *Bali History*, Bali: Cameroon Protestant College.

Glauning, H., 1905, 'Bericht des Hauptmanns Glauning, Leiters der Station Bamenda, über seine Expedition nach Bali, Bameta und dem Südbezirk', *Deutsches Kolonialblatt* 16: 667–72.

―――1906, 'Bericht des Hauptmanns Glauning über seine Reise in den Nordbezirk', *Deutsches Kolonialblatt* 17: 235–41.

Green, Malcolm, 1982, *Through the Year in West Africa*, London: Batsford.

Harter, Pierre, 1986, *Arts anciens du Cameroun*, Supplement to Volume 40 *Arts d'Afrique Noire*, Arnouville: Arts d'Afrique Noire.

Hutter, Franz, 1902, *Wanderungen und Forschungen im NordHinterland von Kamerun*, Braunschweig: Friedrich Vieweg und Sohn.

Jahresberichten, 1903–15, Published Annual Reports, Basel Mission, Basel.

Jeffreys, M.D.W., 1938, 'Carved figures from Bali Cameroon. Correspondence', *Man* 38, No. 186.

―――1957, 'The Bali of Bamenda', *African Studies* 16: 108–13.

―――1962a, 'Some notes on the customs of the Grassfield Bali of Northwestern Cameroons', *Afrika und Übersee* 46(3): 161–67.

―――1962b, 'Traditional sources prior to 1890 for the Grassfield Bali of Northwestern Cameroons', *Afrika und Übersee* 46(3–4): 168–99; 296–313.

Jenkins, Paul, 1996, 'Warum tagen die Missionare Kostüme? Forschungsmöglichkeiten im Bildarchiv der Basler Mission', *Historische Anthropologie* 4(2): 292–302.

―――2004, 'Camera evangelista – camera lucida? Trans-border experiences with historical photographs from a mission archive', in Michael Albrecht, Veit Arlt, Barbara Müller & Jürg Schneider (eds) *Getting Pictures Right: Context and Interpretation*, Köln: Rüdiger Köppe Verlag.

Jenkins, Paul & Christraud Geary, 1985, 'Photographs from Africa in the Basel Mission Archive', *African Arts* 18(4): 56–63 & 100.

Kaberry, P.M. & Chilver, E.M., 1961, 'An outline of the traditional political system of Bali Nyonga, Southern Cameroons', *Africa* 31(4): 355–71.

Keller, Jakob, 1906, 'Eine merkwürdige Sitte in Bali', *Jahresbericht [der Basel Mission] 1905*, Basel Mission: 87–88.

――――1909a, 'Die Bedeutung des Bali-Volkes für die Evangelisierung des Hinterlandes von Kamerun', *Der Evangelische Missionsmagazin*: 157–63.

――――1909b, 'Echo aus Bali', *Der Evangelische Heidenbote*: 91–92.

――――1919, 'Das Lelafest in Bali', *Der Evangelische Heidenbote*, June: 63–66, July: 78–81, October: 116–18.

――――1926, *Goldkörner im heidnischen Urgestein. Ein Vergleich der Sitten und Gebote Israels hauptsächlich im Pentateuch, mit denen der Heiden in Kamerun*, Basel: Missionenstudien N.F. 2.

Keller, W., 1981, *Zur Freiheit berufen. Die Geschichte der Presbyterianischen Kirche in Kamerun*, Zurich: TVZ.

K.H., 1909, 'Missionar Ferdinand Ernst (1896–1909 in Kamerun)', *Der Evangelische Heidenbote*, August: 63–64.

Knöpfli, Hans, 1999, *Sculptures and Symbolism. Crafts and Technologies: Some Traditional Craftsmen of the Western Grasslands of Cameroon. Part 2: Woodcarvers and Blacksmiths*, Basel and Limbe: Basel Mission.

――――2001, *Baskets and Calabashes, Palms and People. Crafts and Technologies: Some Traditional Craftsmen and Women of the Western Grasslands of Cameroon. Part 3: Utensils for Everyday Life*, Basel and Limbe: Basel Mission.

――――2002, *Living in Style. Crafts and Technologies: Some Traditional Crafts-men and -women of the Western Grasslands of Cameroon. Part 4: Handicrafts, Music, and the Fabric of Social Life*, Basel and Limbe: Basel Mission.

Koloss, Hans-Joachim, 2000, *Worldview and Society in Oku (Cameroon)*, Berlin: Beihefte zum Baessler Archive, Neue Folge, Band 10.

Krüger, Christoph, 2003, *Dowayo/Namchi poupées du Cameroun. Les Dowayo et leur culte*, Dusseldorf: U. Gottschalk.

Lederbogen, Jan, 1989, 'Technikgeschichte der Fotografie: Fotoausrüstungen und Fotografieranleitungen für Forschungsreisende', in Thomas Theye (ed.) *Der Geraubte Schatten. Die Photographie als ethnographisches Dokument*, Munich: C.J. Bucher.

Lewerenz, Eduard, 1912, 'Das Versöhnungsfest der Balileute', *Aus den Berichten der Basler Missionare*, 1 (October): 41–43.

Lima Sema, Adolf, 1988, 'The Mungaka language, its development, spread and use', in Vincent Titanji, Mathew Gwanfogbe, Elias Nwana, Gwanua Ndangam & Adolf Lima Sema *An Introduction to the Study of Bali-Nyonga. A Tribute to his Royal Highness Galega II Traditional Ruler of Bali-Nyonga from 1940–1985*, Yaoundé: Stardust Printers.

McNaughton, Patrick R., 1991, 'Is there history in horizontal masks? A preliminary response to the dilemma of form', *African Arts* April XXIV(2): 40–53; 88–90.

Marquardsen, Hugo, 1908, 'Die Tätigkeit des Hauptmanns Glauning in Deutsch-Ostafrika und Kamerun', *Deutsches Kolonialzeitung* 2 May 25(18): 316.

Meek, C.K., 1931a, *A Sudanese Kingdom: An Ethnographical Study of the Jukun-Speaking Peoples of Nigeria*, London: Kegan Paul, Trench, Trubner and Co.

――――1931b, *Tribal Studies in Northern Nigeria*, Two Volumes, London: Kegan Paul, Trench, Trubner and Co.

Michels, Stefanie, 2004, *Imagined Power Contested. Germans and Africans in the Upper Cross River Area of Cameroon 1887–1915*, Münster: Lit Verlag.

Moisel, Max, 1908a, 'Zur Geschichte von Bali und Bamum', *Globus* 93: 117–20.

——1908b, 'Eine Expedition in die Grashochländer Mittel-Kameruns', *Deutsche Kolonialzeitung* 25, 28 March: 217–20, 4 April: 236–38, 11 April: 267–72, 18 April: 278–89, 25 April: 309–10.

Moldenhauer, Robert, 1909, 'Eröffnung eines Sägewerkes im Kameruner Hochland', *Der Evangelische Heidenbote* 13–14.

Mzeka, Paul N., 1990, *Four Fons of Nso': Nineteenth and Early Twentieth-Century Kingship in the Western Grassfields of Cameroon*, Bamenda: The Spider Publishing Enterprise.

Northern, Tamara, 1973, *Royal Art of Cameroon: The Art of the Bamenda-Tikar*, Hanover New Hampshire: Hopkins Center Art Galleries and Dartmouth College.

——1984, *The Art of Cameroon*, Washington: Smithsonian Institution.

Nwana, Elias M., Augustine M. Ndangam & David F. Nti (eds), 1978, *The Lela Festival, The Living Culture of Bali Nyonga*, Volume 1, Bamenda: Privately Printed.

Nwana, Elias M. & Augustine M. Ndangam (eds), 1981a, *A Collection of Some Popular Names together with a Pictorial Presentation of Some Aspects of the Bali Culture. The Living Culture of Bali Nyonga*, Volume 3, Bamenda, Privately Published.

——1981b, *A Portrait of Their Royal Highnesses*, Bamenda: Privately Printed.

Nyamndi, Ndifontah Bernard, 1988, *The Bali Chamba of Cameroon: A Political History*, Paris: Editions Cape.

O'Neil, Robert, 1996, 'Imperialisms at the century's end: Moghamo relationships with Bali Nyonga and Germany 1889–1908', in Ian Fowler & David Zeitlyn (eds) *African Crossroads: Intersections between History and Anthropology in Cameroon*, Cameroon Studies, Volume 2, Oxford: Berghahn.

Pefok, Isaac Fielding, 1962, 'Isaac Fieldong Pefok, B.E.M. A brief autobiography. Recorded by Dr. M.D.W. Jeffreys, MA, Ph.D.' *The Nigerian Field* 27(2): 81–90.

Pradelles de Latour, Charles-Henry, 1995, 'The initiation of the Dugi among the Péré', in Ian Fowler & David Zeitlyn (eds) 'Mama for Story; Studies in the Ethnography of Cameroon in Honour of Sally Chilver', Special Issue, *Journal of the Anthropological Society of Oxford* 26(1): 81–86.

Preston Blier, Suzanne, 1998, *Royal Arts of Africa. The Majesty of Form*, London: Laurence King.

Prinz, Ulrike, 1989, 'Forscher und Fotografen – Kurzbiografen', in Thomas Theye (ed.) *Der Geraubte Schatten: Photographie als ethnographisches Dokument*, Munich: C.J. Bucher.

Ritzenthaler, Robert & Pat Ritzenthaler, 1962, *Cameroons Village: An Ethnography of the Bafut*, Milwaukee Public Museum Publications in Anthropology, No. 8.

Ritzenthaler, Pat, 1966, *The Fon of Bafut*, London: Cassell.

Rubin, Arnold, 1978, 'Buffalo mask, Chamba Nigeria', in Jacqueline Fry (ed.) *Twenty-five African Sculptures*, Ottawa: National Gallery of Canada.

Sargent, Robert A., 1999, *Economics, Politics and Social Change in the Benue Basin c. 1300–1700: A Regional Approach to Pre-Colonial West African History*, Enugu: Fourth Dimension Publishers.

Schachtzabel, Alfred, 1938, 'Professor Dr. Bernhard Ankermann zum 80. Geburtstag', *Sonderbeilage zum Baessler-Archiv* XXI: 22–25.

Schindlbeck, Markus (ed.), 1989, *Die ethnographische Linse: Photographien aus dem Museum für Völkerkunde*, Veröffentlichungen des Museums für Völkerkunde Berlin, NF 48.

Schuler, Eugen et al., 1903, 'Im Lande der Bali. Eine Kundschaftsreise Basler Missionare ins hinterland von Nordkamerun', *Evangelisches Missions-Magazin* 47: 191–214.

Seignobos, Christian, 1998, 'Les Dowayo et leurs taurins', in Christian Seignobos & Eric Thys (eds) *Des taurins et des hommes, Cameroun, Nigeria*, Paris: Editions de l'Orstom, Collection Latitudes 23.

Stelzig, Christine & Johannes Röhm, 2000, 'Der schriftliche Archivbestand des Fachreferates Afrika im Ethnologischen Museum Berlin: Das Projekt seiner Erfassung und Er-schließung', *Baessler-Archiv* NF XLVIII: 107–270.

Stevens, Phillips Jr., 1976, 'The Danubi ancestral shrine', *African Arts* 10(1): 30–37 & 98.

Striebel, Jonathan, 1909, 'Die geheimen Orakel der Balineger', *Der Evangelische Heidenbote*, November: 81–83.

Strümpell, Karl, 1910, 'Vergleichendes Wortzeichnis der Heidensprache Adamauas', *Zeitschrift für Ethnographie* 42: 444–88.

Stumpf, Carl, 1911, *Die Anfänge der Musik*, Leipzig: Verlag von Johann Ambrosius Barth.

Thomas, Trevor, 1938, 'Variations on a theme: analysis of small carved figures from Bali, Cameroons, Africa', *Man* 38(32): 33–37.

Tischhauser, Georg Johan, 1938, 'Carved figures from Bali Cameroon. Correspondence', *Man* 38(187).

—— 1993, *Mungaka (Bali) Dictionary*, compiled by Georg Tischhauser; revised and translated by Johannes Stöckle in cooperation with Samuel Fe Tita Mangwa, Köln: Rüdiger Köppe.

Tischhauser, Georg Johan & Wilhelm Zürcher, 1941, 'Der Wechsel auf dem Königsthron in Bali', *Der Evangelische Heidenbote* November: 154–57.

Titanji, Vincent, Mathew Gwanfogbe, Elias Nwana, Gwanua Ndangam & Adolf Lima Sema, 1988, *An Introduction to the Study of Bali-Nyonga. A Tribute to his Royal Highness Galega II Traditional Ruler of Bali-Nyonga from 1940–1985*, Yaoundé: Stardust Printers.

Vielhauer, Adolf, 1951, *Grundzüge einer Grammatik der Balisprache*, Basel Mission.

Warnier, Jean-Pierre, 1980, 'Trade guns in the Grassfields of Cameroon', *Paideuma* 26: 79–92.

———1985, *Echanges, développement et hiérarchies dans le Bamenda précolonial (Cameroun)*, Stuttgart: Franz Steiner Verlag.

Wente-Lukas, Renate, 1977, *Die materielle Kultur der nicht-islamischen Ethnien von Nordkamerun und Nordostnigeria*, Studien zur Kulturkunde 43, Wiesbaden: Franz Steiner.

Young, Michael, 1998, *Malinowski's Kiriwina: Fieldwork Photography 1915–1918*, Chicago and London: University of Chicago Press.

Unpublished References

BEM Berlin Ethnological Museum; BMA Basel Mission Archive; MS manuscript; TS typescript

Ankermann, Bernhard, 1907, Letter to von Luschan: 21 December 1907 (Bali) BEM 'I/MV Acta betreffend die Reise des Dr. Ankermann nach Kamerun' 798: 54–55.

———1908, Letter to von Luschan: 7 April 1908 (Bamum) BEM 'I/MV Acta betreffend die Reise des Dr. Ankermann nach Kamerun' 798: 106–7, 109.

———1909, Bills from Photolabor Johan Nöller in Rummelsburg, BEM 'I/MV Acta betreffend die Reise des Dr. Ankermann nach Kamerun' 799: 49–50.

Chilver, E.M., 1960, 'Interview: Bafut', 26 June 1960.

———1963, 'Interview with *lela* officers', 22 April 1963, MS, 15 pp.

———1964, revised 1970, *Historical Notes on the Bali Chiefdoms of the Cameroons Grassfields*, Reports prepared for the Bali Historical Society, consisting of: Report No.1 *Origins, Migration and Composition*, MS revised in 1970, courtesy of the author; Report No.2 *Settlement and Composition*, TS 1964. Institute of Human Sciences, Garoua.

———2001, 'Brief notes on royal burial in Bali Nyonga, with some comparisons', MS, 31 pp.

Dah, Jonas N., 1983, 'Missionary Motivations and Methods. A Critical Examination of the Basel Mission in Cameroon 1886–1914', thesis for Doctorate in Theology, University of Basel.

Dorsch, H., 1908, 'Jahresbericht 1907', MS, BMA E-2.25.55.

Fardon, R.O., 1980, 'The Chamba', Volume 2, University College London, University of London Ph.D. thesis.

Fomuso, Buma-Foncham Henri, 1976, 'Sacrifice among the Bali-Nyonga in Mezam Division N.W. Province of Cameroon (A Descriptive Analysis)', University of Yaoundé, dissertation for Licence en Théologie in the Faculty of Protestant Theology.

Göhring, Martin, 1905, Letter to mission committee 1905, MS BMA E-220.390.

Gwanfogbe, Mathew, 1995, 'Changing Regimes and the Development of Education in Cameroon 1886–1996 (with Special Reference to the Basel Mission)', Institute of Education, University of London Ph.D. thesis.

Hummel, Adelheid, 1931, 'Einiges aus der alten Geschichte des Bali Volks', TS BMA E-5-2.7, 2.

Hunt, W.E., 1925, *Assessment of the Bali Clan*, Buea Archives, Cameroon; consulted in 1984 as a typescript copy at the Institute of Human Sciences, Bamenda Station.

Keller, Jakob, 1906, 'Jahresbericht 1905', MS BMA E-2.20, 394.

——— 1912, 'Jahresbericht 1911', MS BMA E-2.34, 56.

——— 1919, 'Das Lelafest in Bali', MS BMA E-10.2, 15.

Lewerenz, Eduard, 1912, 'Das Lelafest der Bali', MS, BMA E-2.37, 50.

Merz, Andreas, 1997, 'Die Politik Bali-Nyongas (Grasland von Kamerun) gegenüber der Basler-Mission und der deutschen Kolonialmacht, anhand von Dokumenten und historischen Photographien aus dem Archiv der Basler Mission von 1889 bis ca. 1910', Lizentiatsarbeit, Historisches Seminar der Universität Basel, Volume 1 text, Volume 2 photographs.

O'Neil, Robert John, 1987, 'A History of Moghamo, 1865 to 1940: Authority and Change in a Cameroon Grassfields Culture', Columbia University Ph.D. thesis.

Rubin, Arnold, 1969, 'The Arts of the Jukun-Speaking Peoples of Northern Nigeria', Indiana University Ph.D. thesis.

Russell, Stuart Wells Jr., 1980, 'Aspects of Development in Rural Cameroon: Political Transition amongst the Bali of Bamenda', Boston University Ph.D. thesis.

Soh, Pius Bejeng, 1975, 'A Study of Lela, a Bali Chamba State Cult of the NorthWest Grassfields of Cameroon', University of Yaoundé, Mémoire de D.E.S. de Sociologie.

Steinegger Nzie, Catherine, 1998, 'Kleider machen Leute: Rekonstruktion der Kleidungsgewohnheiten in Bali-Nyonga von der Mitte des 19. Jahrhunderts bis ca. 1930', Seminararbeit bei Paul Jenkins Historisches Seminar der Universität Basel.

Stelzig, Christine, 2003, 'Afrika am Museum für Völkerkunde zu Berlin 1873–1919. Aneignung, Darstellung und Konstruktion eines Kontinents', University of Leipzig Ph.D. thesis.

Steudle, Friedrich, 1932, 'Jahresbericht 1931', TS, BMA E-5–207, 8.

Striebel, Jonathan, 1909, 'Das Lelafest', MS, BMA E-2.30, 59.

Thomas, Guy Alexander, 2001, 'Why do we need the Whiteman's God? African Contributions and Responses to the Formation of a Christian Movement in Cameroon, 1914–68', School of Oriental and African Studies, University of London Ph.D. thesis.

Tischhauser, Georg Johann, 1975, 'Sitten und Gebräuche der Bali im Grasland von Kamerun', 20 December, 6 pp, Tischhauser Nachlass, TS, BMA E-10.54, 17.

Vielhauer, Adolf, 1930, 'Jahresbericht 1929', TS, BMA E-5–2.4, 51.

Widmaier, Rudolf, 1909, 'Report on the first Bali Christians', 4 January, MS, BMA E-2.30, 57.

Zürcher, Wilhelm, 1940, 'Jahresbericht 1940', TS, BMA E-5.2, 15.

Index